LABYRINTHS & MAZES

LABYRINTHS & MAZES

A Complete Guide to Magical Paths of the World

JEFF SAWARD

A Division of Sterling Publishing Co., Inc.
New York

A GAIA ORIGINAL

Books from Gaia celebrate the vision of Gaia,
the self-sustaining living Earth, and seek to help
its readers live in greater personal planetary harmony.

Conceived by Patrick Nugent

Editors	Linda Sonntag
	Jo Godfrey Wood
Cover Design	Barbara Zaretsky
Design	Sara Mathews
Graphics	Jeff Saward
Production	Jim Pope
Direction	Joss Pearson
	Patrick Nugent

Published by Lark Books, a division of
Sterling Publishing Co., Inc.
387 Park Avenue South, New York, N.Y. 10016

Originally published under the title *Labyrinths and Mazes: The Definitive Guide to Ancient & Modern Traditions*
by Jeff Saward (ISBN 1-85675-183-X)

© 2003 Gaia Books Limited, United Kingdom

Distributed in Canada by Sterling Publishing,
c/o Canadian Manda Group, One Atlantic Ave., Suite 105
Toronto, Ontario, Canada M6K 3E7

Distributed in the U.K. by Guild of Master Craftsman Publications Ltd., Castle Place, 166 High Street, Lewes, East Sussex, England BN7 1XU Tel: (+ 44) 1273 477374, Fax: (+ 44) 1273 478606, Email: pubs@thegmcgroup.com, Web: www.gmcpublications.com

Distributed in Australia by Capricorn Link (Australia) Pty Ltd.,
P.O. Box 704, Windsor, NSW 2756 Australia

Every effort has been made to ensure that all the information in this book is accurate. However, the publisher cannot be responsible for any injuries, losses, and other damages that may result from the use of the information in this book.

If you have questions or comments about this book, please contact:
Lark Books, 67 Broadway, Asheville, NC 28801, (828) 253-0467

Printed and bound by Imago, China
All rights reserved

ISBN 1-57990-539-0

Photographs: title page, the gilded altar of the Watts Chapel in Compton, England;
previous page, a detail from the chapel showing angels holding labyrinths.

Next did Hephaestus depict a dancing circle

Like unto that Daedalus wrought in spacious Knossos

For Ariadne of the fair tresses.

Homer's Iliad, XVIII. 590-592.

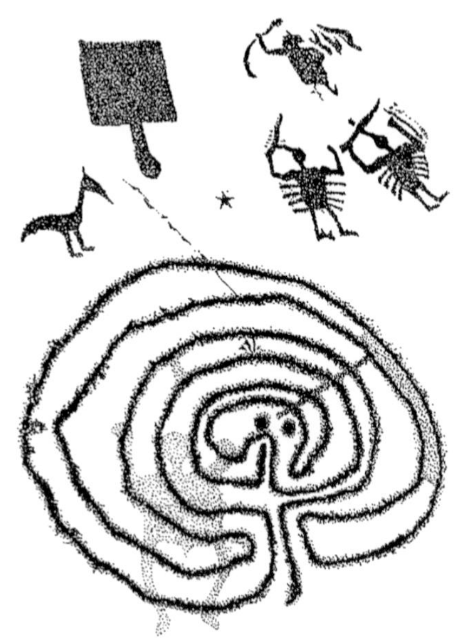

Metric conversion table
1 inch = 2.54 centimetres – 1 centimetre = 0.394 inch
1 foot = 0.3048 metre – 1 metre = 3.2808 feet
1 yard = 0.9144 metre – 1 metre = 1.0936 yards
1 mile = 1.609 kilometres – 1 kilometre = 0.6214 mile

Contents

Introduction

The idea of mazes and labyrinths may conjure up images of paths running between high hedges, a pattern on a cathedral floor, or the legend of Theseus battling with the Minotaur in gloomy passageways deep underground. Yet these are just three snapshots in the long and winding history of mazes and labyrinths, a story that spans thousands of years and is set in places as far apart as the lush jungles of Indonesia, the barren landscapes of the Arctic, and the high deserts of the Americas. The plot is complex, but the story starts with a simple symbol, the labyrinth, found around the world in an amazing variety of forms, many of which are still flourishing to this day. Its development into the familiar puzzle mazes that enliven parks and gardens is only one of the twists in the tale.

People have been walking the winding pathways of labyrinths for thousands of years. Fascination with this archetypal symbol continues to this day.

Entering the Labyrinth

The history of labyrinths and mazes is filled with unexpected twists and turns – not unlike like the designs of mazes themselves. At the heart of this story is an archetypal symbol, universally known as "the labyrinth", that occurs worldwide, in different cultures and points in time, and in places as diverse as Brazil, Mexico, and the American Southwest; across Europe, in Iceland, and in Africa, India, and Indonesia. Throughout this vast range, the labyrinth takes many forms and is constructed in many different materials. While its origins are difficult to trace and remain mysterious, most of the specimens from prehistory and many from the more remote regions of its range, employ exactly the same design: a series of concentric lines, carefully connected, to form the "classical" labyrinth. Many developments of this original design have appeared, better suited to a new usage or cultural context.

The majority of these ancient labyrinth devices are not mazes in the familiar sense – intricate designs with choices of pathways and hidden goals – for they have just one pathway that leads from the entrance to the central goal, albeit via a convoluted course. It was not until the Middle Ages and the time of the Renaissance that unicursal (one-path) labyrinths became a popular feature of garden design and rapidly evolved into the first true multicursal puzzle mazes, usually formed of hedges. Modern mazes, however complex, are direct descendants of the original labyrinth design and here, at the beginning of the twenty-first century, they are evolving into another important phase of labyrinth history.

The classical labyrinth symbol. Unchanged for thousands of years, this simple design has spread around the world and appears in many surprising locations.

The following pages endeavour to give a concise summary of this complicated story, illustrated with important historic labyrinths and mazes from around the world. This story certainly features the current maze and labyrinth revival, but as many hundreds of new examples have appeared since the 1970s, it is difficult to provide anything more than an overview. As with those from the past, only a handful will survive. Those formed of long-lasting materials or fortuitously located are certainly favoured, but others will be preserved by little more than chance. It is important to remember that these same selection criteria have been at work since labyrinths first appeared some 4,000 years ago.

The Labyrinths of Legend

Among the wealth of folklore and tradition linked with labyrinths around the world are stories that tell of a building or even a whole city that was conceived as a labyrinth. Sometimes the labyrinth is symbolic of the walls of a well-defended city from the past, often one that fell by deception or treachery. The following examples include some, but by no means all, of these labyrinths and their legends.

Theseus and the Minotaur

For more than 2,000 years the legend of Theseus and the Minotaur has been associated with the ancient symbol presented as the plan of the labyrinth constructed by Daedalus. Legend tells how King Minos employed the services of Daedalus, the greatest inventor of his generation, to work at his palace at Knossos on the island of Crete. His strangest task was to create a model cow in which Minos's queen, Pasiphae, hid to satisfy her desire for a bull. As a result, the queen gave birth to Asterion, the Minotaur, a creature that was half-man, and half-bull. To conceal his shame, Minos commissioned Daedalus to construct the Labyrinth, an underground network of tunnels leading to a chamber in which the monstrous offspring could be housed, and so designed that anybody who entered would never be able to escape.

The Minotaur craved human flesh, and King Minos obliged King Aegeus of Athens to send a regular supply of seven youths and seven maidens, who would be put into the labyrinth and fed alive to the ravenous beast. When Aegeus' son Theseus came to Crete as part of the tribute, he captured the heart of Minos' daughter Ariadne. In a bid to save his life, she gave him a ball of thread, which he spooled out behind himself as he navigated his course through the labyrinth. Finding the Minotaur in his lair, he killed the unfortunate creature, then retraced his steps back to the entrance by rewinding the thread. Theseus fled from Crete with Ariadne and his fellow Athenian captives, and lived to fight another day.

Discovering that Daedalus had provided Ariadne with the clew of thread and lost him his daughter, King Minos shut the inventor inside the labyrinth with his son, Icarus. However, Daedalus had prepared for this eventuality by inventing wings for them both made of feathers and wax. Daedalus escaped by flying to freedom, but in his youthful enthusiasm Icarus flew too close to the sun, the wax on his wings melted and he plunged to his death.

Though the labyrinth in the palace at Knossos was eventually destroyed by earthquakes and fire the legend of the Cretan labyrinth lives on to this day.

With Athena looking on, Theseus drags the vanquished Minotaur from the labyrinth in this depiction on an Attic red-figure kylix cup produced *c.* 410 BCE.

The Cretan Labyrinth

Built on foundations of earlier buildings on the site, the first major palace at Knossos was constructed *c.* 1930 BCE. Several major earthquakes over the following five centuries caused serious damage and destruction to this and other palaces on Crete, especially the earthquakes and ash-falls associated with the eruption of Thera during the fifteenth century BCE. Rebuilt on each occasion, the Knossos palace was eventually abandoned *c.* 1380 BCE. Evidence suggests that its occupiers knew this structure as the "Labyrinth", but its connection with the labyrinth symbol can be traced back only to the fourth century BCE, although Greek legends about the fearsome Minotaur of Knossos were circulating long before this time.

The excavation of the site by Sir Arthur Evans, from 1900 onwards, revealed the labyrinth for the first time in over 3,000 years and settled any previous argument about the site of the most famous labyrinth of all. Despite recent criticism of Evans' excavation and reconstruction techniques, and his undoubted involvement in the procurement of forged artefacts to satisfy the demands of collectors and museums[1] his work at Knossos was uniquely important. It revealed a previously unknown civilization and artistic tradition to the world and introduced the term Minoan (after the legendary King Minos) to archaeological terminology. His reconstruction of many sections of the Labyrinth, and the frescos that decorated the walls, still allow the visitor to wander around the "Palace of Minos" and speculate on how this most complex of Bronze Age buildings became the labyrinth of legend.

Left: the reconstructed portions of the Knossos Labyrinth provide a glimpse of the splendour of the structure and decoration of this Bronze-Age Minoan palace.

Below: a surviving fragment of the labyrinthine frescos that once decorated the walls of the Palace of Minos at Knossos. It was found during Evans' excavations.

Troy

The story of the Trojan war and the ten-year siege of the city of Troy by the Achaean forces seeking the return of Helen, the abducted wife of Menelaus, was first recounted in Homer's *The Iliad* (eighth or seventh century BCE). Famous among the ancient Greeks and Romans and later throughout medieval Europe, the fabled ruins of Troy are now believed to have been situated at Hissarlyk in northwest Turkey, founded *c.* 3000 BCE. The subsequent occupation levels stretch through to Roman and Byzantine times; ever since excavation of the site began in 1863, controversy has raged over which destruction level represents the Troy of Homeric legend and when that episode took place. The massive defences of the city were finally breached when the Trojans opened the gates and wheeled in the wooden horse, thought to be a peace offering, but actually full of Achaean soldiers. Prior to this Achilles, in a magical attack on the city, had dragged the body of Hector, leader of the Trojans, three times around the perimeter walls.

After the siege, commonly dated to around 1250–1220 BCE,[2] Troy became a legend, symbolized by the labyrinth – the archetypal city of antiquity, invincible to attack, but vulnerable to subterfuge and deceit. The Tragliatella vase from Etruscan Italy (see page 42) provides evidence of the association of Troy with the labyrinth symbol from as early as the seventh century BCE, and the writings of Pliny and others make it clear that the pattern of the labyrinth was understood as a symbol for the defences of Troy in the Roman world. However, it was probably during the later medieval period that the two became synonymous. Many labyrinths constructed of boulders throughout Scandinavia, and of turf in the British Isles and Germany, were named Troy-Town, Troy's Walls or City of Troy, in honour of the fabled city.

Soldiers on horseback ride out from a labyrinth labelled as Troy; the earliest known association of the legend with the symbol comes from the decoration of an Etruscan vase found at Tragliatella.

A stone labyrinth, known locally as *Jeruusalem*, at Kootsaare in Estonia, was excavated and restored in 1986.

Jerusalem

The city of Jerusalem has been an important settlement for thousands of years. The role of the city as the centre of the medieval Christian world was seriously threatened when Saladin seized Jerusalem for the Muslims in 1187. The "lost city" of Jerusalem soon became associated with the labyrinth as a parallel to the legendary city of Troy. Several pavement labyrinths in the cathedrals of northern France were known as "Chemin de Jérusalem" ("Road to Jerusalem"), though there is no documentary evidence for this connection before the eighteenth century. However, the connection is also found in Germany, Finland, and Estonia. Stone labyrinths named after Jerusalem (and other famous cities) are common around the shorelines and islands of the Gulf of Finland (see pages 139 and 146).

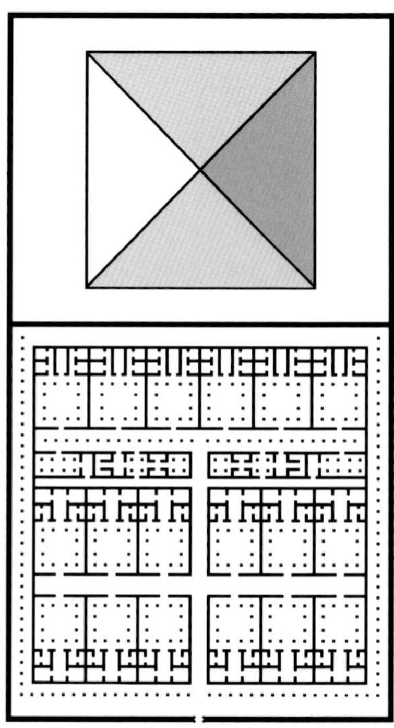

A reconstructed plan of the Egyptian Labyrinth temple and pyramid built for Amenenhet III *c.* 1800 BCE at Hawara.

The Egyptian Labyrinth

The famous Egyptian Labyrinth was actually a huge mortuary temple with accompanying pyramid built at Hawara, near El Fayûm, for the pharaoh Amenemhet III (ruled 1842-1797 BCE). It was first described in detail by the Greek historian Herodotus (*c.* 484–430 BCE), who had clearly visited it. The temple at Hawara reputedly had 3,000 rooms, half below ground, half above, and separate courtyards for each of the administrative districts of Egypt. It is unlikely that its builders viewed it as a labyrinth; Herodotus does not use this term, and the naming of the temple as a labyrinth is down to the Greek historian Diodorus.

Diodorus visited Egypt between 60 and 57 BCE, and although the temple was in ruins at that time, he reported that: "a man who enters it cannot easily find his way out" and further claimed that Daedalus himself modelled the Cretan labyrinth on this building. A century later, further embellishment of Diodorus' description by Pliny (who certainly never visited the site), turned this remarkable building into a legend that later authors accepted without question.[3] When Flinders Petrie excavated the ruins in the 1890s, he discovered that most of the stone had been used to build a Roman town overlying the site. Only the eroded core of the pyramid built adjacent to the temple remains today.

This twelfth-century CE manuscript from Regensburg, Germany, depicts a circular labyrinth labelled *"Urbs Jericho lune fuit assimilata figure"* (the city of Jerico had a moon-like shape).

Jericho

Founded over 10,000 years ago, the ancient city of Jericho in the Jordan Valley northwest of the Dead Sea was rebuilt many times after earthquakes and fires. Although difficult for archaeologists to date, the conquest of Jericho by the Israelites is told in the Bible (Joshua 6). Over the course of six days, the Israelite army circled the walls of the besieged city in silence, as seven priests blew on seven trumpets. On the seventh day the army rose early and circled the defences seven times; all shouted together when the trumpets blew, and the walls of Jericho collapsed. The city was stormed and plundered. Only Rahab and her family were spared on account of her hiding Joshua's spies and providing a cord for them to escape from her window high in the defensive walls of the city – a striking parallel to the story of Ariadne's thread in the legend of the Cretan labyrinth.

From the fourth century CE, Christian pilgrims travelled to Jericho in search of the Biblical city. From the early ninth century Christian manuscripts began to appear depicting classical labyrinths labelled "Jericho". The seven concentric pathways of this labyrinth illustrated the seven circuits made of the city's defences before its fall. Labyrinths with seven walls (therefore only six pathways) accompany a number of Jewish and Syrian manuscripts produced from the eleventh to the eighteenth century. The labyrinths are marked as a plan of the walls of Jericho, and often feature Rahab's house.

Scimangada

In India the labyrinth was both a protective symbol and the plan of military defences of cities and armies at war. The impregnable chakra-vyūha battle formation described in the ancient Indian epic poem *Mahābhārata* subsequently appeared in temple carvings and as a plan for boulder labyrinths (see Chapter 2). The Persian scholar Al-Bīrūnī, writing in the eleventh century, recounted a story of a labyrinth surrounding the fortress of Lanka, from an early version of the *Rāmāyana* epic. The legendary Lanka was said to occupy a position high in the sky above the equator; the real city of Scimangada, whose defensive walls were also represented by a labyrinth symbol (see page 00), was situated in the dense jungle of the Himalayan foothills in modern-day Nepal. This impregnable city was, like many of its labyrinthine counterparts, breached by means of treachery – a citizen revealed the weakest point of the defences. The ruins of Scimangada, destroyed in the fourteenth century and now known as Simraongarh, survive to this day, but they are overgrown and largely obscured by jungle.

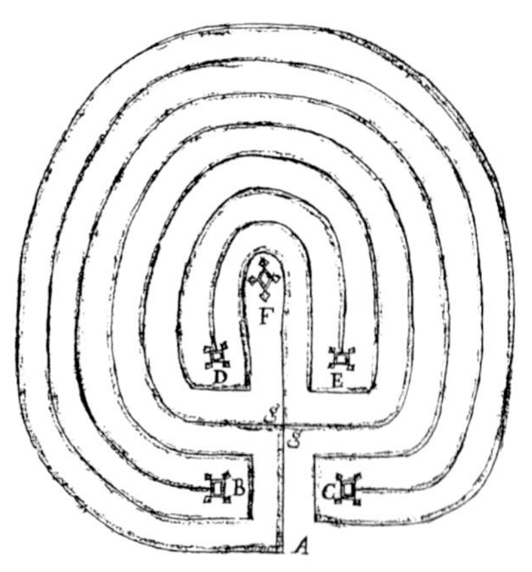

This sketch of a labyrinth inscribed on a stone at Bhaktapur, Nepal, is said to represent a plan of the defences of the legendary city of Scimangada.

Casa Grande

In the Saguaro cactus forest of the Sonora desert, near Coolidge in southern Arizona, stands the remarkable adobe tower house of Casa Grande. It was built by the Hohokam people during the early fourteenth century and abandoned *c.* 1450. The Pima people who subsequently occupied the region knew the ruins as Hottai-ki – the Great House, or Casa Grande, as the Spanish conquistadors named it in the late 1600s. Early travellers occasionally recorded the use of the labyrinth symbol by the Pima, explaining it as a plan of the "big house".[4] It is of considerable interest that a labyrinth, of presumed Piman origin, is engraved on an inner wall of the Casa Grande tower house (see page 70). Separated by thousands of kilometres and thousands of years from Knossos and Troy, where this tradition may have originated, Casa Grande is one of the few buildings in the world to contain the labyrinth symbol that represents it.

A canopy has been erected to protect the fragile adobe walls of the Casa Grande tower house at Coolidge, Arizona against erosion. A labyrinth graffito is carved on an inner wall of Casa Grande.

Constructing the Classical Labyrinth

The first known labyrinth symbol, called the classical labyrinth, has seven concentric pathways surrounding the central goal, and is found dating from prehistory around the shorelines of the Mediterranean Sea and on the Atlantic seaboard of the Iberian peninsular. Across the whole region, and elsewhere throughout the world, the design is, almost without exception, exactly the same. How could this fidelity of form occur in pre-literate societies without an easy way of remembering or recording it?

Starting with the seed pattern (1) as a nucleus, the walls of the labyrinth are built as a series of concentric lines (2 to 9).Once learnt, the technique will produce a perfect labyrinth every time and provides the key to further development of the design.

1

2

3

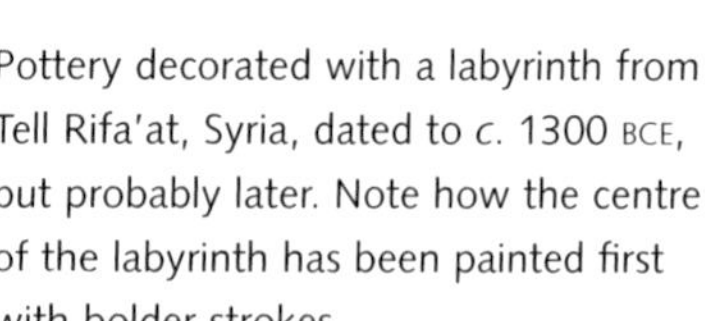

4

Pottery decorated with a labyrinth from Tell Rifa'at, Syria, dated to *c.* 1300 BCE, but probably later. Note how the centre of the labyrinth has been painted first with bolder strokes.

5

The simplest surviving labyrinths, scratched on walls and rocks or painted on pottery, often best preserve details of the freehand construction process. They provide valuable evidence for the widespread use of a "shorthand" transmission technique. The nucleus of the labyrinth – a cross, four angles, and four dots – is drawn first and then the concentric circles are connected to the points around the central core. Conveniently named the "seed pattern",[5] this simple method for reproducing the labyrinth design has been used wherever and whenever the symbol occurs. Easily memorized, it is an ingenious drawing trick that has been passed from person to person, from one culture to another, for thousands of years.

6

7

8

9

The addition of one extra set of angles to the basic seed pattern produces a classical labyrinth with eleven circuits, as seen on this fifteenth-century fresco in Hesselager Church, Denmark.

Expanding the Seed Pattern

Inserting additional sets of angles in the seed will produce labyrinths with more circuits. A different method of connection produces a labyrinth with a spiral at its goal, as seen on this fresco from Seljord, Norway

A fresco from Roerslev Church, Denmark, has the seed and initial circuits painted in a different colour. A further set of angles added to the seed results in a classical labyrinth with fifteen circuits.

A simple form of the labyrinth on a coin from Knossos, Crete, *c.* third century BCE. Just the cross and dots are employed to create a labyrinth with only three pathways surrounding the centre.

Reducing the Seed Pattern

Removing elements from the standard seed pattern will result in labyrinths with reduced numbers of circuits. However, not all of these variants will produce successful designs.

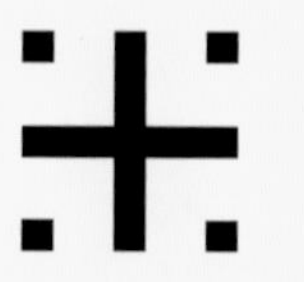

Graffito from Roman Pompeii, dated to *c.* 79 CE. No doubt scratched in a hurry, the corner dots of the seed pattern have been forgotten, resulting in a curious labyrinth with no access to the goal.

A labyrinth stone relief from a temple in Halebid, India, formed from a three-fold seed pattern with a spiral connection in the upper section. This design is known as Chakra-vyūha.

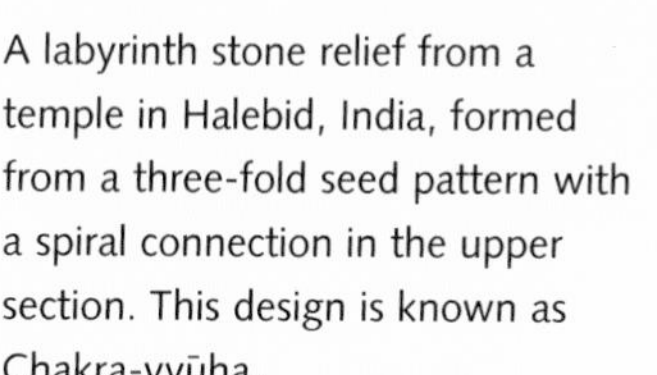

Interesting Variants

Changing the symmetry and structure of the seed can produce some surprising variations, including this complex labyrinth in an Indian magic book.

An early twentieth-century Pima woven basket from Arizona. This unique example is based on a star-shaped, five-fold seed pattern that produces nine pathways surrounding the goal.

Family Tree and Timeline

The evolution of labyrinths and mazes can be simplified to show the five major groups depicted in the family tree opposite. Numerous other smaller branches representing local variations on the basic types are omitted for clarity. The accompanying timeline includes many of the key events in the history of labyrinth and maze development.

Historic Labyrinths and Mazes Worldwide

The task of mapping the distribution of mazes and labyrinths across their 4,000-year history is by no means straightforward. Some examples are difficult to date, and others do not fit neatly into any particular category. Areas of high concentration contrast with areas of emptiness, and while this reflects the historic spread of the concept, it probably also reflects a lack of documented information from certain regions. The key alongside each region gives page numbers for specific information on each group of labyrinths and mazes.

Europe
First labyrinths see pages 36-49
Roman labyrinths see pages 52-57
Labyrinths in churches see pages 82-117
Turf labyrinths see pages 120-135
Stone labyrinths see pages 138-151
Garden labyrinths and mazes see pages 154-169

Labyrinths in Southern Russia
see page 150

American hedge mazes
see pages 174-177

American Southwest labyrinths
see pages 68-75

Hedge maze Sierra Leone
see pages 172-173

Labyrinth artifacts Ecuador
see pages 78-79

Labyrinth geoglyphs Peru
see pages 78-79

Labyrinth inscriptions Brazil
see pages 78-79

Zulu labyrinths South Africa
see page 67

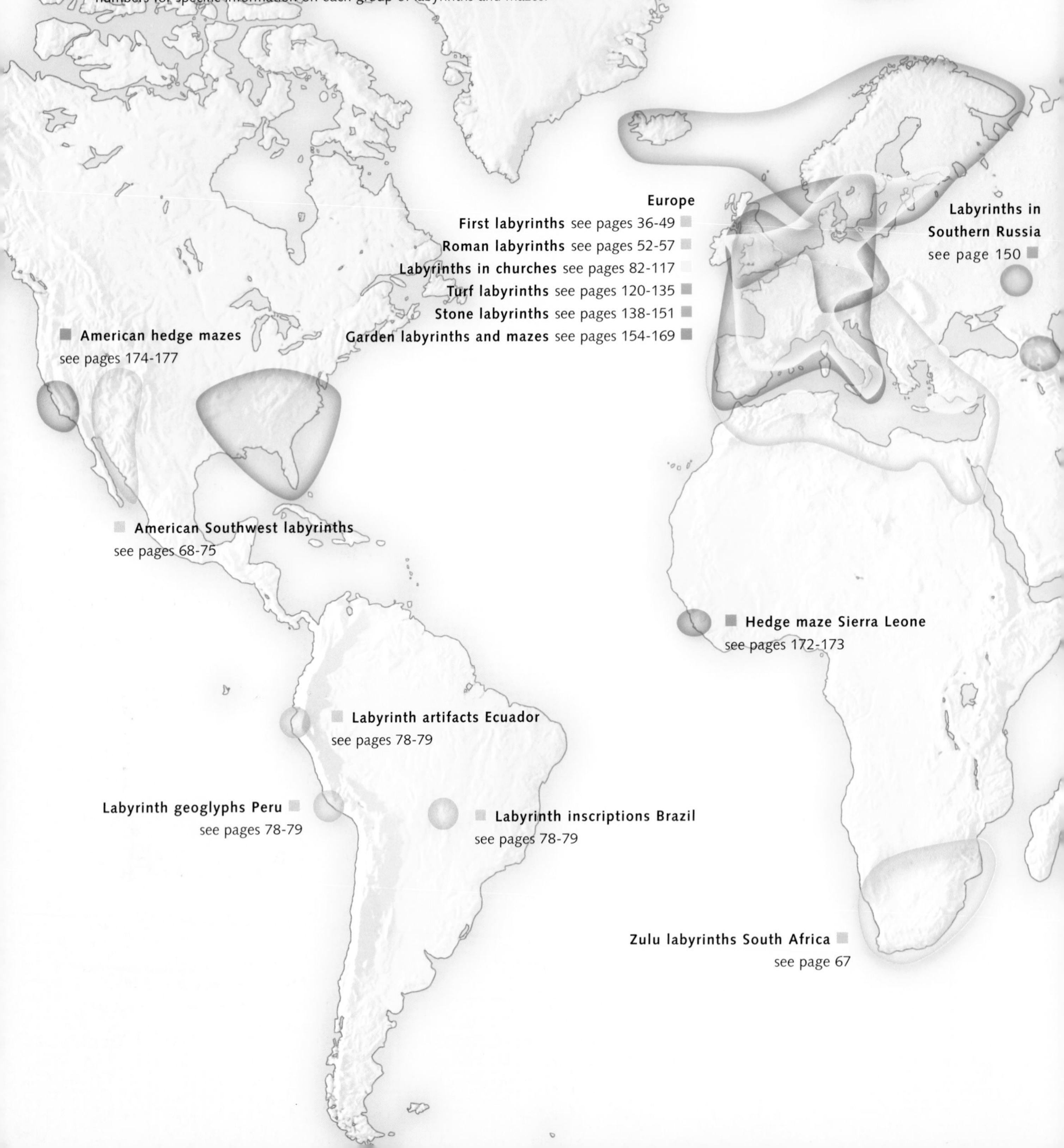

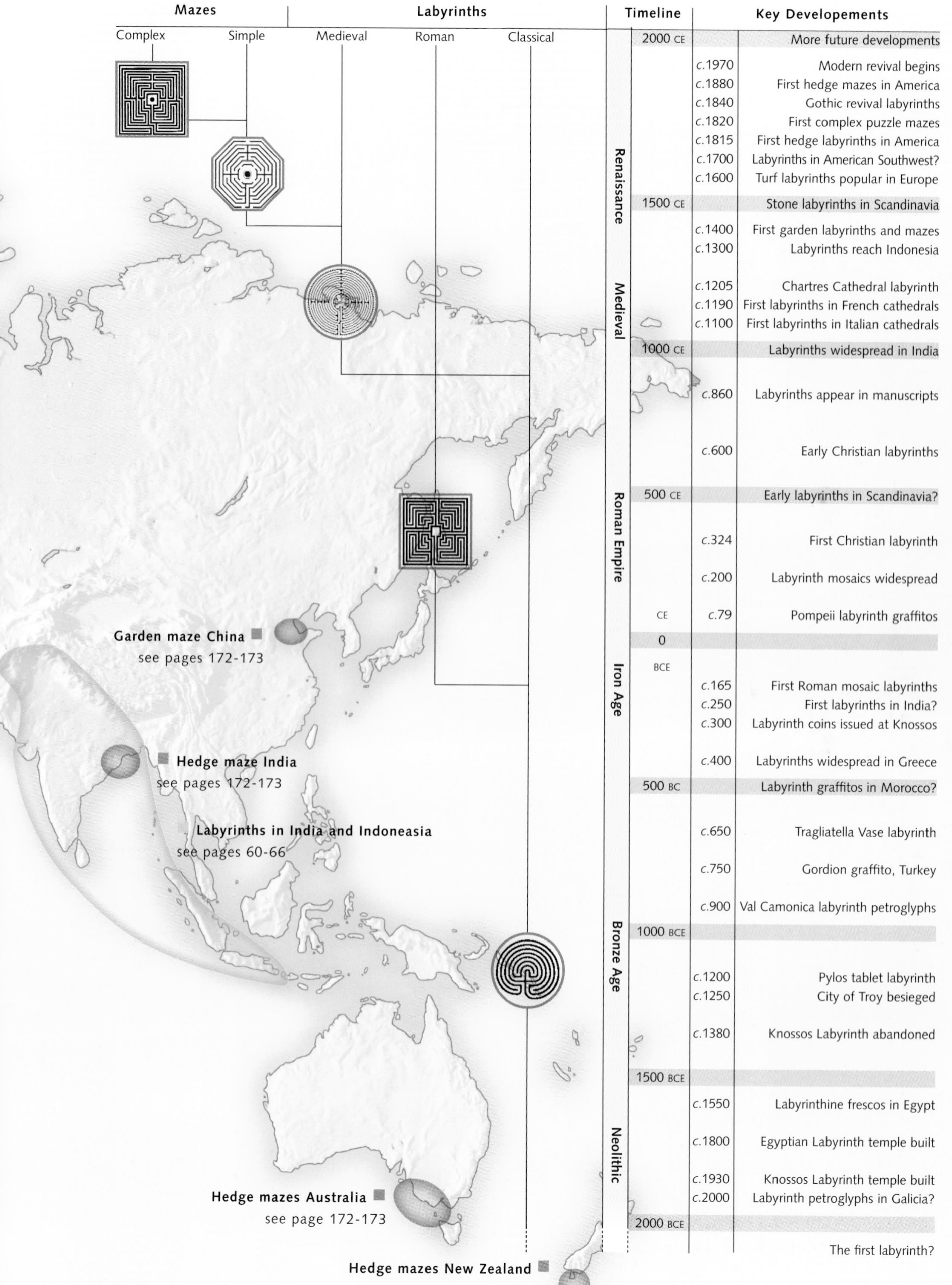
Mazes
Labyrinths
Complex
Simple
Medieval
Roman
Classical
Timeline
Key Developements
2000 CE More future developments
c.1970 Modern revival begins
c.1880 First hedge mazes in America
c.1840 Gothic revival labyrinths
c.1820 First complex puzzle mazes
c.1815 First hedge labyrinths in America
c.1700 Labyrinths in American Southwest?
c.1600 Turf labyrinths popular in Europe
Renaissance
1500 CE Stone labyrinths in Scandinavia
c.1400 First garden labyrinths and mazes
c.1300 Labyrinths reach Indonesia
c.1205 Chartres Cathedral labyrinth
c.1190 First labyrinths in French cathedrals
c.1100 First labyrinths in Italian cathedrals
Medieval
1000 CE Labyrinths widespread in India
c.860 Labyrinths appear in manuscripts
c.600 Early Christian labyrinths
500 CE Early labyrinths in Scandinavia?
Roman Empire
c.324 First Christian labyrinth
c.200 Labyrinth mosaics widespread
CE
c.79 Pompeii labyrinth graffitos
0
BCE
Iron Age
c.165 First Roman mosaic labyrinths
c.250 First labyrinths in India?
c.300 Labyrinth coins issued at Knossos
c.400 Labyrinths widespread in Greece
500 BC Labyrinth graffitos in Morocco?
c.650 Tragliatella Vase labyrinth
c.750 Gordion graffito, Turkey
c.900 Val Camonica labyrinth petroglyphs
1000 BCE
Bronze Age
c.1200 Pylos tablet labyrinth
c.1250 City of Troy besieged
c.1380 Knossos Labyrinth abandoned
1500 BCE
c.1550 Labyrinthine frescos in Egypt
c.1800 Egyptian Labyrinth temple built
Neolithic
c.1930 Knossos Labyrinth temple built
c.2000 Labyrinth petroglyphs in Galicia?
2000 BCE
The first labyrinth?
Garden maze China
see pages 172-173
Hedge maze India
see pages 172-173
Labyrinths in India and Indoneasia
see pages 60-66
Hedge mazes Australia
see page 172-173
Hedge mazes New Zealand
see pages 172-173

Origins and Meanings of the Labyrinth

When, where, and how did the first labyrinth symbol appear? Current research suggests it originated in southern Europe around 4,000 years ago during the late Neolithic or Early Bronze Age, but this perception is subject to revision as new discoveries provide further evidence. A century ago the oldest known example of the labyrinth symbol was to be found on a decorated jar from Etruscan Italy, dated to the seventh century BCE. The discovery in 1957 of a clay tablet inscribed with a labyrinth at Pylos in Greece pushed this earliest date back to *c.* 1200 BCE. In the late 1990s, reappraisal of the dating of petroglyphs in northwest Spain, including a number of labyrinths, suggested that some of these may date to *c.* 2000 BCE. However, these earliest representations provide next to no clues to explain the origin and purpose of the labyrinth as a concept or a symbol in its own right.

The origin of the word "labyrinth", from the Greek *labyrinthos*, has been the subject of much speculation and discussion. The often quoted derivation from *labrys* "house of the double axe", was first proposed by the German archaeologist Maximillian Meyer in 1892. It was given considerable credence by the discovery of numerous double axe heads, as votive objects and scratched on stones, during Sir Arthur Evans' excavation of the Minoan palace at Knossos. This interpretation was championed by Evans as proof that he had found the labyrinth of Greek legend, but it cannot be substantiated, as labrys is a word from the Carian language of Asia Minor (modern day Turkey). It was certainly never used on the island of Crete in Minoan times, where a double axe was known as *wao*, or *pelekys* in the early Greek language. Besides, similar double axes occur at a number of other Minoan palaces, temples, and other cult sites, none of which is labelled "labyrinth".

The literal meaning of *labyrinthos* is "structure of large stones"[6] – the big stone house – appropriate for a large palace and temple complex such as the building at Knossos. And there is evidence that the Knossos complex was known as the labyrinth long before Homer identified it as the site of King Minos' Palace and the scene of the Minotaur legend. Found among the ruins of the Minoan palace was a clay tablet (reference Gg 702) dating from *c.* 1400 BCE, about twenty years before the destruction of the palace, inscribed with Linear B script (an early written form of the Greek language) that records: "To Potnia of the Labyrinth [*da-pu-ri-to-jo*], 1 pitcher of honey." The offering of honey to the Potnia, the lady or goddess, is a common dedication; the interest lies in the term "*da-pu-ri-to-jo*", which is probably something like *laburinto* in modern pronunciation.[7] Assuming that the Potnia was the lady of the house, this is evidence that the building was known to its occupants as the "Labyrinth".

Despite this, there is no sign of the labyrinth symbol among the numerous finds from Knossos, or any of the other Minoan palaces on Crete. The famous labyrinth-inscribed Knossos coins date from 1,000 years later. Fragments of frescos decorated with meander patterns and recovered from the collapsed walls of the palace are the only trace of labyrinthine forms, apart from the complex arrangement of subterranean corridors, rooms, and courtyards that form the structure of the building. Such labyrinthine frescos are not unique to Knossos. A fragment with a similar pattern was discovered in the Minoan palace at Phaistos, also on Crete. Recent excavations at the Hyksos city of Avaris, in Egypt, have uncovered far better preserved frescos with the same labyrinthine patterns, this time accompanying bulls with youths leaping over their horns. This is familiar imagery at Knossos, but a surprising find in Egypt. Dating to *c.* 1550 BCE, these frescos were clearly executed by artists from Crete[8] and suggest that the combination of labyrinthine patterns and bulls, which lay at the heart of the Minotaur legend of later Greek tradition, was already well known and widespread at this time.

It is surprising among all this imagery to find no examples of the labyrinth symbol itself. The earliest example from the eastern end of the Mediterranean comes from the Mycenaean palace at Pylos in Greece. It is a doodle on the back of another Linear B tablet, this time from around 1200 BCE (see page 41). The labyrinth symbol was known much earlier than this, if the evidence of labyrinth petroglyphs dating to *c.* 2000 BCE in Spain is to be believed. Of course, it is possible that the symbol and the story were simply not connected at this time, but the labyrinth coins issued from the fourth to first centuries BCE by the Hellenic Greek settlement at Knossos, suggest that the Greeks were fully aware of the connection. The first direct evidence of a link between the symbol and the story comes from the Roman world. A labyrinth graffito at Pompeii is labelled "*Labyrinthus Hic Habitat Minotaurus*" (see page 46) and depictions of Theseus battling the Minotaur feature at the centre of numerous labyrinth mosaics (see pages 52-7). Maybe the explanation that solves this apparent conundrum still awaits discovery.

The earliest proven association of the labyrinth symbol with a physical structure, in this case a whole town, comes from the same Etruscan jar that a century ago provided the earliest example of the symbol. Found in 1877 in a tomb from the seventh century BCE at Tragliatella, near Cerveteri in Italy, it bears a small labyrinth, inscribed as part of a larger composition on the body of the jar (see page 42). The labyrinth is labelled "TRUIA", which many commentators have taken to signify the legendary city of Troy.[9] The battle for Troy and its eventual demise, famously celebrated by Homer in *The Iliad*, was probably first written down during the eighth century BCE, based on an oral tradition handed down from the very real events of five centuries earlier. Clearly the labyrinth symbol, with its single point of access leading by the longest, and therefore most defendable route to the centre, was identified with Troy at this early time. The association continued to be popular throughout the Greek and Roman worlds and later in medieval Europe, indeed anywhere where the Homeric legends were read or retold.

Knossos and Troy were not the only places linked to the labyrinth symbol. Roman writers also identified the huge temple built by Amenemhet III at Hawara, Egypt, as a labyrinth. In Christian and Jewish mythology, both Jericho and Jerusalem have taken the symbol as an emblem of the defences around the sacred city. The same symbolism is also encountered in descriptions of the fabulous palace prison of Shamaili in Afghan legend, the fabled city of Scimangada in Nepal, and several other tales from the Indian sub-continent (see Chapter 2). In Indonesia, the labyrinth is described as the abode of spirits that trouble the tribal peoples of Sumatra. As far away as the American Southwest, the symbol is presented as a plan of the pathway leading to the hidden home of the father of the tribes.

All of this may go some way to explaining the origin of the word and the early perceptions of the concept, but it still leaves unanswered the question of how the labyrinth symbol first appeared. Many theories have been advanced, but none is ultimately provable. The first person to have created the labyrinth symbol is unlikely to have recorded the fact, but simply shown it to a friend or neighbour, who, impressed by the neat drawing trick, passed it on. Nevertheless, it is interesting to try to trace the thread back to its source. So here, in no particular order of merit, are some of the theories.

The tunnels and caverns of underground cave systems have long been associated with the concept of the labyrinth. As far back as the first century BCE, the Roman writer Catullus mentions the caves at Gortyna on the island of Crete, actually an underground quarry system that provided stone for the Minoan palaces at both Knossos and Phaistos. The caverns at Gortyna were popularly thought to be the location of the legendary labyrinth until the discovery of the Minoan palace at Knossos by Arthur Evans.[10] Today the connection is hardly mentioned, but the symbolism of caves as entrances into the body of Mother Earth remains a potential explanation of the origin of the labyrinth symbol. It corresponds well with the image of the Minotaur's lair, but how such confusing tunnels could have become equated with a regular geometric symbol remains unexplained.

Labyrinthine shapes and structures also occur in nature – in the gill patterns of fungi, the folds of coral and the complex passageways of underground colonies of ants and termites. Any of these natural forms may have provided inspiration for the creator of the first

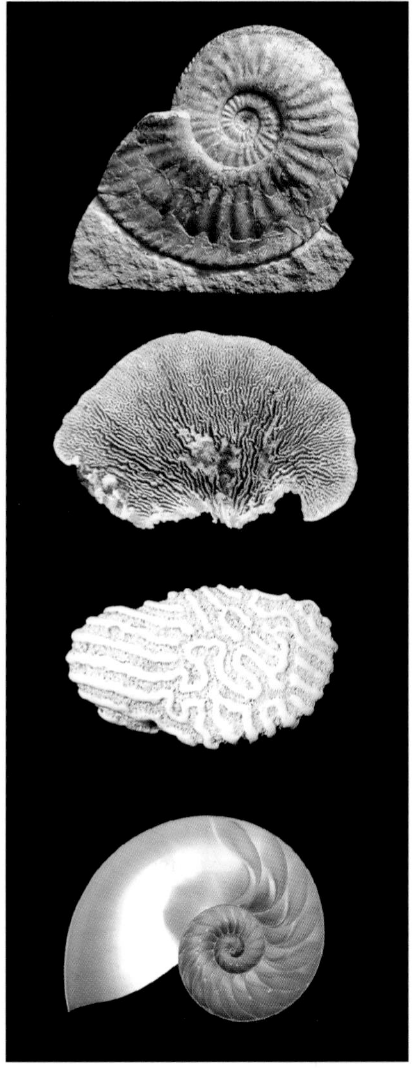

Labyrinthine and spiralling forms often occur in nature. From the top: a Jurassic *Amaltheus* ammonite; *Daedalea quercina*, the Maze-gill fungus; the folds of a *Meandrina* brain coral colony; the internal structure of the shell of *Nautilus pompilius*.

labyrinth symbol, although the transition from a random natural pattern to a geometric symbol is difficult to visualize. Early art forms are often naturalistic – the Palaeolithic cave paintings of southern Europe for instance – and while the labyrinth symbol may have been conceived to denote natural forms, it seems more likely that it was developed from other simpler geometric forms and symbols.

Spirals are among the earliest abstract symbols found in human art. Mammoth ivory, decorated with spirals by Siberian hunters some 23,000 years ago has been found at Mal'ta, near Lake Baikal, and spirals are a common symbol in primitive art around the world. They too are widespread in nature – in the coils of snail shells, ammonites and the nautilus, as well as in the radiating patterns of seed heads and pine cones. In fact the formation of the classical labyrinth symbol from the seed pattern involves little more than constructing a spiral through the points that make up the seed – or overlaying the seed with a spiral. And yet developing the precise symbol of the classical labyrinth from a simple spiral seems to be a feat that would hardly happen accidentally.

Meanders are another ancient symbol with an even closer link to the labyrinth. The earliest meander symbols are also to be found on objects of mammoth ivory from Ice Age sites in Europe and Siberia. An ivory bracelet from Mezin in the Ukraine, dated to *c.* 13,000 BCE, is covered with interlocking meanders. Similar designs on figurines of birds from the same location show a variety of repeating meander patterns. The meander and the closely related double spiral remained popular decorative elements throughout early Neolithic Europe. Their widespread use on cult objects, figurines of goddesses and animals, and models of temples from the Danube basin and the Aegean and Adriatic coastal cultures from *c.* 6000 to *c.* 3000 BCE provides other potential points of origin for the labyrinth symbol.[11]

Less obviously, the double meander, often better known as the Greek key pattern from its frequent use as a decorative border on later classical Greek pottery, is topographically identical to the classical labyrinth. Pin down one end of the double meander and swing the top corners through 180 degrees in both directions and the labyrinth is formed, as if by magic. Any craftsperson, working with meanders as decoration on pottery or basketry, and seeking to expand the symbol to fill a frame or border is likely to encounter this transformation sooner or later, either by accident or experiment. However, to date, no example of the labyrinth has been found among the preserved ceramics from the Neolithic of southern Europe.

Distinctly labyrinthine patterns occur on clay tablets and other objects dating to the second millennium BCE from Mesopotamia – modern Iraq. Divination was an important practice in the region, especially the art of extispicy, in which the internal organs of

The double meander transformed into a labyrinth. Any artist expanding the meander to fill a frame or border will inevitably discover this process; it was certainly familiar to Roman mosaic designers over 2,000 years ago.

Small clay Babylonian divination tablet from Mesopotamia (*c.*1800 BCE) inscribed with a pattern that is superficially close to the true labyrinth design, but has both entrance and exit.

sacrificial rams were inspected for distinctive features that might reveal details of the future. Explanatory tablets with depictions of the folds of the intestines are frequently likened to labyrinths, although these meandering designs invariably have both entrance and exit.

Concentric circles surrounding a central cup or depression, called "cup and ring marks", are a common feature of Neolithic rock art along the Atlantic seaboard of Europe. Indeed, such symbols occur in primitive art around the world. As far back as 1893, the German researcher Ernst Krause suggested that labyrinths evolved directly from such designs. This is a simple and attractive theory, but the concentric circles of the cup and ring marks require an offset of the axis of the labyrinth to produce a correct connection. This offset is not apparent in any of the prehistoric labyrinth petroglyphs so far discovered. Indeed, the labyrinths found in Galicia, Spain and Val Camonica, Italy, as well as others of less certain dating from elsewhere in southern Europe, the Near East and North Africa, all appear to be drawn quite perfectly from the familiar seed pattern. Once again, it is difficult to see how the labyrinth symbol could have developed and become so standardized across this vast area, if cup and rings marks had been its origin.

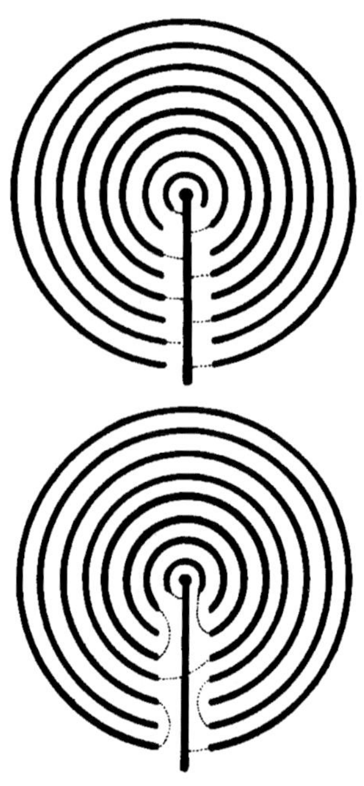

The German researcher Ernst Krause first suggested that the concentric circles of Neolithic petroglyphs could be easily re-connected to create a labyrinth; indeed the oldest known labyrinths are found among prehistoric rock art.

Petroglyghs are by nature durable, but maybe the labyrinth was more commonly employed in medium that has not survived the passage of time. Its occasional transference to rock faces or pottery may be an incidental, albeit fortunate, occurrence. The occasional juxtaposition of labyrinth symbols with figures involved in ritual activities has lead to suggestions that the labyrinth started as a dance pattern, marked on the ground with sticks or stones.

Petroglyphs from Spain and Italy hint at labyrinths as hunting magic. Riders on horseback, a procession of armed youths and copulating couples accompany the labyrinth engraved on the Etruscan jar from Tragliatella. All hint at rituals that must have taken place around the unknown labyrinth forms of prehistory. The Roman historian Virgil (70–19 BCE) records that a complex ritual of young men riding horses around the pattern of the labyrinth took place in his time, at events to honour the dead, and to celebrate the founding of cities.[12] Long before this, in Homer's *Iliad*, reference is made to "a dancing floor like unto that which in wide Knossos Daedalus fashioned of old for fair-tressed Ariadne". The description goes on to describe a dance performed by young men and maidens, holding each other's wrists, as they wound back and forth in circles with tumblers whirling up and down between them. Homer is not specific, but many have taken this to be a dance in the pattern of the labyrinth.

Later Greek historians and poets, including Callimachus (third century BCE) and Plutarch (*c.* 45–*c.* 120 CE), tell us about a dance known as the Geranos, or crane dance. It was celebrated around an altar on the island of Delos, in commemoration of the escape of Theseus from the Cretan labyrinth. Once again, lines of youths and maidens, grasping each other's wrists, or holding a rope (Ariadne's thread), would follow a dance pattern said to imitate the circling passages of the labyrinth. Today these dances have been revived to once again celebrate the story of Theseus and Ariadne. One remaining mystery surrounds the reason for this dance to be named after the crane (*Grus grus*), a large, long-legged bird of marshlands and wet fields. Although not native to Greece, breeding in Asia Minor and Northern Europe, cranes do pass through the region on migration and occasionally stop off in spring, when their remarkable mating dance may be witnessed. A pair of birds will circle each other, calling loudly, and with leaps and bows toss sticks into the air above their heads. Perhaps the labyrinth symbol was somehow conceived to replicate the circling dance pattern of the cranes.

Dances in imitation of animal and bird courtship were once common in this region and many survived into Greek tradition.[13] The Geranos may have originated in the earliest civilizations in the region; votive statuettes of long-necked bird goddesses, decorated with meander patterns, were common among the prehistoric cultures of the Danube basin and the Aegean coasts.[14] Among the curious figures surrounding one of the labyrinth petroglyphs at Val Camonica (see page 40) is a bird, possibly a crane, and two figures wearing plumed cloaks and pointed masks, holding sticks aloft – perhaps an early depiction of a ritual crane dance around the circuits of the labyrinth. Such ceremonies, passed on by oral tradition and then lost, remain a mystery, but some of the earliest labyrinth depictions do hint at a heritage of dances and rituals across prehistoric southern Europe.

Other theories have linked the coils of the labyrinth with the complex movements of the sun and the planets against the background of the sky.[15] Explaining the looping paths of the planets, especially Mercury, taxed the mind of many learned astronomers from the time of the Greeks onward. The similarity of the concentric paths of the later medieval labyrinth designs to the successive shells of the Ptolemaic universe was certainly not lost on medieval scholars (see page 90), but none of these celestial patterns quite replicates the outline of the labyrinth. They may provide a correspondence to modern eyes, but there is no contemporary evidence to suggest that this might be the source of the symbol.

Perhaps, after all, the labyrinth started life as a simple drawing trick to scratch in the dust and pass on to others in awe of your skill. Whatever the truth, the successive layers of meaning and tradition that the labyrinth has accrued, like the encircling pathways that guard the secret at its core, have carried this simple symbol to new lands, for new purposes, for four millennia or more.

Terminology and Definitions

In dealing with a subject as varied and complex as labyrinths and mazes, it is essential to be clear about termminology and definitions. The first task is to clarify the difference between a labyrinth and a maze. While the two terms are often used interchangeably, historians and enthusiasts are often passionate about which is which. If you look up the words in a good dictionary, you will probably conclude that a maze is a labyrinth and a labyrinth is a maze. The *Oxford English Dictionary* gives the following definitions.

"Maze: a network of paths and hedges designed as a puzzle for those who try to penetrate it; a complex network of paths or passages; a labyrinth. (From Middle English, originally as *mased* (adj.): related to amaze: surprise greatly; overwhelm with wonder, from Old English *amasian*, of uncertain origin.)"

"Labyrinth: a complicated irregular network of passages or paths etc.; an intricate or tangled arrangement; a maze. (From French *labyrinthe* or Latin *labyrinthus*, from Greek *labyrinthos*, in earliest use referring to the maze constructed by Daedalus in Greek Mythology to house the Minotaur.)"

From this source it would seem that no real difference exists between the two. Yet across the modern English speaking world, and especially in Britain and America, complex puzzle designs are commonly referred to as mazes and simpler single-path designs are popularly known as labyrinths. Throughout much of the non-English-speaking world, no such distinction exists. Practically every maze mentioned in this book would be called a "labyrinth", for the word "maze" is a peculiarly English word of medieval origin that refers to a state of confusion. Clearly, to be confused, let alone amazed, there must be some element of choice in the pathway that you are trying to follow, some opportunity for bewilderment. Many current commentators within the field have taken this as a point of definition: to qualify as a maze, a design must have choices in the pathway.

Clearly, this category will include many of the modern installations in entertainment parks and tourist attractions, which exist solely for the purpose of perplexing visitors, as well as the traditional hedges mazes in public parks and private gardens around the world. But what are we to make of the plans of the earliest documented hedge

Maze definition
To qualify as a maze, a design must have choices in the pathway. (Hedge maze, Williamsburg, USA)

mazes? Many of these were planted to designs in early printed books and on the floors of cathedrals, which have but one path that leads inexorably from the entrance to the goal, albeit by the most complex and winding of routes.

These designs were known at the time of their creation as "labyrinths", a term that had been in circulation for several thousand years; they were a development of simpler labyrinth designs that likewise had been in existence for millennia. All these designs have just a single path, however confusing its twists and turns might seem. This has also been taken as a definition: to qualify as a labyrinth a design should have but one path. Though the dividing line between what constitutes a maze or a labyrinth can sometimes become blurred, by and large these definitions apply throughout this book.

Labyrinth definition
To qualify as a labyrinth, a design should have but one path.(Pavement labyrinth, Sens Cathedral, France)

While this debate is easily resolved, much more heated discussion has surrounded attempts to establish a workable system of classification for different types of labyrinths and mazes. The development of mathematics and scientific classification since the time of the Renaissance has not only provided a framework for the analysis of design styles, but also driven the development of the current generation of puzzle mazes.

As early as 1736, the Swiss mathematician Leonhard Euler published his studies of simple maze puzzles and explained the rules for solving them. His famous "Seven Bridges of Königsberg" puzzle is a classic example. Further studies during the nineteenth century by mathematicians and maze designers including William Hamilton, Earl Stanhope, and Lewis Carroll, introduced new principles for maze design, with increasing levels of complexity, many of which are commonplace in today's installations.[16] In 1922 W.H. Matthews attempted to analyse the structure of mazes according to how the pathways were connected, and established the terms "unicursal" (single-path) and "multi-cursal" (many-pathed) to distinguish labyrinths from mazes.

During the second half of the twentieth century various systems have been proposed to define the individual forms of labyrinths and mazes. They were often either over-simple or over-complicated and confusing to the general reader.[17] The system used in this book relies largely on the structural differences of labyrinths, classified according to their cultural origin, and the structural complexity of mazes. The next section of the book offers a guide to the different design categories and their construction.

Labyrinth Classification

The classical labyrinth is simply constructed from an easily remembered seed pattern (see page 16), a trick that has clearly been instrumental in its wide dissemination. This is by far the world's commonest form of labyrinth, and remains popular to this day. Simple amendments to the seed pattern allow different versions of this form to be created quickly and easily and such varieties, often with eleven or fifteen circuits, are common in northern Europe and especially in Scandinavia. Several variants used in historical contexts are distinctive enough to deserve sub-categories of their own.

Circular and square varieties of the classical labyrinth design. Mirror image forms will result in the first pathway turning either left or right. Both forms are common and may simply be a consequence of the handedness of the creator.

The Classical Labyrinth

The archetypal labyrinth design consists of a single pathway that loops back and forth to form seven circuits, bounded by eight walls, surrounding the central goal. It is found in both circular and square forms, without structural design differences. As only the method of execution is different, the two styles do not justify separate classification. Practically all labyrinths prior to the first few centuries BCE are of this type. Found throughout Europe, North Africa, the Indian sub-continent, and Indonesia, this is also the design that occurs in the American Southwest and occasionally in South America.

The form is often inappropriately known as the "Cretan labyrinth",[18] a term that implies an origin on the island of Crete. Although its subsequent association with the legendary labyrinth at Knossos is well documented, the design certainly predates the legend and has not been found at Knossos prior to the fourth century BCE.

The classical labyrinth is also known as the "seven-circuit labyrinth" among modern writers, especially in America. This too is confusing, for other labyrinth types can have seven paths and classical labyrinths may occasionally have more or fewer than seven. The term "classical" has gained widespread acceptance in recent years and is to be preferred, as it correctly implies the original form and is free from association with any particular location or region – appropriate for a design that is found worldwide.

Classical Baltic

Found throughout Scandinavia and also in northern Germany, but principally around the shorelines of the Baltic Sea, this labyrinth is also known as the "Baltic Wheel" or "Wheel", after an important example in Hanover, Germany (see page 131). A relatively simple reconnection of the upper part of the classical seed pattern produces a double spiral at the centre with separate entrance and exit paths. These labyrinths are ideal for continuous processions and games where two or more walkers enter the labyrinth, and this purpose is often reflected in associated traditions and folklore.

A Baltic type labyrinth cut in turf on the Dransberg hill at Dransfeld, Germany. The double spiral at the centre allows a quick exit from the labyrinth.

The stone labyrinth at Baire Gauni, near Chinnakottur in Tamil Nadu, India, is laid out in the Chakra-vyūha style commonly encountered throughout India.

Classical Chakra-Vyūha

An unusual development of the classical labyrinth, found primarily in India, is based on a three-fold, rather than a four-fold seed pattern and is often drawn with a spiral at the centre. It is referred to in Indian tradition as Chakra-vyūha, a magical troop formation created to ensure victory at the battle of Kurukshetra in the *Mahābhārata* epic (see page 61). Occurring in a number of forms, it is frequently encountered in magical documents, as a charm for protection during childbirth.

Other Classical Labyrinths

Other labyrinths based on three-fold and occasionally on two-fold or five-fold seed patterns are found in various locations. A unique five-fold classical labyrinth with nine circuits recently discovered on a Pima basket from Arizona[19] demonstrates the many varieties of labyrinth that can be created with a full understanding of the construction process. A number of labyrinths with blundered designs, including errors created by unskilled hands, should also be included in this category.

A Pima handwoven basket, made *c.* 1910, decorated with an unusual nine-path variant of the classical design created from a five-fold seed pattern.

Roman Labyrinths

A typical Roman labyrinth design of the simple meander type, laid in the early fourth century CE at Harpham, England.

While the classical labyrinth was known throughout the Roman Empire, the popular use of the labyrinth as a design element in mosaic flooring resulted in a number of developments, all classifiable as "Roman" varieties. These labyrinths are of considerable interest as they represent the first real attempts to create new forms of the genre and the first major changes to a symbol that had already been in circulation for nearly 2,000 years. Several researchers have attempted classifications of Roman designs, based on their mathematical[20] or geometrical[21] properties.

Daszewski's categories are by far the most practical for popular use and allow the majority of the sixty or so Roman labyrinths to be designated as meander, serpentine, or spiral types. The meander is actually formed from four classical labyrinths (although sometimes other numbers are employed) reduced to a quarter of their normal area and subsequently rejoined to form a continuous labyrinth with a distinctive four-fold symmetry. Kraft further divides meander forms into simple and complex types, although the construction principal remains the same. Similar labyrinths with their individual quadrants composed of serpentine or spiralling pathways form the basis of the serpentine and spiral varieties (see page 50).

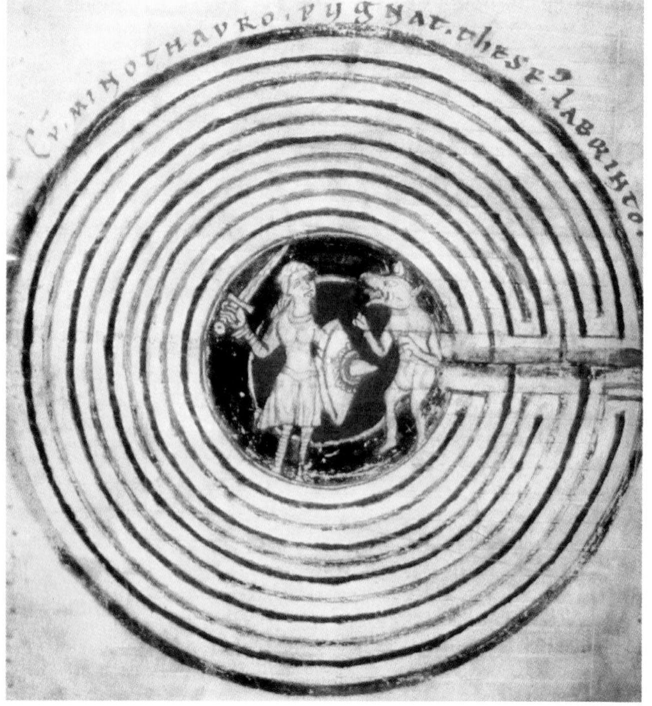

The Otfrid labyrinth design, here showing the battle between Theseus and the Minotaur, in a late twelfth-century manuscript from Regensburg, Germany.

The Otfrid Labyrinth

An important though short-lived labyrinth form, the Otfrid is based on the classical seed pattern, but with an additional set of turns inserted to create an eleven-circuit labyrinth. First found in a Christian manuscript compiled by Otfrid of Weissenburg during the ninth century CE (see page 87), this design probably provided the impetus for the development of the much more influential medieval design.

The Medieval Labyrinth

First developed during the ninth century CE, the medieval labyrinth combined the eleven circuits of the Otfrid labyrinth with the four-fold symmetry of the Roman labyrinth to produce a design better suited for use in a Christian context. By the twelfth century this form was common in manuscripts and began to appear in the decoration of churches and cathedrals in Italy. Spreading to France in the thirteenth century, it soon became the principal form throughout much of southern and western Europe. The famous use of this labyrinth at Chartres Cathedral has led many writers to term this design the "Chartres" labyrinth. For exact replicas of the labyrinth at Chartres, this term is acceptable, although inappropriate otherwise, as this design was in widespread circulation long before it was employed at Chartres. Although others have used the term "medieval Christian", "medieval" accurately portrays the context of this labyrinth, and does not exclude those examples that appear in secular contexts.

An ornate form of the medieval labyrinth, as inlaid in the floor of Chartres Cathedral, France, *c.* 1205.

The turf labyrinth at Boughton Green, England, had a basic medieval design with various changes to the circuits and the centre replaced by a spiral.

Medieval Varieties

As with the classical labyrinth, a considerable number of variations on the basic theme of the medieval labyrinth have been recorded. Circular, square, and polygonal forms are common and need no separate classification. Some examples display deliberate attempts to produce a different design – with more or fewer circuits, different methods of connecting the pathways, or alterations to fit available space or a specific purpose. Others are clearly the result of incorrect construction or inaccurate restorations of previous designs. This is especially the case with turf labyrinths, which are prone to deterioration.

The current revival of interest in the medieval labyrinth, especially in America since the mid-1990s, has resulted in the development of a number of new variations, often with fewer circuits to enable them to fit confined locations. Some are based directly on the labyrinth in Chartres Cathedral and many have been given specific names by their creators, but most of these titles exist primarily to establish copyright.

Medieval St Omer

One particular medieval group deserves separate recognition – the St Omer labyrinth. Its pathway seems to be a random meandering design, although it can be proved that the pattern was developed from the standard medieval form.[22] The original example constructed in the fourteenth century at the Abbey of St Bertin in St Omer, northern France, was copied and further developed on several occasions and has proved popular again in the nineteenth and twentieth centuries.

The St Omer pavement labyrinth.

Maze Classification

With a history stretching back to the late Middle Ages, puzzle mazes, like labyrinths, were simple at first, then underwent periods of rapid development. While various types of mazes have been proposed and described by modern authorities,[23] five basic types can be clearly identified.

A simply connected maze design with limited choice of paths, planted at Krenkerup, Denmark, in 1877.

Simply-Connected Mazes

Developed as they were from medieval labyrinth designs, the earliest mazes were made by rearranging the walls of a labyrinth to create a pathway with choices, often including a number of dead-ends or blind alleys, as well as a path that leads eventually to the goal. The most important part of a maze are the walls that contain the paths. For the majority of early mazes, and many recent examples, however complex the design may appear, the maze is formed with one continuous wall that has many junctions and branches. If the wall surrounding the goal is connected to the perimeter of the maze at the entrance, the maze can be solved by always keeping one hand in contact with the wall, however many detours that may involve. These "simple" mazes are correctly known as "simply-connected".

Multiply-Connected Mazes

At the height of their popularity between the sixteenth and eighteenth centuries, many complex mazes were created, but the majority were simply-connected. It was not until the early nineteenth century that the principle of isolating the goal of the maze from the perimeter to defeat the "hand-on-wall" method and increase the level of difficulty was truly understood (see page 164). Any maze with the goal set within an island of barriers, physically unconnected to the rest of the maze, qualifies as multiply-connected. The best examples contain islands within islands and, paradoxically, can be developed into very intricate mazes with very few dead-ends that are nonetheless extremely difficult to solve. This principle has been eagerly developed by modern maze designers (see Chapter 6), and many professional installations are now of this type.

The hedge maze planted during the 1820s at Chevening House, England, was one of the first consciously designed to provide a more complex puzzle and thwart the "hand-on-wall" rule.

A modern three-dimensional wooden panel maze at Labyrinthia, Denmark.

Three-Dimensional Mazes

Although the majority of traditional puzzle mazes with walls of hedging plants or other materials appear three-dimensional, the pathway running through the maze is essentially only two-dimensional, even if the maze contains raised mounds or platforms. While the concept of truly three-dimensional mazes has been around since the nineteenth century, they existed only on paper until the early 1980s, with the introduction of bridges to add complexity and interest to the panel mazes then common in New Zealand, Australia and Japan.[24] Bridges are also a common addition to the huge maize mazes that have become popular since the mid-1990s. The introduction of a third dimension allows the islands of a multiply- connected maze to be totally isolated from each other, with the only link via a bridge (or underpass). In some mazes, successful progress to the goal depends on reaching a series of points within the maze in the correct order.

A conditional movement maze. The object of Steve Ryan's "Freeway Maze" is to enter the intersection and exit on the opposite return carriageway without making any U-turns and avoiding the stalled cars (red spots) blocking a number of routes.

Conditional Movement Mazes

Long established as a theoretical concept, mazes with rules – conditional movement mazes – have become a reality since the 1980s. The next move is dictated by the overall rules or by instructions given at the visitor's current position, allowing extremely complex puzzles to occupy a very limited space. Often constructed in modern materials, these mazes can offer an entertaining intellectual challenge and have proved popular in educational contexts, particularly to illustrate complex mathematical and scientific concepts.

Interactive Mazes

High-tech mazes where the design responds to the actions of visitors are an increasingly common feature at amusement parks and other tourist attractions. They often incorporate computer-timed barriers and other innovative devices such as motion sensors and mechanisms that determine the physical characteristics of the walker. Interactive mazes first appeared in the closing years of the twentieth century and no doubt herald future leading-edge maze design.

The Darwin Maze at Edinburgh Zoo, Scotland, contains many interactive features installed along the seemingly simple paths.

Chapter I

Ancient Origins

Thousands of years ago, hunters on remote hillsides in southern Europe, scribes in palaces, and artisans in workshops around the shores of the Mediterranean Sea began to scratch a simple symbol on rocks and pottery. The knowledge of how to draw this symbol was passed on, from person to person, from one settlement to the next. In time it would become associated with some of the greatest structures of prehistoric Europe, the Near East, and northern Africa. The labyrinth, as it was known in ancient Greece and the Roman Empire, soon became a common device across southern Europe. The first two thousand years of labyrinth history is often mysterious and difficult to trace, but is littered with fascinating artefacts each marked with this characteristic symbol.

The labyrinth symbol, one of a pair carved on a rockface in Rocky Valley, England. While the labyrinth design is thousands of years old, dating rock carvings of this type is often very difficult.

To find the oldest examples of the labyrinth symbol we must look for them on a medium that can survive for thousands of years without relying on exceptional circumstances for preservation. Labyrinths laid on the ground, carved on wood, painted on skins, or woven into fabrics are unlikely to have endured. But by carving on stone and moving rocks to create monuments, the Neolithic artists of Europe have ensured the survival of their art and invention.

Prehistory: Petroglyphs and Artefacts

While the celebrated cave paintings of Palaeolithic Europe are essentially pictographic art, the art forms of the Neolithic are far more abstract. The animals and hunting scenes are still present, but spirals, interlocking and concentric circles, and geometric designs predominate, carved on rocks, boulders, and construction stones. This rock art – called petroglyphs – is found along the Atlantic coastline from Scandinavia, down through the British Isles and Brittany to the Iberian Peninsular and out to the Canary Islands. Extending into the Mediterranean, comparable styles are found on the western Mediterranean islands and also in the valleys leading into the Italian Alps. In the Bronze Age the abstract symbols and hunting scenes of earlier times gradually give way to images of weapons and warfare. Carvings incorporating depictions of daggers and axes reflect the new metal-working technologies.

Almost identical symbols occur at different locations, but they do not necessarily date from the same time. Carvings inside burial structures, such as the passage tombs of Carrowmore, Loughcrew, and the Boyne Valley in Ireland can be dated securely to the same period, though in some cases carvings are appropriated into later monuments. Open-air carvings on rock outcrops are far more difficult to date and could stem from various episodes of activity. The earliest examples of rock art can be placed around 3500 BCE; other examples, especially those in Italy, are dated as recently as 500 BCE.

The design of spirals carved on to the entrance stone of the passage tomb at Newgrange, Ireland, is one of the finest examples of Neolithic rock art. It is dated to *c.* 3200 BCE.

Cup and ring carvings, such as these at Achnabreck in Argyll, Scotland, dating from the Neolithic or early Bronze Age, can often appear very labyrinthine in form.

Recent research points to petroglyphs of Neolithic and early Bronze Age Europe as the most plausible source of the first labyrinth symbols. This idea is not new. Various writers have pointed out the similarity between the ubiquitous "cup and ring" designs of this period and the pattern of the classical labyrinth. Whether one form evolved from the other, or whether the labyrinth symbol was developed separately, remains unclear. Conflicting dates and interpretations, and the limitations of precision that apply to dating rock art make looking for the "first labyrinth" a difficult task.

One contender for first labyrinth symbol is incised on an inner chamber wall of the Neolithic tomb known as Tomba del Labirinto at Luzzanas, Sardinia. It is often dated with the construction of the tomb to *c.* 2500–2000 BCE. Cut into soft stone and known locally as *domus de janus* (fairy houses), such burial chambers are widespread in Sardinia. They are sometimes decorated with reliefs of bulls' heads or architectural features. A rock-cut tomb at S. Andrea Priu, carved to resemble the interior of a traditional wooden building, is cut into a cliff face beneath a life-sized statue of a bull. The careful decoration in these tombs, created by hammering and scraping with stone tools, is quite unlike the hastily scratched lines of the Luzzanas labyrinth. This was probably engraved with a metal tool, as was the later Roman graffiti also found in these tombs. Some believe that the Luzzanas labyrinth was inspired by the Minotaur myth and dates from the same time as these graffiti. Until a scientific technique for dating graffiti is developed we will not know whether it is Roman or Neolithic; 2,000 or 4,000 years old.

The labyrinth graffito inscribed on the wall of the Tomba del Labirinto at Luzzanas, Sardinia. Its dating is uncertain, but it could be of Roman origin.

The labyrinth-inscribed Hollywood Stone from County Wicklow in Ireland (see page 83), often claimed to date from *c.* 2000 BCE, is surely early Christian or even medieval. Close study of the incised lines forming this labyrinth, carved on a granite boulder, betrays the use of a metal chisel, something that did not exist 4,000 years ago. Likewise, two sharply incised labyrinths carved into a soft slate outcrop in Rocky Valley in Cornwall, England, are described on an official plaque attached to the rock face as: "Early Bronze Age, 1800–1400 BCE". This dating was attributed in the late 1940s on the grounds that the carvings resembled Bronze Age carvings elsewhere in Britain. The local historian responsible hoped to prove prehistoric links between Cornwall and the Mediterranean. The carvings are to be found behind the ruins of an eighteenth-century mill, abandoned by the 1880s. Several inscriptions are carved into the stonework, mostly names and dates of the mill's owners. The curious location, and the lack of wear to the carvings on a stone prone to weathering, strongly suggest that the labyrinths are no more than 250 years old.[1]

The smaller of the two labyrinths on a rockface behind Trewethett Mill in Rocky Valley, England. They probably date from the eighteenth or nineteenth century CE.

There are always problems associated with dating isolated rock inscriptions. Without accompanying archaeological evidence, text, or other symbols nearby to provide clues, a classical labyrinth on its own could date from any period. Most dating techniques are based on how designs and symbols change over time – but of course, this form of the labyrinth never changes.

loses the sharp edges and marks of the carving tool, until a design carved hundreds of years ago looks no different from one carved thousands of years ago.

The labyrinth carved on the Pedra do Labrinto near San Xurzo de Mogor, Spain, is accompanied by the ubiquitous concentric cup and ring motifs.

However, labyrinth petroglyphs of genuine prehistoric origin are to be found in Europe, their antiquity proven by their association with other undoubtedly ancient symbols. Perhaps the most exciting of these are the collection of labyrinths and labyrinthine designs on rock outcrops in the provinces of Pontevedra and Vigo, along the coastline of Galicia in northwest Spain.

A perfectly drawn labyrinth with a deep cup-like depression at its centre on the aptly named Pedra do Labrinto near San Xurxo de Mogor, Marín, is accompanied by a number of concentric "cup and ring" marks. This is one of the most distinctive symbols to appear on these ancient rock art panels. Nearby is another labyrinth on an outcrop known as the Pedra dos Campiños. It is flawless in design, though the remainder of the slab has been removed by quarrying and we do not know what carvings accompanied the labyrinth. The Pedra do Outeiro do Cribo at S María de Armenteira, near Meis, was only discovered in 1979 and is better preserved. Here the labyrinth accompanies three stags. A rider on horseback on the same outcrop is a later addition, obviously carved with a metal tool.

A labyrinth on the Pedra do Outeiro do Cribo, at Santa Maria de Armenteira, is adjacent to deer with imposing antlers. The rider on horseback is a later addition.

Labyrinthine designs appear on several rock art panels in this region. They are close enough to perfect labyrinths to be interpreted as failed attempts to construct one, perhaps by someone not wholly familiar with the technique. Or they may represent "prototypes", in an exercise to establish the design. Two such designs occur adjacent to a magnificent stag on the Laxa de Rotea de Mendo at Campo Lameiro. Both appear unfinished, as if they were abortive attempts to make the correct pattern. Two more, at the Outeiro das Laxes rock art site at Vilaboa, are much closer to the correct form, with looping paths that fail to connect around the centre. The extensive rock art site at Parada, near San Isidro de Montes, swarms with deer and stags, and mixed in among them are five labyrinths, some more successfully drawn than others.

The association of a number of these Galician labyrinths with carvings of deer is of great interest. The prehistoric inhabitants of this area obviously hunted in the hills where many of these carvings are found beside paths still used by the livestock that roam the area today. The deer carved on the rock outcrops, sometimes accompanied by lines of carved hoof prints, skirt around the circular motifs and labyrinths in the same manner that the animal tracks in the landscape skirt the pools and bogs in the valleys below. The correspondence between the symbolism of the rock art and the landscape is striking, though by no means a literal map. The petroglyphs seem to be hunter's art, magical symbols for the hunt.[2] Perhaps the labyrinth symbolized a place to trap prey or treacherous ground to be avoided.

Archaeologists cataloguing rock art sites in the region have recently discovered another perfectly drawn example at Chan do Rei, near Marzán, and a fascinating example on the outcrop known as Pedra Escrita, near Burgueira, which has been defaced with Christian crosses in historic times. Compare this with a labyrinth-inscribed stone built into the wall of a twelfth-century chapel at Arcera, on the north coast of Spain (see page 84), which may have been an earlier inscription simply reused as building stone. The central cross of the Arcera labyrinth shows signs of later emphasizing in an attempt to "Christianize" the symbol. It seems that the same fate was suffered by the symbol on the Pedra Escrita.

For many years the Galician labyrinths have been ascribed to the late Bronze or early Iron Age. This dating was arrived at by comparing them with the labyrinths at Val Camonica in the Italian Alps, dated to *c.* 750–500 BCE. However, recent reappraisal suggests an earlier date for the rock art of Galicia.[3] The discovery of rock art panels overlaid by other datable features has provided valuable clues. The analysis of objects, tools, and weapons appearing among the symbols also allows comparison with similar objects found in securely datable burial sites nearby. The conclusion is that the rock art of Galicia belongs to the late Neolithic and early Bronze Age. This places these labyrinths somewhere during the late third or the early second millennium BCE and makes them the earliest examples currently known. They could well be as much as a thousand years older than any labyrinth that can be confidently dated.

The labyrinths that occur on the extensive rock art panels at Val Camonica in northern Italy are far better known than those in Galicia, largely due to the efforts of Emmanuel Anati. His pioneering work to record the 15,000 or more carvings that decorate numerous rock outcrops along the sides of this Alpine valley started in 1956 and continues. At least three true labyrinths have been found and a further three derivatives have been recorded. The majority are found around Capo di Ponte; the example at Luine is situated further south near Boario. These labyrinth petroglyphs are attributed to the early Iron Age, c. 750–500 BCE.[4] However, the complex juxtaposition of carvings that range from the Neolithic to later Etruscan and Roman periods makes it difficult to be certain of the carving sequence for many of the rock surfaces in Val Camonica.

The extensive petroglyph panel at Parada, near San Isidro de Montes, contains five labyrinths, some more accurately carved than others.

Recently discovered on an outcrop known as Pedra Escrita, near Burgueira, is this ancient labyrinth, which has been defaced in more recent times with Christian crosses. Similar superstitious "conversions" of pre-Christian symbols are known from other petroglyph sites in Europe.

The best known of the labyrinths appears among the 800 or more carvings on the extensive rock face at Naquane. This labyrinth is unusual, for instead of showing the walls, it is the pathway that is carved into the rock. Surrounding the labyrinth, and possibly carved in context with it, are an animal (a sheep or pig), a long-legged bird (a crane or heron), and three warriors. One warrior holds a spear and shield, the other two are fighting with swords above their heads and wearing strange plumed costumes. A line drawn from the centre of the labyrinth points directly to these two figures. What ritual or dance is being played out here and what is its connection with the labyrinth? As with so much of the symbolism contained in this ancient rock art, we can only guess. Above the labyrinth is a number of "paddles", of a style dated to the sixth century BCE. Anati and others claim to see a pair of eyes at the centre of the labyrinth. Another figure, in a helmet, overlaps the lower left portion of the paths, but it is difficult to say which carving was made first. The perfect preservation of many of these carvings on rocks, ground and polished by glaciers, allows us to see each mark made by tools and hammer stones. It seems that they were soon covered by overgrowth, otherwise erosion would have dulled the detail.

The well-known labyrinth petroglyph at Naquane in Val Camonica, Italy, is unusual in that the pathway of the labyrinth is depicted, rather than its walls. The labyrinth is surrounded by animals and warriors.

The labyrinth on the rock face at Campanine, carefully inscribed with an obvious seed pattern at its core, is accompanied by several carvings of axe heads, two of which appear to frame the entrance to the labyrinth. Another, at Luine, faces upwards, and is accompanied by two figures holding a spear and axes. Two labyrinths at Zurla are poorly drawn attempts to represent the pathway of the labyrinth, not the walls. The larger example is above a figure with raised arms, the second, smaller labyrinthine design appears unfinished. A crowd of warriors surrounds the final example at Dos del Merichi, also labyrinthine in design rather than a true labyrinth. Once again the path is depicted, but the lines near the entrance meander wildly. Is this an unsuccessful attempt at drawing the design, or just a more free-form interpretation? Zanettin's rendition of the design[5] suggests that the line of the path issues from the shield or bow held by a running figure to the left of the field: several warriors with huge spears stand to the upper right. This whole panel shows remarkable animation and portrays a vivid battle scene.

At Dos del Merichi a labyrinthine motif is clearly associated with a crowd of warriors brandishing spears and axes. How the labyrinth relates to this battle scene is open to interpretation.

Most of the Val Camonica labyrinths accompany depictions of warriors in battle, real or ritual, with spears, swords, and shields from the later Bronze or Iron Age. This is a marked contrast with the labyrinths in Galicia, where most accompany depictions of wild animals. Perhaps this represents a different purpose for the labyrinth in the two communities or a different date of origin.

Despite the apparent popularity of the labyrinth with the rock artists of Val Camonica and Galicia, the design has so far not been found elsewhere along the Atlantic seaboard. However, a labyrinth petroglyph has been reported at a rock-art site north of Taouz in southeastern Morocco.[6] Several other labyrinths may exist at other sites around Taouz, but further research is needed to confirm this. Carvings of chariots, which are usually dated among the rock art of the region to *c.* 500–200 BCE, accompany the confirmed labyrinth.

A labyrinth appears among other motifs, dated to *c.* 500–200 BCE, at a rock art site near Taouz in Morocco. This is possibly the earliest record of the labyrinth in North Africa.

While the labyrinths carved on the rock faces provide tantalizing clues to the early origins and purposes of the labyrinth motif, they offer little evidence that can securely date them. For more accurately datable labyrinths, we must turn to the work of archaeologists,[7] who have discovered a number of labyrinths scratched or painted on pottery and other objects that they have excavated. With radiocarbon dating, items found in sealed tombs or accompanying burials, where organic material is found, can be dated to within a narrow window of time. For labyrinths scratched as graffiti on buildings, the history of the building can often provide valuable clues.

The earliest example of the labyrinth symbol so far discovered, for which an accurate date can be determined, comes from southern Greece. It is on the reverse of a clay tablet from the Mycenaean palace at Pylos, the traditional home of King Nestor, who with Menelaus raised the fleet of "long black ships" to assist in the siege and subsequent downfall of Troy. Found in 1957 during excavation of the storerooms of the palace, it was one among the many hundreds of similar tablets that had been preserved by being baked in the fire that destroyed the palace *c.* 1200 BCE. These clay tablets were the means by which the palace accounts were kept, recording deliveries of goods, sales of produce, and demands for tributes and supplies from the surrounding province. The front of the labyrinth tablet is inscribed with Linear B text, an early ideographic script used throughout the Mycenaean world between the sixteenth and twelfth centuries BCE, and records the names of ten men, followed by the ideograms for one or two goats. Presumably it records the delivery of goats to the palace during the course of one day. The square labyrinth scratched on the reverse is a doodle, executed during an idle moment when there were no more goats to be recorded. The construction of the labyrinth is quite perfect, so much so that it is difficult to discern how the scribe started the design, although it seems likely that the central cross and angles were scratched first.

The oldest securely datable labyrinth so far discovered is inscribed on a clay tablet, found in the ruins of the Mycenaean palace at Pylos in southern Greece. This doodle was created by an unknown scribe around 1200 BCE.

The association of the labyrinth symbol with a tablet inscribed with Linear B script is of interest. Written records, in cuneiform script, first appear in ancient Mesopotamia around 3200 BCE, and hieroglyphics appeared in Egypt around 3100 BCE. But it was not until around 1800 BCE that writing was first used in the Bronze Age world of Minoan and Mycenaean Greece, initially in Linear A and then Linear B script, as increasing trade necessitated the keeping of accounts and records. As a test of drawing skill, a trick transcending language differences to be taught to a fellow trader in a distant port, it is easy to see how the labyrinth symbol might have become widespread by the time the unknown bookkeeper at Pylos drew it to pass the time of day. The labyrinth was probably seen as an amusement; later civilizations imbued it with deeper significance.

Another frequently nominated candidate for the earliest-dated example of the labyrinth is the pair of labyrinth-decorated pottery fragments excavated in 1960 at Tell Rifa'at in Syria. Although found at a level dated to about 1200 BCE, the excavation notes record that these sherds were "out of place, provenance disturbed". The two fragments form much of the lower half of a small bowl, originally about 6 in (15 cm) high. The bowl is wheel-made and of good quality, although the decoration is relatively crude and hand-painted in matt black. The two labyrinths on the bowl are both damaged, but the best preserved was drawn from the familiar seed pattern (see page 16). A horse and some curious figures that have been interpreted as imitations of Syriac or Arabic letters accompany them. If these are imitations of writing, the bowl cannot date to the Bronze Age. Without further scientific testing of the pottery it is impossible to rule out a later date – there is certainly Roman disturbance on the site.

Two labyrinths are painted on this bowl found during excavations at Tell Rifa'at in Syria. Often dated to *c.*1200 BCE, the bowl may be of Roman origin.

A secure date can be provided, however, for a pair of labyrinth graffitos scratched on a building excavated at Gordion, Turkey, capital of the ancient kingdom of Phrygia and burial place of King Midas. The back wall of the building, which was erected *c.* 750 BCE, was soon covered in a variety of graffiti, including warriors, houses, dogs, several birds, and two labyrinths. The larger example shows obvious drawing errors due to hasty construction. Later activity obstructed the back wall and the subsequent destruction and collapse of the building, around 690 BCE, fortuitously preserved these doodles, created by folk with time on their hands.

The labyrinth graffito scratched on a wall among the ruins of Gordion in Turkey can be securely dated to *c.*750 BCE.

The depiction of a labyrinth on a wine jar discovered in 1877 in an Etruscan tomb at Tragliatella, Italy, dating from *c.* 660–630 BCE, is well known and has been much debated. The incised decoration that runs around the vessel shows a complex scene of characters making offerings, a row of armed youths, two copulating couples, and armed soldiers on horseback running from a labyrinth with the word "TRVIA" inscribed in the outermost circuit. Conflicting interpretations have been given for the decoration on this vessel. One[8] suggests that it depicts the judgement of Paris, son of the Trojan King Priam, handing an apple to Aphrodite in return for Helen – the small figure standing between them with the label "MI VELENA" ("this Helen"). It was the abduction of Helen, the most beautiful woman in the world, that sparked the Trojan War. The war is symbolized by the warriors on foot and horseback, and the city of Troy ("Truia") by the

Dating from the mid-seventh century BCE, the body of the Tragliatella vase is inscribed with a complex collection of characters making offerings, two copulating couples, a row of armed youths, and two soldiers on horseback riding away from a labyrinth inscribed with the word "TRVIA" in the outermost circuit. Originally scratched through the applied slip, the design is now only faintly visible. The interpretation of this extraordinary scene has been the subject of much debate.

Silver coins minted at Knossos between 300 and 70 BCE. A number of interesting variants of the classical labyrinth symbol are found among this extensive series of issues, produced by the Hellenic trading settlement that was established on the site of the legendary labyrinth.

labyrinth in the distance. An alternative reading[9] equates the scene with the story of Theseus. This time the figures represent Ariadne and her nurse presenting the clew of thread to Theseus before he sets off into the labyrinth to kill the Minotaur. The remaining figures presumably represent Athenian youths. The label "Truia" is explained as a derivation of the Latin verb *amptruare*, here meaning "arena". Another view[10] interprets the ceremony as an enactment of the *Ludus Trojæ* (Game of Troy), a theatrical ritual carried out at funerals and the founding of fortifications and settlements, described in detail by Virgil six centuries after this pitcher was made. This popular connection between the labyrinth and the fortifications of Troy (and indeed other fabled cities) has continued throughout the history of the symbol in Europe.

Without doubt the most familiar labyrinths from antiquity are those on the bronze and silver coins minted at Knossos. Nearly a thousand years after the Minoan palace complex had been razed by earthquakes and fire, the Hellenic settlement at Knossos started to issue coins *c.* 425 BCE. The inhabitants wanted to commemorate their town's illustrious past, for the earliest coins (425–360 BCE) were decorated with the Minotaur on the obverse (head) and meander–swastika devices on the reverse (tail). Between 360 and 300 BCE combinations of male and female heads, bulls' heads, meander frames, and patterns predominate until around 300 BCE, when the first issues decorated with the labyrinth on the reverse appear. These soon became the common reverse pattern and were issued until the Roman period, around 70 BCE. The vast majority of the labyrinths on these coins are square (only one issue with the head of Apollo on the obverse has a circular labyrinth) and nearly all have the entrance facing upwards. A number of interesting variants from the standard classical labyrinth have been noted on this extensive series of coins. Labyrinths with three, five, and seven pathways all occur, as do blundered designs with errors and dead ends. Perhaps some of the engravers at work in Knossos were not fully conversant with the correct technique, while others understood the process enough to create correctly connected alternatives.

The labyrinth also appeared on clay seals applied to documents issued in Knossos and the town of Itanion in eastern Crete. Two labyrinth seals were excavated in 1978 in the ruins of an archive house at Kallipolis in Greece, among 500

or more seals that were fired and preserved when the building was burnt down during the destruction of the city in 279 BCE. Originally applied to papyrus scrolls and documents, the example issued at Knossos has a square labyrinth, just as depicted on the coins, with the label "KNOSION". The seal from Itanion shows a naked youth holding a spear, leaning on a square labyrinth in the background. The labyrinth on both seals probably declares the Cretan origin of the documents to which it was applied.

It is interesting to note that for about a century before labyrinth coins were issued at Knossos, the city's coins showed the Minotaur and various meander devices to symbolize the legendary labyrinth that formerly existed there. There must have been many, many thousands of Minotaur and labyrinth coins minted over the 300 years or so that they were in circulation, although today they are rare and command high prices. These coins would have circulated far and wide, especially those struck in silver. It is not difficult to imagine how they carried the labyrinth to lands where the symbol had been previously unknown. The fascination with the design on the reverse has ensured their desirability ever since. One such coin, which found its way into the collection of Queen Kristina of Sweden (1644–54), inspired her to produce a medal copied from the coin.[11]

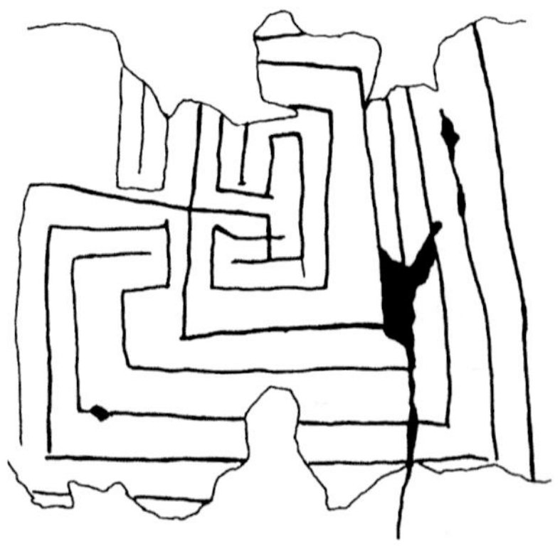

This labyrinth doodle, inscribed on a roof tile found among the ruins of the Acropolis in Athens, contains a curious drawing error at its centre.

A labyrinth graffito from the Hellenistic world comes from one of the most famous sites in classical Greece – it is a broken gable tile decorated with a square labyrinth that was discovered amongst the ruins of the Acropolis in Athens. Manufactured at the beginning of the fourth century BCE, the labyrinth is on the upper surface of the tile, and was scratched on before the tile was painted and fired, presumably by a workman during an idle moment. The design has a number of errors at its centre, caused by an incorrect connection of the seed pattern. The artist has started the labyrinth in exactly the same way as on the Pylos tablet, 800 years earlier (see page 41), but has made the first connection to the right of the seed, instead of from the top, resulting in a lop-sided labyrinth. Another square labyrinth, scratched on a wall in the House of the Tritons on the island of Delos, can be dated to between 125 and 88 BCE, when the house was destroyed in a raid. Despite the connection between Delos and labyrinth mythology – it was here that Theseus performed the geranos dance after escaping from Crete – this tiny depiction of the labyrinth, less than 2 in (4.5 cm) square, is just a doodle.

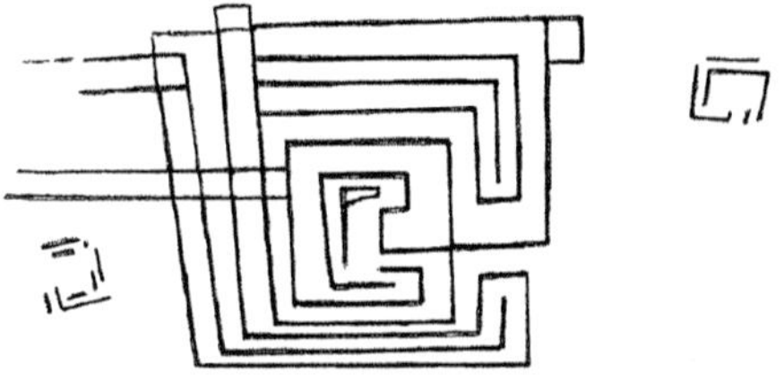

Painted low down on a pillar supporting the roof of the El-Salamuni quarry near Achmin, Egypt, this graffito is probably the first evidence of the labyrinth symbol in Egypt.

A labyrinth graffito rendered in red paint on a pillar in the old quarry of El-Salamuni, cut deep into a hillside north of Achmin, Egypt, is the first evidence of the labyrinth symbol in Egypt. The centre has been subtly altered to create the "ntr" hieroglyph – the symbol for "god". The quarry reaches back some 250 ft (75 m) into the hillside and was in use until the thirtieth dynasty, during the fourth century BCE. The labyrinth graffito, painted low on a pillar left in to support the ceiling, may date from when the quarry was being worked, but was more likely painted after the site was abandoned. It is difficult to date this graffito, but it is probably from a period of Hellenistic influence in the area during the fourth to second centuries BCE. It has been suggested[12] that it was created by a Greek inhabitant who thought the quarry sinister, the dwelling place of a dangerous divinity like the Minotaur's lair.

The only other labyrinth symbol recorded in Egypt can be seen on a paving slab in the Ptolemaic temple at Kom Ombo, constructed during the reign of Ptolemaios VI Philometer (181–146 BCE). Worn by the passage of feet, this otherwise perfect classical labyrinth is located in the corridor on the southeast side of the temple. A number of other slabs also bear graffiti of obvious antiquity and, while it is impossible to say when this labyrinth was cut into the floor, it may well be of Roman origin.

Similar Roman labyrinth graffitos are known from Pompeii, the Italian town destroyed by an eruption of Mount Vesuvius in 79 CE. The excavation of the buildings has revealed many exceptional decorative objects. This snapshot of Roman life also preserved the graffiti that adorned the walls of buildings before anybody had a chance to erase them. Two circular labyrinths are among numerous other graffitos scratched on the south wall of a narrow passage behind the smaller of Pompeii's two theatres. The larger labyrinth, 10 in (26 cm) across, is of classical design, although the brackets are set at an unusual angle. The smaller, only 6 in (14 cm) wide, lacks the dots at the four corners of the seed pattern. Consequently, the labyrinth has only five pathways and dead-ends, the same mistake that can be seen on coins from Knossos. The Pompeiian labyrinths are next to each other; perhaps the smaller labyrinth was a first attempt and the "artist", realizing the mistake, re-drew the larger labyrinth in correct form alongside.

A third example at Pompeii is scratched on a pillar at the front of the house of Marcus Lucretius on the Via Stabiana. Square, with the entrance facing upwards, it is accompanied by an inscription: "LABYRINTHUS HIC HABITAT MINOTAURUS" ("the labyrinth, here lives the Minotaur"). It is popularly assumed that this was meant to be a reference to the disposition of the owner of the house. Evidently it was scratched shortly before the eruption that destroyed Pompeii, or surely it would have been

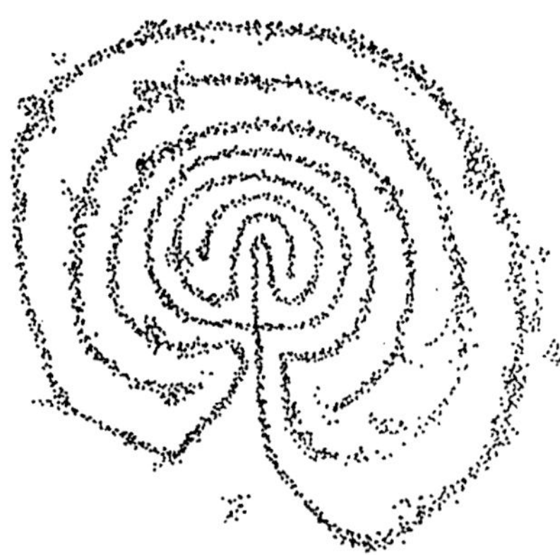

This labyrinth graffito from Egypt, carved on a paving slab in the Ptolemaic temple at Kom Ombo, is difficult to date, but could be of Roman origin.

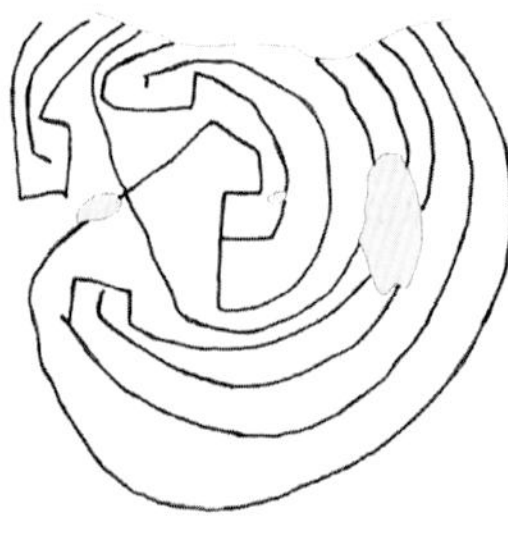

Above: two labyrinths scratched on the back wall of a theatre in Pompeii, Italy. The smaller example has been incorrectly drawn – the entrance does not connect to the centre.

Below: the famous labyrinth graffito from a pillar in front of the house of Marcus Lucretius at Pompeii. Clearly these graffitos at Pompeii date to just before the destruction of the town in 79 CE.

removed. The remarkable survival of these labyrinths from Pompeii shows that the disfigurement of public buildings was just as much a problem 2,000 years ago as it is today. The defacement of Marcus Lucretius' pillar proves that the Minotaur legend was popular with the Romans and provides the first written connection between the classical labyrinth symbol and the Cretan labyrinth myth.

Not all the labyrinths from the Roman world have such scurrilous origins. A classical labyrinth carved on the end of a stone slab from Quanawat in Syria, and now stored in the Louvre Museum in Paris, was formerly a piece of architectural decoration. It was probably a capstone for a votive niche from a temple or tomb, although its original location is not recorded. Alongside the incised labyrinth appears a scorpion and a curious sinuous figure interpreted as a snake. An inscription on the front of the block records in Greek script that it was made by "Tawelos, son of Rabbis, son of Socheros". Comparison of the symbols on this stone with a similar Syrian inscription from Soueida[13] suggests that the labyrinth from Quanawat is a benevolent symbol, a defence against the harmful and poisonous creatures of the desert.

Also from the far east of the Roman Empire is a finely executed labyrinth carving still lying amongst the ruins at Side, the former Roman town and sea port of Pamphylia, on the southern coast of Turkey. Although now in two pieces on the ground, the stone was formerly a piece of decorative carving on the ceiling of a richly

Lying among the ruins of the Roman town of Pamphylia at Side, Turkey, this carved block from the ceiling of a public building has a design quite different from the classical labyrinths encountered so far.

A stone slab, probably part of a votive niche, from Quanawat, Syria, now in the Louvre Museum in Paris.

ornamented room in a public building, possibly the gymnasium; it is dated from the middle of the second century CE. The paths of the labyrinth line a bowl-shaped recess and surround a flower carved in high relief at the centre of the bowl. While the workmanship is far superior to any examples we have previously encountered, perhaps the most surprising feature is the design of the labyrinth itself. Far more complex than the classical labyrinth, its distinctive four-fold symmetry represents a new departure in labyrinth design. Its complexity is shared by many more labyrinths from Roman cities, towns, and villas, for it was a common feature of the exquisite Roman art of mosaic; and leads us to the next group of labyrinths we will study.

Scattered across southern Europe and North Africa, around the shores of the Mediterranean and the Atlantic seaboard of Spain, the first labyrinths span a period of over 2,000 years. Throughout this time the design hardly changed; the classical labyrinth, easily drawn from memory, remained the predominant form. Also marked on this map are the legendary labyrinthine cities of Troy and Jericho and the Egyptian labyrinth at Hawara.

The First Labyrinths

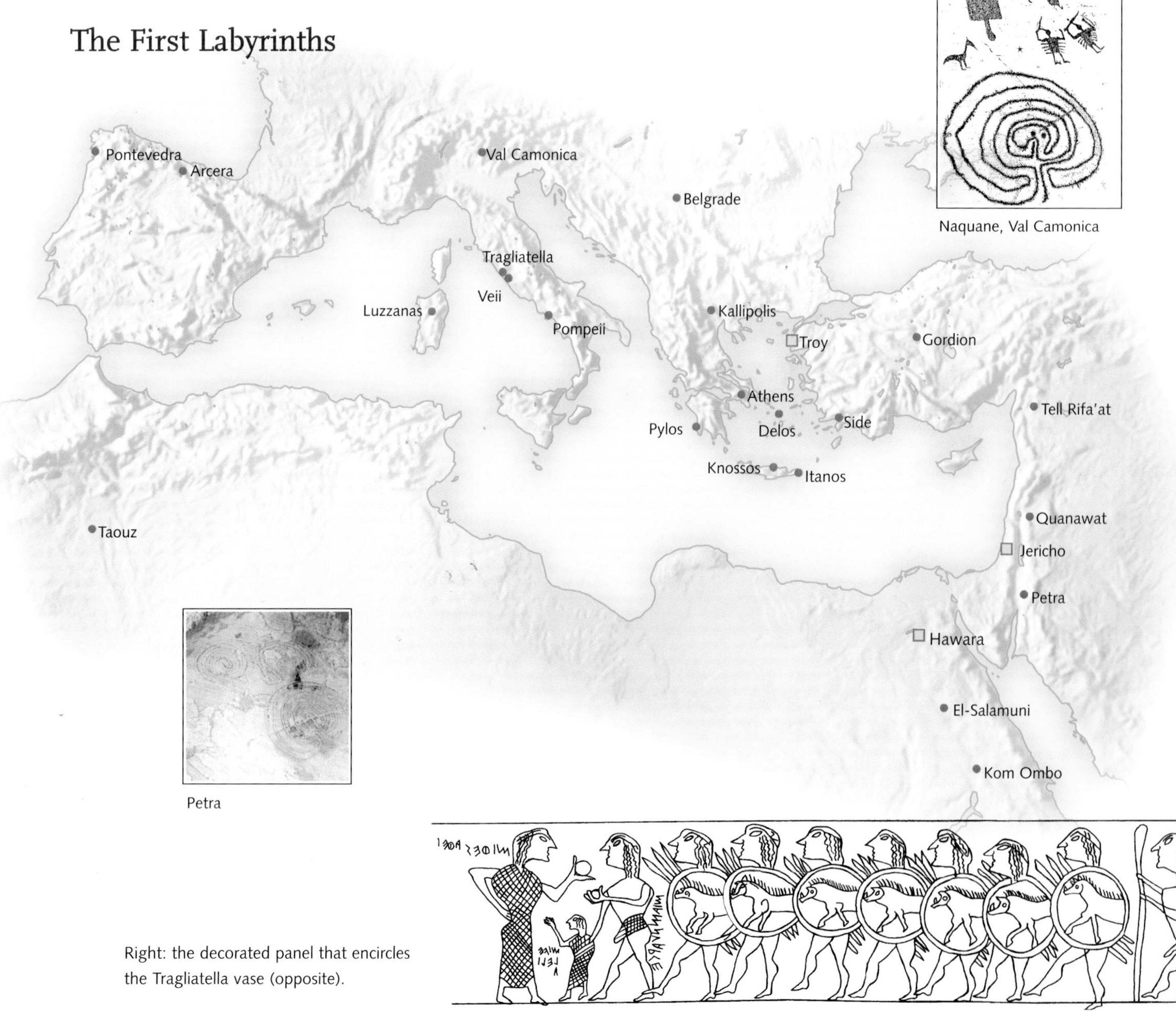

Naquane, Val Camonica

Petra

Right: the decorated panel that encircles the Tragliatella vase (opposite).

Location	Type	Dating	Comments
Spain			
Arcera	Rock inscription	?	Neolithic or early Christian?
Pontevedra			
Pedra do Labrinto	Rock inscription	*c.* 2000 BCE	Labyrinth with cup and rings
Pedra dos Campiños	Rock inscription	*c.* 2000 BCE	Flawless labyrinth
Pedra do Outeiro do Cribo	Rock inscription	*c.* 2000 BCE	Labyrinth with stags
Laxa de Rotea de Mendo	Rock inscriptions	*c.* 2000 BCE	Two incomplete examples
Outeiro das Laxes	Rock inscriptions	*c.* 2000 BCE	Two labyrinthine designs
Parada	Rock inscriptions	*c.* 2000 BCE	Five labyrinths with stags
Chan do Rei	Rock inscription	*c.* 2000 BCE	Perfect labyrinth
Pedra Escrita	Rock inscription	*c.* 2000 BCE	Defaced with Christian crosses
Sardinia			
Luzzanas	Rock inscription	?	In Neolithic tomb, Roman graffiti?
Italy			
Pompeii	Graffitos on walls	*c.* 79 CE	Three labyrinth graffitos
Tragliatella	Inscribed on pottery	*c.* 660-630 BCE	Complex design with labyrinth
Val Camonica			
Naquane	Rock inscription	*c.*750–500 BCE?	Labyrinth path with warriors
Campanine	Rock inscription	*c.*750–500 BCE?	Labyrinth with axeheads
Zurla	Rock inscriptions	*c.*750–500 BCE?	Two labyrinthine designs
Dos del Merichi	Rock inscription	*c.*750–500 BCE?	Labyrinthine design with warriors
Luine	Rock inscription	*c.*750–500 BCE?	Labyrinth with warriors
Veii	Pottery decoration	Roman	On vase fragment (unpublished)
Serbia			
Belgrade	Inscribed on a tile	2nd/3rd C. CE	In Belgrade museum?
Greece			
Athens	Graffito on roof tile	*c.*400 BCE	Originally on roof of Acropolis
Delos	Graffito on wall	*c.*125–80 BCE	Courtyard of House of Tritons
Kallipolis	Clay document seals	*c.*280 BCE	On papyri from Knossos and Itanos
Pylos	Clay tablet graffito	*c.*1200 BCE	The oldest securely dated example
Crete			
Knossos	Coins	*c.*285–70 BCE	Many examples recorded
Turkey			
Gordion	Graffitos on wall	*c.*750 BCE	Two labyrinths on wall plaster
Side	Architectural carving	mid-2nd C. CE	Roman meander design
Syria			
Quanawat	Carving on masonry	Roman	Capstone of votive niche
Tell Rifa'at	Pottery decoration	?	Dated *c.*1200 BCE, maybe Roman
Jordan			
Petra	Rock inscriptions		
Egypt			
El-Salamuni	Painting in quarry	?	3rd C. BCE or later?
Kom Ombo	Graffito on pavement?	Roman graffito?	On temple floor
Morocco			
Taouz	Rock inscription	*c.*500–200 BCE	Possibly several examples?

Constructing the Roman Labyrinth

1 The classical labyrinth

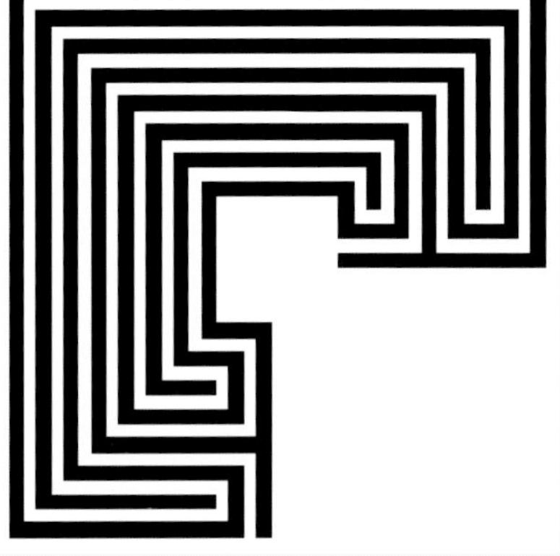
2 Reduced to three quarters

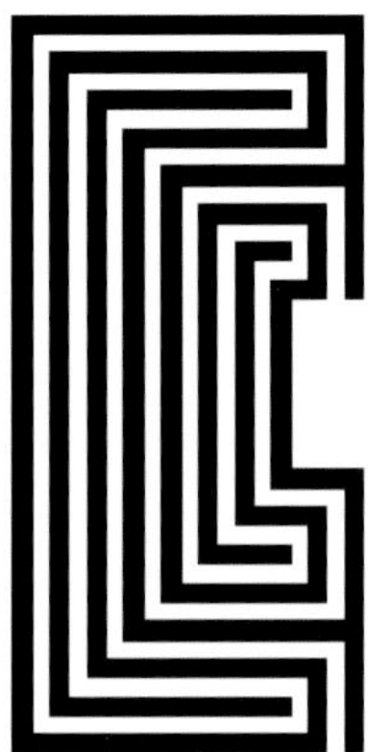
3 Reduced to half

The popularity of the Theseus and the Minotaur story and the motif used to signify it throughout the Roman Empire, have left us with a wealth of examples of the labyrinth symbol for study. By far the most common and dramatic of the preserved labyrinths from this period are those that appear as design elements on the mosaic floors of villas and public buildings.

The designs commonly employed in the majority of mosaic labyrinths appear to be quite different from the earlier classical design (1), but are in fact a simple development from it. Most consist of a number of reduced classical labyrinths (2–4), usually four, arranged as quarters of a larger design (5) with a connecting pathway added (6) to create a new labyrinth (7). The resulting path that leads through the labyrinth traces out the entire course of the first section, then the second, and so on, until it finally loops into the centre.

This represents the first real development of the labyrinth symbol from its original form and marks the start of a long process that leads ultimately to the multitude of complex multicursal designs that are used today in puzzle mazes.

A further development that took place in Roman times was the construction of labyrinths formed by stacking together other meandering patterns. Ranging from simple serpentines and spirals to complex meanders that double back on themselves, all produce appealing designs, but the labyrinths are mostly relatively simple.

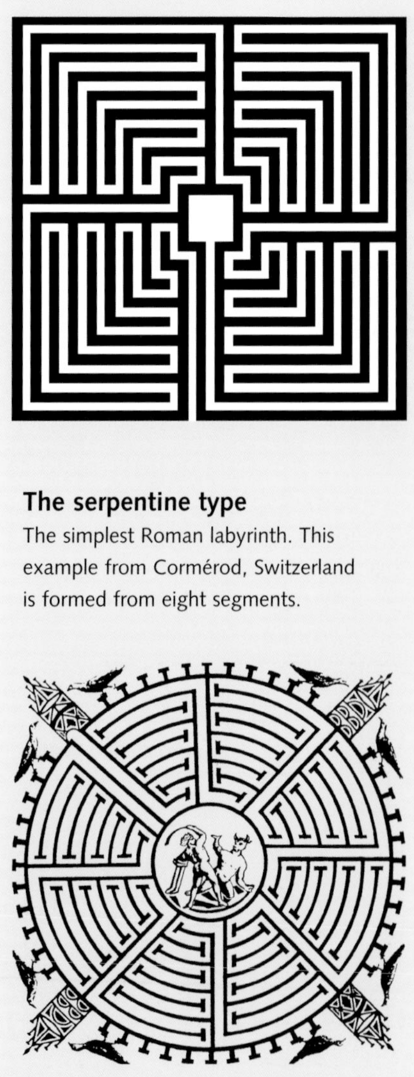
The serpentine type
The simplest Roman labyrinth. This example from Cormérod, Switzerland is formed from eight segments.

4 Down to a quarter

5 Four quarters repeated

6 The final connecting path is added

7 Creating a simple meander labyrinth

The spiral type

Two examples are known, both from Algeria, including this late example from the Christian basilica at Al-Asnam.

The simple meander type

The commonest of Roman labyrinths, this example from Harpham, England is formed with three coils.

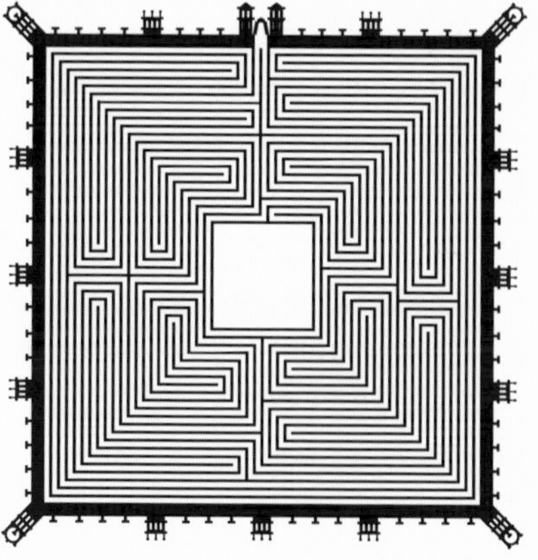

The complex meander type

This complex labyrinth from Pula, Croatia, has separate entrance and exit paths.

Dating from *c.* 165 BCE, the recently discovered *opus signinum* pavements at Mieza in Greece contains this damaged labyrinth, the earliest known example so far discovered. It is also the first example of the new form of Roman labyrinth, which has a more complex design than its classical predecessor and is better suited to the regularity of mosaic layouts.

Roman Labyrinth Mosaics

Both the labyrinth symbol and the myth of the Minotaur were widely known at the time of the Roman Empire, and the appearance of the labyrinth among Roman graffiti points to a knowledge of the classical design in a broad cross-section of society. The popular use of more complex geometric forms of the labyrinth in mosaic pavements has provided us with the largest selection of examples from this time, as over sixty are recorded[14]. Dating from *c.* 165 BCE to *c.* 400 CE, they are found throughout the Roman Empire, from Portugal in the west to Cyprus in the east, and from northern England to North Africa. Many of these labyrinth mosaics, discovered during excavations of Roman villas, towns, and settlements, are damaged or fragmentary, but a good number survive intact or can be reconstructed from the surviving sections to allow study of their designs.

The earliest known mosaic labyrinth is located at Mieza in Macedonia, Greece. A product of the Roman settlements in this region, it was probably constructed around 165 BCE, and was uncovered during excavation work between 1981 and 1983. The style, typical of early Roman mosaics, is thought to have been developed in the Phoenician city of Carthage during the fourth century BCE. It was formed by laying small cubes of coloured stone or glass called tesserae into mortar mixed with crushed terracotta to produce a pattern set into a distinctive red brick floor.

The classical labyrinth was occasionally represented in mosaic. Two are found among the preserved Roman ruins at Coimbra, Portugal. A square example (above) has an additional wall added adjacent to the entrance to make the labyrinth fit within a square frame. A small circular labyrinth (below) is installed in the corner of a room, where symmetry is less of a concern.

A small mosaic – only 12 in (30 cm) across – from the late second or early third century CE, is found in the Casa de Cantaber at the remarkable Roman ruins of Conimbriga, in the modern-day Portuguese city of Coimbra. The problem of incorporating the basic asymmetry of the classical labyrinth design into a square frame is sidestepped here by putting the "circular" form in the corner of the room, just inside the doorway. The placing of a trident and a symbol of concentric circles in at other entrances to the room suggests that the labyrinth was seen as an apotropaia, a device intended to guard the doorway. Another example from Conimbriga, dating from the first half of the third century, is one of a pair of juxtaposed labyrinths in the Casa dos Repuxos. Here, adding an extra pathway and drawing the entrance out to the side of the frame has solved the problem of asymmetry.

Slightly earlier in the second century, the labyrinth mosaic at Salinas de Rosio, Spain, has wider paths in the outermost coils at either side of the entrance in a not altogether satisfactory attempt to restore balance to the overall design. A final small example, found on the floor of a large first-century building at St Côme, near Nîmes in France, has a most unusual design. An accompanying inscription, which identifies this as the work of "Pythis, son of Antiochus", has taken the centre of the labyrinth and rotated it ninety degrees to produce an untidy design, but an interesting example of the willingness of the mosaic artist to experiment.

A curious version of the classical labyrinth from St Côme, France.

The reasons for this shift towards a more complex design may include the need for a regular geometric pattern that was adaptable for mosaic. Although no examples have survived, we know from contemporary sources that mosaic craftsmen had pattern books, not just for the process of construction, but also as samples to show prospective clients. Collections of designs would have been assembled in scrolls, but no two mosaics are alike and the artists were adept at producing endless variations on a theme to fit the varying shapes and sizes of the rooms they were paving. Labyrinth mosaics range in size from under 3 ft (1 m) to 20 ft (6 m) or more, and the new designs of the period were ideally suited to fit or fill available space.

Roman mosaic labyrinths were too small to have been walked, and would have provided visual and contemplative exercise only. Possibly the sole exception is a curious "half-labyrinth" that adorns the Roman baths at Makthar in Tunisia. Here a narrow pathway winds to the centre, where it loops back and forth, maybe in an allusion to Ariadne's thread.

Surrounded by crenulated walls and towers, this labyrinth from Cremona, Italy, guards a goal containing Theseus battling with the Minotaur, a common theme for depiction at the centre of mosaics.

Mosiac labyrinths are often located near entrances or just inside doorways, suggesting an apotropaic protective function. In addition, they are frequently surrounded by renditions of walls and towers to give the impression of being enclosed, like a town or city, inside defensive fortifications. As many of the labyrinths are square, this coupling of labyrinth and defensive walls echoes the often square, four-fold division of Roman towns and fortifications. It enforces the protective function of the labyrinth as a symbol representing the security and stability of the Roman Empire.

One of the few labyrinth mosaics that is large enough to walk, the example from Makthar in Tunisia also has an unusual semi-circular design with the pathway prominently marked.

The labyrinth mosaic discovered in an underground hypogeum at Sousse in Tunisia in 1860 has, regrettably, since been broken up and destroyed.

A number of these mosaic labyrinths are found in bath houses. These examples were designed not only to provide decorative design but perhaps also as a topic for conversation. There is even one example known from within a Roman tomb, created in *c.* 200 CE at Sousse in Tunisia. Before crossing the labyrinth in the underground hypogeum, the visitor is warned by an inscription that runs either side of the doors at the labyrinth entrance: "*Hic inclusus vitam perdit*" ("Whoever is locked in here will lose his life").

The central goals of mosaic labyrinths are often works of art in their own right and were sometimes imported as separate items from workshops that specialized in high quality decorative mosaic. While a simple decorative flower adorns the centre of the labyrinth from Harpham in England, and a representation of a house fills the centre of the labyrinth at Pont-Chevron in France, the labyrinth at Ostia, near Rome, bears an unusual representation of the Roman lighthouse in Ostia harbour. But the story of Theseus and the Minotaur appears at the centre of most Roman mosaic labyrinths. In some the story is alluded to by the simple placement of a bull's head or Theseus's club; elsewhere a basic scene of Theseus battling the Minotaur suffices. A few show the finest work of the mosaic artists, with lifelike renditions of Theseus and the downtrodden Minotaur in splendid detail. The specimens from Cormérod, now in the Miséricorde Building of the University of Fribourg, Switzerland, and from a large villa at Loig, near Salzburg, now in Vienna Museum, are among the finest. The latter is also surrounded by scenes from the story of the escape from Crete – a veritable illustrated tableau of the labyrinth myth.

Without doubt the most remarkable central goal of all is to be found in the beautifully preserved mosaic in the ruins of the House of Theseus at Nea Paphos on Cyprus. Dating from the late third century, but repaired during the fourth century following an earthquake, this labyrinth is unusual for its circular form and 20-ft (6-m) diameter. Unique in its design and vibrant colours, a guilloche

A simple decorative flower fills the centre of the labyrinth mosaic excavated at Harpham, England. The mosaic is preserved, although in poor condition, in a museum in Hull.

Although poorly displayed, the labyrinth in the House of Theseus at Nea Paphos in Cyprus is surely one of the most spectacular examples of all with the full pantheon of characters from the Minotaur myth depicted in the central roundel.

One of the two labyrinths preserved at Nea Paphos, this example is only 20 in (51 cm.) in diameter, and forms part of a much larger decorative pavement.

ribbon pattern winds the length of the path, leading to a large central roundel that depicts the pantheon of characters from the story of the Cretan labyrinth. This most stunning of mosaic labyrinths disappoints only by being housed in a wooden shed, with plastic sheeting to keep out the weather.

The popular association of the labyrinth with the myth of Theseus and the Minotaur had far-reaching effects, for this tradition carried through into the pavement labyrinths built in the cathedrals of medieval Europe. In fact the first labyrinths in a Christian context are two mosaics from as far away as Algeria (see Chapter 3). How the labyrinth, so intimately linked with the pagan hero Theseus, gained acceptance with the Christian Church and went on to become an important symbol in Christian iconography is a fascinating story. However, before we can follow this thread further, we must first investigate the story of how the labyrinth appeared in remote corners of the world, far away from the influences of Roman civilization and the subsequent European cultures that arose after the decline of the Roman Empire.

Found in 1815 in the bath house of a large Roman villa at Loig, near Salzburg, Austria, and now preserved in the Vienna Kunsthistorisches Museum, this elaborate labyrinth mosaic is accompanied by scenes depicting Theseus and Ariadne, as well as the Minotaur.

Roman Mosaic Labyrinths

Destroyed and buried examples marked in italics

Location	Design type	Size (m)	Shape	Date	Comments
Algeria					
Al-Asnam	Spiral type	2.5	Square	*c.* 324 CE	Central word square
Annaba	Serpentine	7.4 x 5.8	Rectangular	150–200 CE	Preserved in bath house
Cherchel	Simple meander	1.8	Square	*c.* 200 CE	Partially preserved
Dellys	Spiral type	3.8	Square	*c.* 200 CE	Found in bath house
Tametfoust	?	3.5 x 3.5	Octagonal	4th C. CE	Tree in centre panel
Tigzert	?	?	Square	*c.* 450 CE	Destroyed
Austria					
Salzburg	3-coil meander	4.2	Square	275–300 CE	Now in Vienna museum
Bosnia					
Stolac	Complex meander	4.2	Square	c. 300 CE	Centre in Sarajevo museum
Croatia					
Pula	Complex meander	4.3	Square	2nd C. CE	Very complex design
Cyprus					
Pula	1-coil meander	6.0	Circular	Late 3rd C. CE	Preserved in situ
Nea Paphos	Serpentine	0.5	Circular	2nd C. CE	Detail in large pavement
England					
Cirencester	2-coil meander	1.95	Square	Early 4th C. CE	Buried for protection
Cirencester	1-coil meander	*c.*6.0?	Square	2nd C. CE	Labyrinth border, buried
Fullerton	Simple spiral	3.2	Square	4th C. CE	Crude design, buried
Harpham	3-coil meander	3.0	Square	Early 4th C. CE	In storage at Hull museum
Keynsham	Classical?	?	Square?	?	Buried, awaiting excavation
Oldcotes	3-coil meander	2.9	Square	3rd C. CE	Excavated 1870, reburied
France					
Chusclan	2-coil meander	3.0	Square	150–200 CE	Wall and tower surround
Pont-Chevron	2-coil meander	0.84	Square	150–200 CE	Small, but well preserved
St Côme	Classical	0.45	Square	Late 1st C. CE	Now in Nimes museum
St-Cyr-sur-Mer	Serpentine	0.28	Circular	1st C. CE	Two small labs. in pavement
Sainte-Colombe	?	?	?	?	No information available
Verdes	2-coil meander	10.2 x 9.2	Circular	200–250 CE	Fragment in Château de Blois
Vienne	2-coil meander	6.0?	Circular	200–250 CE	Now in Lyons museum
Greece					
Mieza	2-coil meander	?	Square	Late 2nd C. BCE	Earliest known example
Italy					
Brindisi	4-coil meander	5.2	Square	200–250 CE	Fragment in Brindisi museum
Cremona	2-coil meander	1.0 x 0.9	Square	1–50 CE	Now in Cremona museum
Giannutri	Complex meander	4.5	Square	150–200 CE	Surviving in situ
Ostia	2-coil meander	3.75	Square	*c.* 150 CE	In the Palazzo Imperiale
Piadena	2-coil meander	1.35	Square	25–50 CE	Dying Minotaur at centre
Pompeii	4-coil meander	?	Square	80–60 BCE	Villa di Diomede, destroyed
Pompeii	3-coil meander	2.1	Square	80–60 BCE	Casa del Labirinto
Pompeii	2-coil meander	2.1	Square	60–40 BCE	House in Region VIII
Pompeii	2-coil meander	?	Square	*c.* 50 CE	Now destroyed
Rome	4-coil meander	*c.*4.0	?	*c.* 100–180 CE	Wall and tower surround
Rome	?	*c.*5.0?	Square?	*c.* 130 CE	Destroyed 1935
Libya					
Gurgi	?	?	Square	*c.* 200 CE	Centre in Tripoli museum
Shahhat	2-coil meander	*c.*5.0	Square	*c.* 200 CE	Centre in Cyrene museum
Sabrata	Serpentine	3.0	Circular	1st C. CE	Badly damaged when found
Portugal					
Coimbra	Classical	0.3	Circular	175–225 CE	In corner of room
Coimbra	Classical	1.5	Square	200–250 CE	Next to example below
Coimbra	2-coil meander	1.5	Square	200–250 CE	Bull's head at centre
Coimbra	3-coil meander	3.4 x 3.1	Square	Late 2nd C. CE	Wall and tower surround
Sardinia					
Nora	?	?	Square	*c.* 200 CE	Only fragments discovered

The more than sixty mosaic labyrinths discovered across the Roman Empire span a 500-year period and display a range of shapes, sizes, and designs, representing the first real attempt to develop the labyrinth symbol.

Caerleon

Coimbra

Location	Design type	Size (m)	Shape	Date	Comments
Serbia					
Gamzigrad	2-coil meander	2.8	Hexagonal	*c.* 300 CE	Unique 3 sector design
Sicily					
Solunto	?	?	Circular	*c.* 125–100 BCE	Fragment of *opus signinum*
Taormina	Complex meander	6.5 x 6.0	Square	*c.* 150 CE	Wall and tower surround
Spain					
Altafulla	?	?	?	*c.* 230 CE	Preserved, but unpublished
Córdoba	?	4.2 x 4.0	Square	150–200 CE	Only central panel survives
Italica	2-coil meander	3.5	Square	*c.* 150 CE	Surviving in situ
Merida	2-coil meander	*c.*3.0	Circular	2nd/3rd C. CE	Surviving in situ
Pamplona	?	?	Circular	*c.* 150 CE	Centre in Pamplona museum
Salinas de Rosio	Classical	2.75	Square	Late 2nd C. CE	Preserved in situ
Switzerland					
Avenches	1-coil meander	0.7	Circular	*c.* 250 CE	Now in Avenches museum
Baugy	?	?	Circular	?	Noted 1802, destroyed
Cormérod	Serpentine	4.2	Circular	200–225 CE	Now in Fribourg museum
Orbe-Bosceaz	3-coil meander	3.5	Square	*c.* 200 CE	Preserved in situ
Tunisia					
Dougga	5-coil meander	4.8	Square	150–200 CE	Now in Bardo museum, Tunis
El Djem	3-coil meander	2.36	Circular	175–225 CE	Wall and tower surround
Henchir el Faouar	Serpentine	4.8	Square	Early 4th C. CE	Still in situ
Henchir Kasbat	4-coil meander	3.8 x 3.1	Rectangular	Late 3rd C. CE	Now in Bardo museum, Tunis
Makthar	5-coil meander	16.5 x 7.8	Semicircular	199 CE	Unique design, surviving
Sousse	Complex meander	5.6 x 3.4	Square	200–250 CE	Found in underground tomb
Wales					
Caerleon	3-coil meander	2.4	Square	*c.* 100 CE?	Fragment in Caerleon mus.

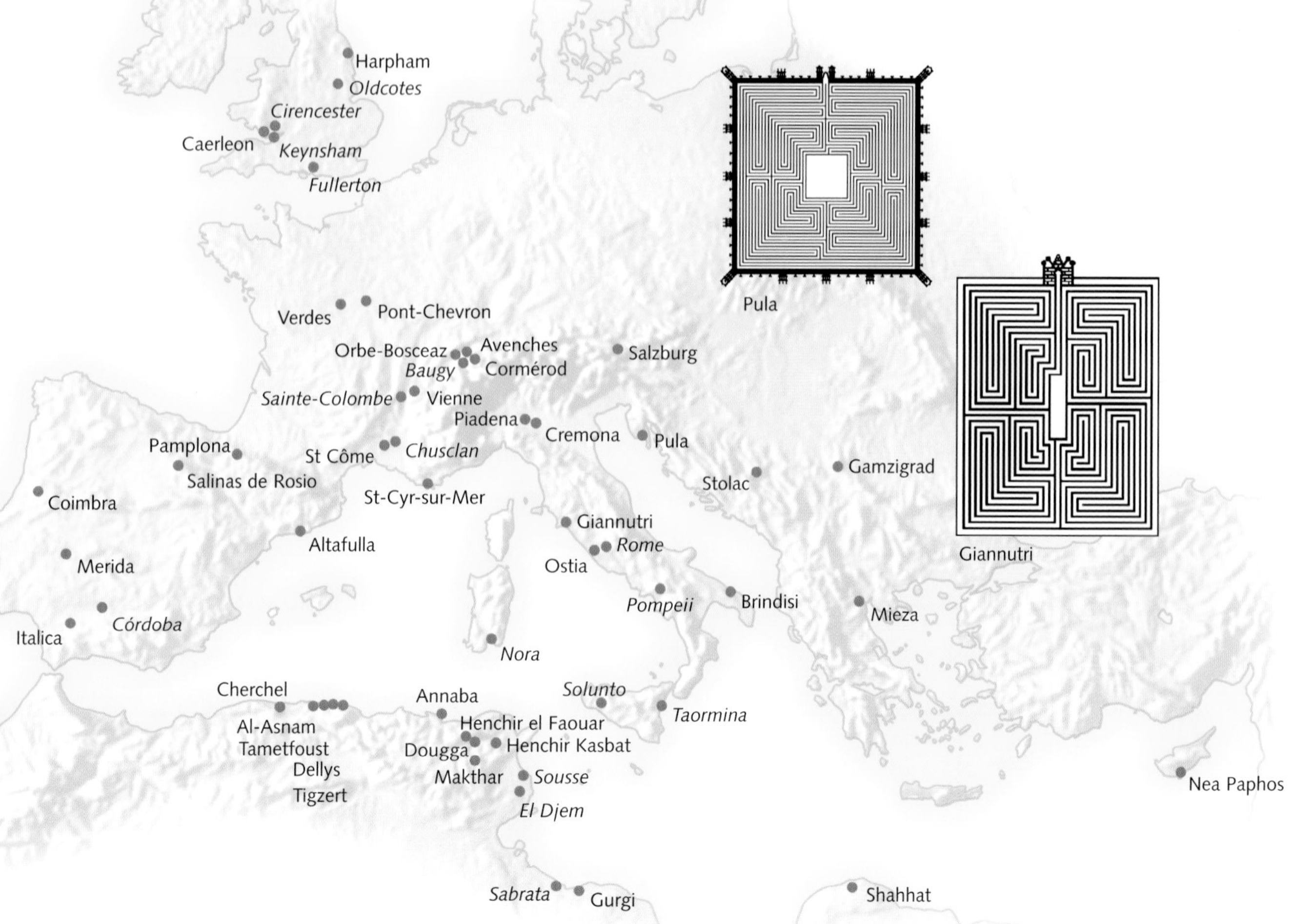

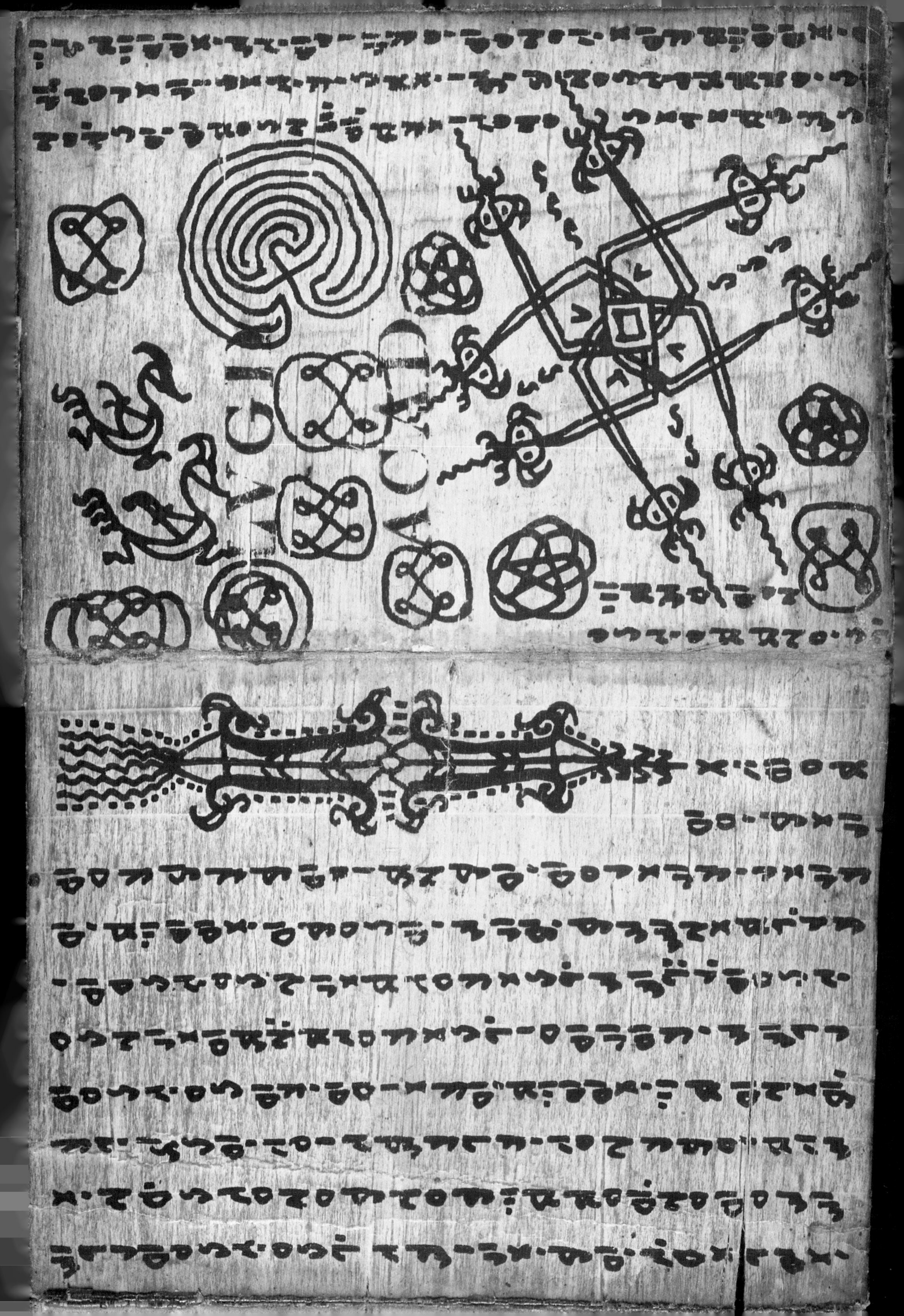

Chapter 2

Asia, Indonesia, and the Americas

Hundreds of years ago, the magicians of the Batak tribes living in the remote highlands of Sumatra were troubled by a mischievous spirit that pestered their villages. Their books of magic charms recommended drawing a labyrinth to send the spirit back home. In India, the labyrinth was a charm to ease the pain of childbirth and an invincible formation for troops in the great battles of the ancient epics, first written down over 2,000 years ago. In the deserts of the American Southwest are labyrinths representing the abodes of ancestors, and in the jungles of Brazil are labyrinths as yet unsolved. All share one thing in common: they have the exact same design. How the same symbol comes to be used in such far-flung regions of the world is a puzzle that still evades explanation.

A small classical labyrinth depicted in a magical text written on tree bark, from Sumatra. How the labyrinth symbol found its way from Europe to the distant jungles of Indonesia, and to other remote corners of the world, is one of the most mysterious aspects of the labyrinth story.

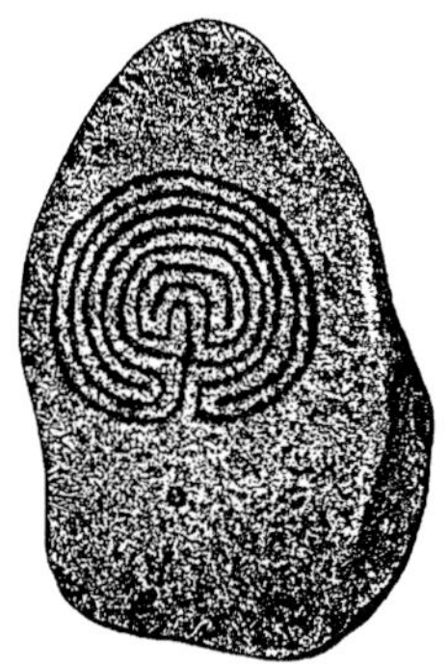

Far beyond the bounds of Europe, the labyrinth symbol has been documented across southern Asia, as far east as Java, in parts of Africa, and perhaps most surprisingly in North and South America. When and how the labyrinth first found its way to these far-flung outposts is often difficult to determine, although new discoveries and research are now beginning to piece together the story.

A classical labyrinth carved on a dolmen shrine at Padagula in the Nilgiri Hills, India (above), is said to date to 1000 BCE, but this is debatable and unproven. Likewise, a labyrinth recently discovered at Pirla in Goa (below), requires further research before a secure date can be ascribed to it.

The Labyrinth in Asia

The labyrinth symbol is found across a wide swathe of southern Asia, particularly in the Indian sub-continent and in parts of Indonesia that were influenced by trade with India. More common in Hindu and Buddhist contexts, it is also occasionally found in the Islamic world.

The labyrinth probably first reached Asia around the fourth century BCE, when the campaigns of Alexander the Great forged contacts between India and Europe. Nearly all the labyrinths in the sub-continent are classical, or locally developed forms of it, which seems to confirm that the symbol reached India before the development of its design really took off in Europe. The absence of Roman and medieval labyrinth designs in Asia also suggests that no cross-fertilization of ideas took place subsequently.

Unsubstantiated claims date some Asian labyrinth carvings to as far back as 1000 BCE. These include a perfect classical labyrinth carved on a dolmen shrine at Padugula in the Nilgiri Hills[1] and one recently discovered at Pirla in Goa.[2] However, the earliest reliable evidence for the labyrinth in Asia is a painting in a cave at Tikla in Madhya Pradesh, India, dated to around 250 BCE. In Pakistan, a carving on a boulder by the Indus at Shatyãl can also be dated to the first few centuries CE.[3] It is accompanied by numerous Buddhist figures and symbols at a resting spot on the Great Silk Route, which linked India to central Asia and was followed by pilgrims and traders alike. Eighteenth- and nineteenth-century labyrinths are also known in northern Pakistan, including a series of labyrinth carvings in the prayer rooms of mosques. They are usually found low down on pillars to enable contemplation while sitting at prayer. Several such labyrinths in the Mosque of Lamūtai have unfortunately been destroyed in recent years as old timber mosques are demolished for rebuilding in modern materials.

Carved near the base of a wooden pillar in the old mosque at Tal in northern Pakistan, this labyrinth is one of several recorded in mosques in this area. Some of them have been destroyed in recent years.

During the eighteenth century, the Vatican sent numerous missionaries to Nepal and Tibet. Their reports and letters provide a wealth of information. Father Cassiano da Macerata, travelling between 1740 and '45, made an account of a labyrinth carved on a stone in the royal palace at Bhaktapur in Nepal.[4] The design was said to represent a plan of the walls defending the fabled city of Scimangada, which were eventually breached, despite their strength. Cassiano, who had visited the overgrown site of the city deep in the forest at modern Simraon south of Kathmandu, describes the walls enclosing it. "A labyrinth which it was impossible to enter except at a single spot, and after having entered there one had to pass beneath four fortresses, which were evenly distributed from place to place within the enclosures of the labyrinth."

Cassiano goes on to retell the local legend of how an aggrieved minister of the King of Scimangada plotted the monarch's downfall. He revealed the weakest point in the city walls to the attacking army of a rival Muslim emperor, with disastrous consequences for the city and its inhabitants. This description is accompanied by a sketch of the city's defences and is drawn as a perfect classical labyrinth. Forts are marked at the ends, the city is at the centre, and the point of the fatal breach is marked where the four walls cross at the core. Cassiano implies that he based his sketch on the inscription on the stone in the palace at Bhaktapur; unfortunately the whereabouts of this stone are unknown.

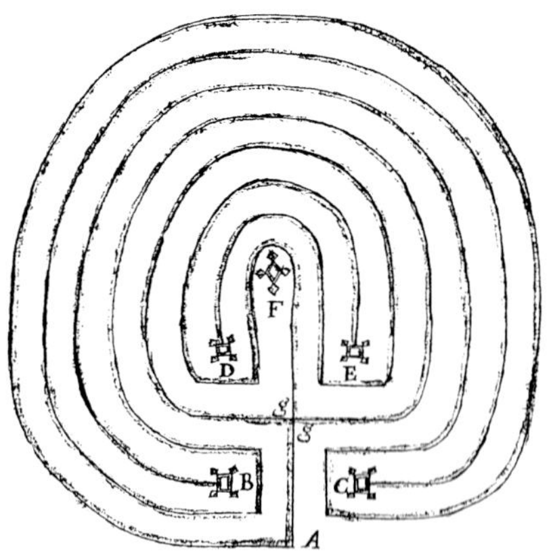

Cassiano's sketch of the design carved on a stone in the royal palace at Bhaktapur, Nepal, which is said to represent the defences of Scimangada. The forts at the ends of the walls and the city at the centre are marked, as is the weak point in the defences (the centre of the seed) where the invading army breached the walls.

Another depiction of Scimangada was recently discovered during restoration work at the temple of Dattatreya in Bhaktapur.[5] It is a curious swastika–labyrinth painted on a wooden ceiling panel in a large first-floor meeting room. It shows the complex defences of the city, with warriors, chariots, and elephants parading around the walls. A similar swastika-labyrinth pathway is to be found laid out on the ground in the form of 500 or more votive lingas, within the enclosure of the temple of Paśupatinātha in Nepal.

The extensive overgrown ruins of Scimangada remain largely unexcavated. Historical sources record that the city was founded in 1097 and was the seat of a powerful dynasty until it was destroyed in 1325. A high inner wall, surrounded by concentric earthen walls and ditches, is still visible. The defensive walls were intended as a metaphorical labyrinth, so we should not expect to find an actual labyrinth at the site. Cassiano records that ancient coins also bore the labyrinth symbol, but no examples have been found.

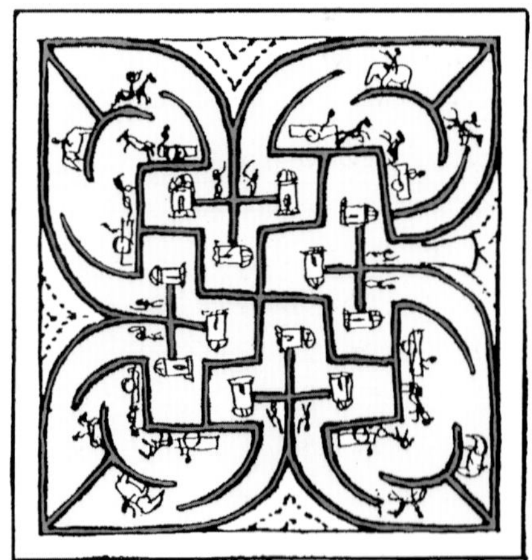

Another depiction of the defences of Scimangada, this time represented as a labyrinthine swastika device, recently discovered in the Dattatreya temple in Bhaktapur.

The parallels between the story of the fortifications and fall of Scimangada and the cities of Troy and Jericho are striking, but there is no need to look to European or Middle Eastern sources for origins, as the labyrinth has a long tradition in the legendary literature of India. An allusion in the Indian *Mahābhārata* epic has ensured a wide knowledge of the labyrinth throughout the continent. The content of the *Mahābhārata* was clearly influenced by the campaigns of Alexander the Great in the late fourth century BCE, although the text was probably added to until the first few centuries CE.

At the battle of Kurukshetra, the magician Drona endeavours to ensure victory for the Kaurava army by devising a troop formation called chakra-vyūha (wheel battle formation), which "the gods themselves could not enter". However, Abhimanyu, the sworn enemy of Drona and the only other person who knows the chakra-vyūha plan, joins the fray on the side of the Pandavas. He knows the way in and kills many enemies. But never having learnt the route out he is killed at the centre by arrows from all sides.

Whether chakra-vyūha and the labyrinth symbol were associated from the earliest origins of this story or not, they certainly were by the late twelfth or thirteenth century, when two depictions of the battle were carved on the friezes of the Hoysaleshvara and Kedareshvara temples at Halebid, Mysore. Both show an army arranged in labyrinth formation, although the design is a modified classical labyrinth with the central section replaced with a spiral – a variant common in India and rightly called the "chakra-vyūha type".

Another fascinating labyrinth tale is found in a document from Afghanistan. Accompanying a simple drawing of the labyrinth symbol is a text that tells the story of the House of Shamaili. Once there were seven princes, the sons of King Namazlum, all of whom hoped to marry the beautiful Shamaili, daughter of King Khunkhar the Bloodthirsty. The King kept his daughter imprisoned in a secret room hidden deep inside the palace and had promised her hand to the first suitor to set eyes on her. The first six princes tried to catch a glimpse of Shamaili, but got lost in the twisting passageways leading to her room, and the king killed them all for their pains. The seventh brother, Prince Jallad Khan, disguised himself as a magical dancing statue, which so delighted the king that he had it taken to Shamaili's room. Under the cover of darkness, Prince Jallad Khan revealed his true identity and exchanged rings with the Princess, who wept for joy at being discovered by such a handsome suitor. The happy pair were duly married. Prince Jallad Khan then put out the eyes of King Kunkhar the Bloodthirsty to avenge the death of his brothers. This story bears striking similarities to the story of the fall of Troy and many of the other ancient labyrinth myths.

The labyrinth has been recorded in several Indian manuscripts from the seventeenth century onwards, particularly from Rajasthan and Gujarat.[6] Many appear on Tantric drawings as protective magical charms; several are designed for easing labour pains and ensuring an easy birth. The pregnant woman puts saffron on a metal plate, draws a labyrinth in it with her finger, rinses the plate and drinks the water. The labyrinth symbolizes the baby's one-way passage out of the womb. Labyrinths have also been recorded as tattoo patterns in southern India and are found in the design copybooks of wandering Korowa tattoo artists.[7] In Tamil Nadu, labyrinths are still employed as protective devices known as kolam – elaborate patterns traced in rice flour on a freshly scrubbed doorstep. They serve as an offering to Lakshmi, the goddess of rice, earth, and wealth, to stop evil spirits from entering, and to ensure good fortune to those within.

A simple (and incorrectly connected) labyrinth that accompanied an account of the story of Shamaili's House collected in Afghanistan during the twentieth century.

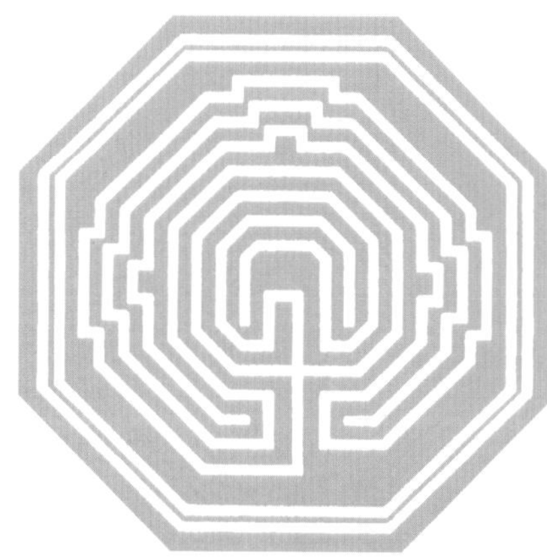

A traditional Kolam pattern from Tamil Nadu, India. Traced out with rice flour on the thresholds of houses in the region, the labyrinth is said to provide magical protection for the household.

This labyrinth pattern, from a design copybook carried by a wandering Korawa tattooist in southern India, was collected during the 1930s.

A large labyrinth formed from mounded boulders, known locally as Lakshmana-mandal, at Sitimani, near Bijapur in Madras.

Perhaps the most surprising form of labyrinth encountered in India is the stone and boulder labyrinth found in the regions of Madras, Orissa, and Tamil Nadu. Two small examples in Tamil Nadu are located at Baire Gauni north of Chinnakottur and near the ruined city of Kundani in Hosur Talug. Made of lines of stones embedded in the ground, both are of the chakra-vyūha design. A larger example of the chakra-vyūha type, near Bijapur in Madras, is known locally as the Lakshmana-mandal and has walls made of mounds of rocks. A remarkable labyrinth near the temple of Rhanipur Jharial, north of Titlagarh in Orissa, was supposedly laid out by the male yogis who gather here to venerate the sixty-four female yogis to whom the temple is dedicated. A photograph taken in 1977[8] shows the design to be of the classical type. Some experts have commented on its similarity to labyrinth designs from the American Southwest, but we should not take them too seriously. The age of these stone labyrinths is completely unknown, though their location in the vicinity of standing stones and other ancient structures may imply considerable antiquity. These Indian labyrinths offer potential for further research and exciting finds.

A labyrinth formed from stones near Baire Gauni, which is near Chinnakottur in Tamil Nadu. The design (22 ft/6.6 m in diameter) is of the chakra-vyūha type widespread in India, with a spiral at the centre.

In his study of India of 1045, the Iranian geographer Abū'l-Rayhān Al-Bīrūnī illustrates a classical labyrinth and records it as a plan of Rāvana's fortress at Sri Lanka. This same labyrinth features in the *Rāmāyana* epic, in which the demon Rāvana abducts Sita, wife of the hero Rama, and holds her hostage in the impenetrable fortress. With the help of an army of monkeys, Rama attacks the labyrinthine fort and rescues his wife.

The island of Sri Lanka, off the southern tip of India, has several recorded labyrinths. They appear in wall paintings from the eighteenth century in the temples of Mädavala and Arattana in the districts of Kandy and Nuwara Eliya, in the central highlands of the island. Both are accurately drawn classical labyrinths, representing the Vanga-giriya (Crooked Mountain), a place of banishment for Prince Vessantara, a figure from Buddhist mythology. He was exiled for seven months to live with his wife and children in two huts deep in the jungle, and the track leading to them was so overgrown that they had to walk in single file. This is another occasion where the labyrinth symbol helps tell a story.

Below: The banishment of Vessantara on the crooked mountain, represented by the labyrinth, from the Buddhist story of Vessantara Jātaka, is shown on this fresco painted *c.*1755 in a temple at Mädavala, Sri Lanka.

The labyrinth was also carried across to the eastern shores of the Indian Ocean, probably from the seventh century BCE onwards, when India started to trade with Indonesia. The design occurs frequently

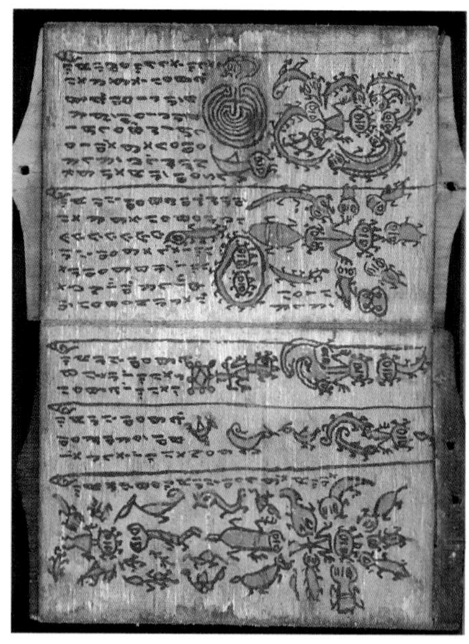

A classical labyrinth painted on tree bark in a book of magical charms from northern Sumatra, given as a charm against evil spirits. Collected in 1853, this and the example on page 58 were produced by the Batak tribes living around Lake Toba. They knew the labyrinth as the abode of Si Jonaha or Djonaha, a rogue from the spirit world who troubled the tribe.

amongst the magical symbols and devices used by the Bataks around Laka Toba, in the remote volcanic highlands of northern Sumatra. Long feared as a ferocious tribe of headhunters, their isolation was broken only in the mid-nineteenth century, first by missionaries and then by Dutch traders. Labyrinths were particularly used in magical texts, painted on sheets of bark bound into books, and on votive objects; one is carved on a magician's staff. At least two labyrinths accompanying appeals for protection from evil spirits are called "Jonaha's Wall". All these texts and ritual objects date from the mid- or late nineteenth century and were collected by Dutch traders – most are now in European museums.

Several labyrinths have also been carved or painted on ceremonial huts and rice barns in Sumatra, especially in Permatang Purba, where two examples appear on the timbers and support pillars of the royal palace. The majority of these Sumatran labyrinths are seven-path classical in design and are carefully drawn; the artists had learnt the traditional method. Rather more surprising are records, but alas no plans, of turf labyrinths, similar to those in England and Germany, cut during the 1930s on hillocks in villages north of Lake Toba. These labyrinths were formed from a simple trench and kept open by repeated walking. The design was explained as the refuge of Djonaha, a rogue and prankster in Batak mythology, whose exploits resemble the Elder Brother labyrinth story from Arizona (see p.68). The Sumatran labyrinths clearly derive no direct influence from their European counterparts, nor is the story connected to the American labyrinth tradition; instead they illustrate the universal adaptability of the symbol to local needs and materials.

The furthest export of the labyrinth tradition so far recorded is to the Indonesian island of Java, where several hoards of gold finger rings engraved with the labyrinth symbol have been discovered. They are of Hindu influence and date from the ninth to the fifteenth centuries. Some of the engraved labyrinths are perfectly executed using the seed pattern technique. Others display blunders, evidence that while the artisan was familiar with the symbol, he lacked understanding of the technique.

Although China and Japan have no records of permanent labyrinths, they did employ a labyrinthine device for a fascinating practical purpose. Time-keeping in ancient China was an elaborate process developed over centuries and involving the use of water, fire, and even mercury, to regulate huge mechanical clocks. These were used to monitor and predict astronomical events, to determine the time of ritual observances, and to check the accuracy of the calendar.

Domestic time-keeping often involved the burning of graduated incense sticks. For the timing of ceremonies in Buddhist temples, an ingenious series of graduated incense burners was developed between

Several labyrinths have been reported carved or painted on timbers and pillars of ceremonial huts and rice barns in Sumatra, especially in the village of Permatang Purba. Each of the pillars supporting the palace of the former kings of the region is decorated with the magical symbols of one of the kings; one pillar is decorated with several small labyrinths.

A gold ring found in 1882 with a hoard of gold and silver objects at Guranting in southwest Java. Difficult to date precisely, this and similar gold rings found in Java are commonly dated between the ninth and fifteenth centuries CE. While the engraver of this ring clearly knew how to construct the labyrinth from the familiar seed pattern, a small connection error has occurred during the engraving process.

the eighth and eleventh centuries CE. Powdered incense, formed into a meandering, labyrinthine path, was burnt on hard wooden plates and in metal bowls. Small bamboo flags burned and grains of particular incenses released their aromas as the smouldering pathway reached their position in the sequence, marking the timing of particular points in the ceremonies.

The precise formulas developed for slow-burning incense resulted in some remarkable temple clocks that would burn accurately for up to a hundred days. Some of the incense trails on these clocks resemble the designs of some Roman mosaic labyrinths, which share the need to stack the maximum length of pathway into the minimum area. While a few impressive time-keeping devices survive in temples and museums, smaller domestic versions of these "incense seals", or *hsiang lu*, were produced until the late nineteenth century. Although by this time they served a more decorative and contemplative purpose, they continued to employ traditional labyrinthine patterns for the incense pathway, which was formed with a moulded metal template. In Japan similar incense clocks comprised a deep tray of lacquered wood, which was filled with wood ash. A perforated wooden template was used to lay the incense powder on top of the ash in the shape of a meandering swastika.

During the eighteenth and nineteenth centuries the influences of European trade and colonialism brought Western time-keeping methods to China and Japan, making the incense clocks obsolete. Travellers from the West also introduced multicursal garden mazes into China. By the mid-nineteenth century they had reached Australia and even New Zealand, but this is part of a different strand of the story (see Chapter 5).

The labyrinthine pattern formed from powdered incense in a Chinese *hsiang lu* clock (left), ready for lighting, and the perforated metal template through which the incense trail is poured (right). This example is possibly from the Shanghai workshop of the Buddhist scholar Ting Yün, who manufactured a number of *hsiang lu* as incense burners for the home altar or for scholars' desks during the 1870s. A perforated cover is fitted over the tray containing the smouldering incense trail, which burns for some twelve hours.

Indian Sub-Continent and Indonesia

Destroyed examples marked in italics

Location	Type	Comments
Pakistan		
Lamūtai	Wooden sculptures	Two labyrinths on pillars of mosque prayer room
Mānkyāl Bālā	Inscription	Carved on door frame of mosque
Shatyāl	Rock inscription	Dated to first few centuries CE?
Tal	Wooden sculpture	Carved on pillar of mosque prayer room
Ūtrōt	Wooden sculpture	Formerly on prayer room pillar, destroyed 1980
Nepal		
Bhaktapur	Stone carving	Reported 1740, whereabouts now unknown
Bhaktapur	Ceiling decoration	Recently restored in the temple of Dattatreya
India		
Baire Gauni	Stone labyrinth	Small labyrinth of uncertain age
Halebid	Temple wall inscription	12th–13th C., on Kedareshvara temple
Halebid	Temple wall inscription	12th–13th C., on Hoysaleshvara temple
Ondavalli	Inscription in temple	Graffito on floor of temple, age uncertain
Padugula	Rock inscriptions	Five labyrinths carved on a shrine, age uncertain
Pirla	Rock inscription	Recently discovered, age uncertain
Rhanipur Jharial	Stone labyrinth	Huge labyrinth near ancient temple
Sitimani	Stone labyrinth	Large labyrinth formed with mounds of stone
Tikla	Cave painting	Dated *c.*250 BCE, the earliest evidence for the region?
Sri Lanka		
Arattana	Temple wall painting	Painted mid-18th C.
Mādavala	Temple wall painting	Painted 1755
Sumatra		
Pematang Purba	Inscriptions & painting	Decoration on timbers of Royal Palace
Batak region	Paintings & carvings	Items collected in 19th C., now in museums
Java		
Guranteng	Inscribed finger rings	Found 1882, 9th–15th C., now in museums
Malang	Inscribed finger rings	9th – 15th C., now in museums

The labyrinths found across this region occur in a variety of forms and their history can be traced back over 2,000 years. However, they are not well documented, and undoubtedly more examples await discovery. Included in this table and map are permanent labyrinths, inscriptions, and sculptures, and labyrinths recorded on portable objects, which are often now found in ethnographic collections and museums. Not included are documents and manuscripts containing labyrinths, which are particularly common in India.

Below: an inscribed bamboo tube, collected during the nineteenth century in the Batak region of Sumatra, decorated with a Batak magical text and a labyrinth.

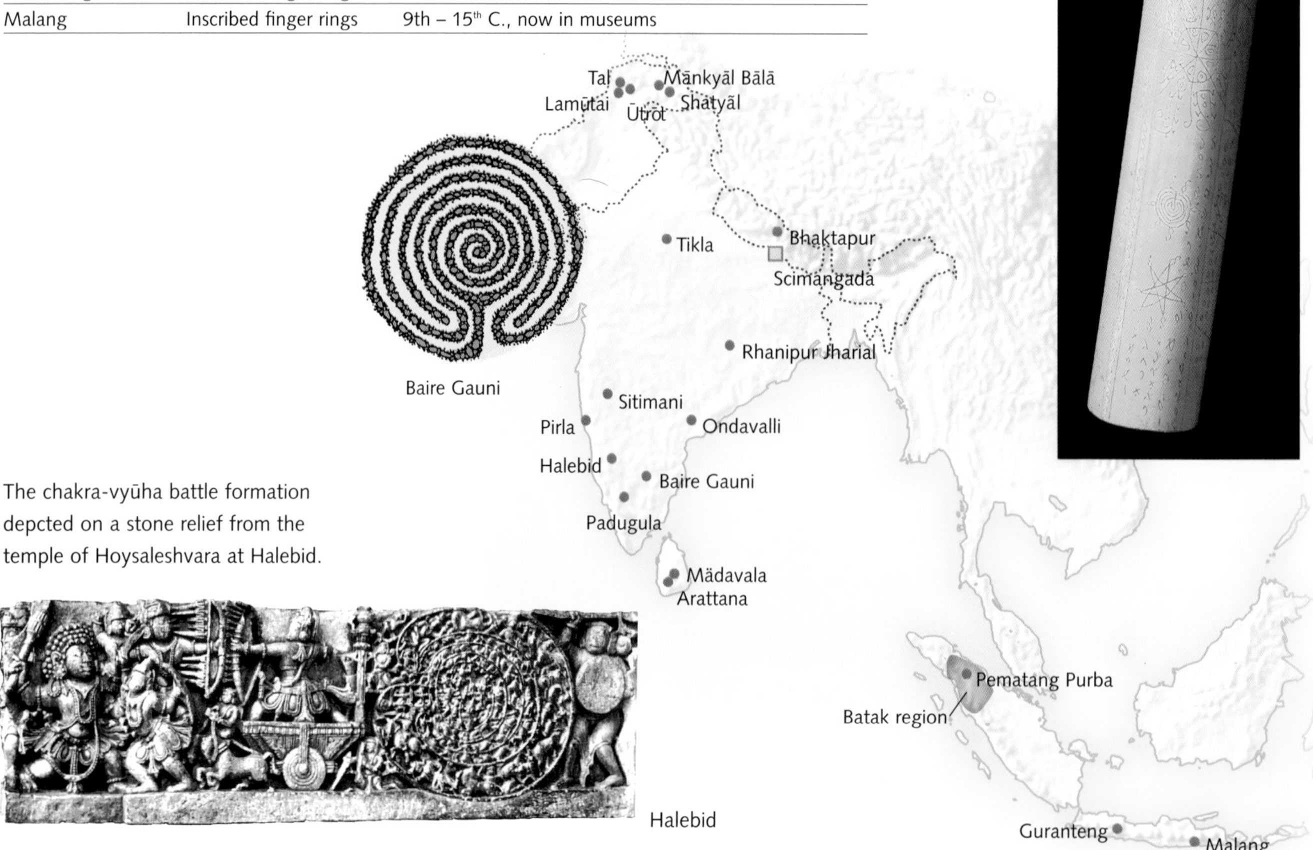

The chakra-vyūha battle formation depcted on a stone relief from the temple of Hoysaleshvara at Halebid.

The Labyrinth in Africa

The labyrinth symbol is widespread throughout North Africa, with examples dating from prehistory as well as from the Roman Empire, but there are no labyrinths recorded in central Africa. However, in southern Africa missionaries working among the Zulu in the early twentieth century documented a labyrinth game practised by the boys, designed to prepare them for hunting and herding in adult life.

L.H. Samuelson's book, *Some Zulu Customs and Folklore* (1912), records that the Zulu were fond of maze patterns, known as *usogexe*, which they drew on the ground with a finger or with saliva blown through a straw. Samuelson records the pattern that the Zulu boys drew. It was a curious maze-like design known as *tshuma sogexe*, with two goals at the centre, one of which was the royal hut. The creator of the pattern would challenge another boy to use a grass stem to trace the correct route to the royal hut. Any errors or failure to reach the correct hut would be greeted with a shout of "*Wapuka sogexe!*" ("You are done for in the Labyrinth!") and the player would be forced to go back to the start and begin the game again.

The labyrinthine design known as tshuma sogexe, traced in the dust by Zulu boys, recorded by L.H. Samuelson during the early twentieth century.

Another description of Zulu labyrinths published by Dudley Kidd in 1906 adds a few extra details. The clever boys marked labyrinths in the sand with amazing rapidity, while the others looked on, waiting to be challenged to find the way to the hut. A remarkable photograph of a young Zulu boy drawing his labyrinth accompanies this account. Kidd records that adults also practised this game while smoking hemp, blowing bubbles of saliva through a hollow stem on to the ground to form the labyrinths and using further armies of bubbles to try to breach the chieftain's defences. The suggestion that the Zulu's labyrinthine designs represented the barricades around the chief's hut, the central point of their tribal territory, provides parallels with the story of Troy. Protecting settlements with labyrinthine defences, real or symbolic, is a common theme. The Ovambo people, who herd cattle and grow millet in northern Namibia, still surround their encampments with stockades of thorny branches. These can be moved to change the passageways to the leaders' huts and livestock – which deceives predators as well as raiders during tribal conflicts.

Dudley Kidd published this unique photograph of a young Zulu boy tracing a circular labyrinth in the sand in 1906.

The existence of the labyrinth tradition in an area so remote from other labyrinth regions poses a question. Is this an independent development of the labyrinthine concept or do the symbolism and stories derive from sources in northern Africa? The southwards migration of Bantu-speaking peoples at the end of the first millennium CE could have spread knowledge of the labyrinth. The original source was possibly the Arabian and Indian traders who regularly travelled the seaports of eastern Africa. As the Zulu have no written history and little evidence has survived of the details of their migration routes, this may be an insoluble question.

Labyrinths in the American Southwest

In the beginning there was only darkness, inhabited by Earthmaker and Buzzard. Earthmaker rubbed dirt from his skin and held it in his hand, from which grew the greasewood bush. With a ball of gum from this bush, Earthmaker created the world. As Buzzard created the mountains and rivers with the passage of his wings, the Spider People sewed the earth and the sky together.

In time Earthmaker brought about a race of people in the desert. They lived for several generations, but they all became sinful except for one, Iitoi, the Elder Brother. Earthmaker saw that Iitoi was true and told him that a flood would kill all the people. The Creator placed Iitoi high on the sacred mountain Baboquivari and let him witness the disaster. Afterwards Iitoi helped create the Hohokam people, from whom the Tohono O'odham descended. He helped teach them the right way, and they lived in harmony for many years.

But in time some of the people turned on Iitoi and killed him. His spirit fled back atop Baboquivari, where he remains to this day. From time to time Iitoi's spirit, in the form of a small man, cunningly sneaks into the villages and take things from the people. Despite their attempts to catch him, the twisting path he takes returning to his home always confuses them. Thus in the labyrinth one can see Iitoi on the pathway and trace the mysterious and bewildering turns he makes on the journey back to his mountain home, Baboquivari.

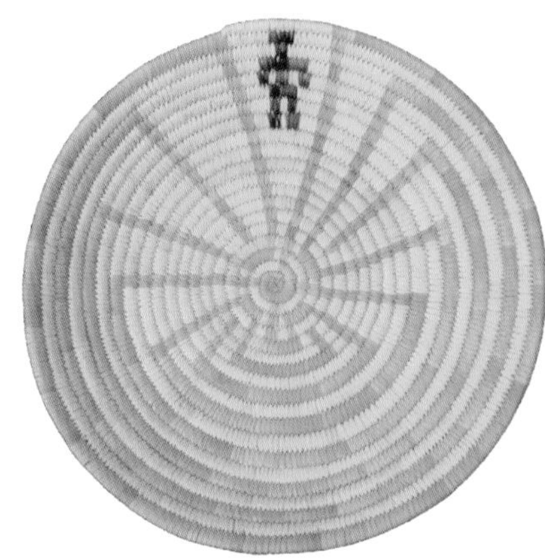

Above: the labyrinth design on a Tohono O'odham basket from southern Arizona. The figure standing at the entrance is Iitoi, the founding father of the tribe; the pattern represents the winding pathway that leads to Iitoi's home, on the top of Mount Baboquivari (below).

So runs the creation myth of the Tohono O'odham people of southern Arizona, well known for their woven baskets decorated with a design known as the Man in the Maze. Perhaps the biggest surprise of our story is the extraordinary appearance of the labyrinth symbol in the Americas. The maze on the baskets of Arizona is the very same classical labyrinth encountered in Europe and Asia; how and when it reached the New World remains the single biggest question of labyrinth research today.

Most of the "ancient" labyrinths of North America are to be found in the high deserts of Arizona and New Mexico in the United States and in the Sonora region of northwest Mexico. The intriguing ruins of Chaco Canyon, Mesa Verde, and other important sites bear witness to the people who once lived in these remote regions – the Uto–Aztecan-speaking Anasazi, Hohokam, and Mogollon tribes. These cultures flourished from the first few centuries CE until *c.* 1200–1400. They mastered the art of farming in an arid climate and produced sophisticated basketry and pottery to store precious food and water. The remains of extensive irrigation systems and networks of long-distance tracks, discovered by archaeologists during the twentieth century, all point to advanced societies that had trade and cultural contacts with the Aztec culture flourishing in Mexico at this time. These highly developed ancient peoples were the ancestors of today's basket-weavers.

Two tribes, the Tohono O'odham and the Pima, employ the labyrinth extensively in their mythology and craftwork. The Tohono occupy a large area of arid desert south of Tucson, Arizona, and the Pima live around the Gila and Salt rivers near Phoenix. Both tribes are considered descendants of the Hohokam (a Tohono name that means "the old ones"). The Hopi of northern Arizona, descendants of the Anasazi, and the Yaqui, originally from Sonora, but now scattered throughout the southwest, also have a long tradition of using the labyrinth. Though it is not a popular design among the Puebloan peoples of New Mexico today, labyrinth petroglyphs in this area show that it was certainly known in the past.

Basket-making skills have been developed and passed down among these people over thousands of years, and the Man in the Maze design has become widespread since the early twentieth century. The baskets are woven from dried grasses, leaves, and plant fibres. While early baskets were purely functional, the influx of settlers and traders in the late nineteenth century created a market for baskets designed also to please the eye. Although not mentioned in early studies of southwestern basketry,[10] the labyrinth design was described as common by Breazeale (1923), who said it was usually woven by the younger members of the tribe.

The basketry labyrinth appears at first sight to be quite different from the classical style, but is in fact the same, with seven paths and eight walls around the goal. Apparent differences occur because the basket is woven in a spiral, from the centre out, with the design built up successively as weaving progresses, rather than overstitched as decoration after completion.

How the labyrinth became such a popular motif is unclear. While Spanish sources cannot be ruled out, geometric designs have always been a feature of Pima and Tohono O'odham basketry and

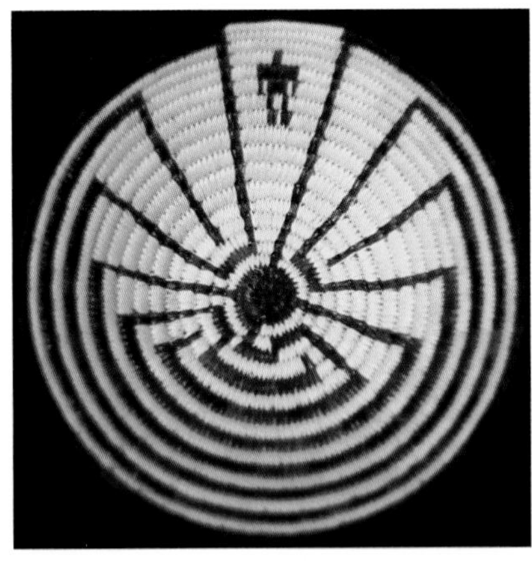

The basket labyrinths appear at first sight to be quite different from the classical style, but are in fact identical, with seven paths and eight walls surrounding the goal. Woven from the centre outwards in a continuous spiral, the design is built up as the basket progresses, not overstitched. The difference in form is a consequence of adapting the labyrinth to the circular medium of basketry.

This unique Pima basket, made *c.*1910, with nine paths instead of seven, is developed from a star-shaped, five-fold seed pattern. It is proof that the unknown weaver was fully conversant with the structure of labyrinths a century ago, long before modern studies of the subject were published. Other variants of the labyrinth possibly await discovery in collections of native basketry from the American Southwest.

appear in descriptions of their craft from the 1850s onwards. Complex meander patterns are a particular favourite, and when employed in a circular medium such as basketry, they inevitably lead to the labyrinth symbol. The recent discovery of a Pima basket dated *c.* 1910 in a private collection[11] provides an early example of the woven labyrinth and a dramatic demonstration that the weaver fully understood the seed pattern. This design is not based on the usual central cross, but around a five-spoke star pattern, so that the labyrinth has nine paths and ten walls.

The labyrinth appears quite frequently as a motif on the distinctive silver jewellery produced by several tribal groups in the Southwest. This Hopi overlay belt buckle renders the motif in an unusual oval form.

Since the 1960s and '70s many hundreds of Man in the Maze baskets have been produced for the tourist market and are now scattered around the world – probably one of the most widespread manifestations of this ancient design. Each one is slightly different, as they are all handmade. They range from plaques less than 3 in (7 cm) across up to baskets 24 in (60 cm) in diameter. The shallow baskets are traditional, but wall plaques and waste-paper baskets are recent adaptations to cater for the tourist market. Demand is such that imported replicas are appearing. The labyrinth is also found on the jewellery produced by Pima, Tohono O'odham, and Hopi silversmiths, however most examples date from the last fifty years or so.

Although the labyrinths on baskets and jewellery are all from the last century, there is evidence of a much earlier knowledge of the design in the region. The example often cited as the oldest, if only because it is the best known, is the labyrinth carved on a wall of the Casa Grande tower house ruins near Coolidge, Arizona. This four-storey clay and mortar building was constructed by the Hohokam people in the early fourteenth century, but abandoned by *c.* 1450. The labyrinth graffito is unlikely to date to the occupation period – it would be the only decoration on the originally polished limed walls – but the labyrinth clearly shows more weathering than the names and dates of more recent visitors. It was probably scratched into the wall after the wooden floors had collapsed, to judge from its location low on the wall of the first floor, by a visitor sometime during the sixteenth to eighteenth centuries.

The Hohokam tower house known as Casa Grande, near Coolidge, Arizona, was built during the fourteenth century CE and abandoned *c.* 1450. This classical labyrinth scratched on the inner wall was probably added later, possibly by a Piman visitor, for whom the symbol would have signified the plan of the "big house" or Hottai-ki.

Further confirmation is provided by a small sketch in a hand-written manuscript, the

Rudo Ensayo of Father Juan Nentvig, a Spanish priest who travelled the region between 1761 and 1762. It depicts a labyrinth drawn in the sand with a stick by a Piman, who stated that it was the plan of a one-time great building. Nentvig was not familiar with the labyrinth; he certainly didn't understand how to draw it, to judge from his clumsy sketch.

In the Piman tongue the labyrinth was known as Siuku Ki, the House of Siuku (also written as Se-eh-ha), the founder of the tribe. Piman children are known to have played a game known as "Tcuhiki" that used the labyrinth as its plan, but regrettably all details of it are now lost. Tradition records that the Siuku Ki was located somewhere in the South Mountains near Phoenix and that the winding passageways of his house kept Siuku well protected from his enemies.[12] However, the design is also cited as a plan of Motecuhzoma's House (in reference to the Aztec kings of that name), the Hohokam tower house complex at Casa Grande. This use of the labyrinth symbol as the abode of a famous figure, often from the mythical past, is of course familiar in both Europe and Asia.

The Tohono O'odham refer to the labyrinth as the House of Iitoi. In their creation myth related earlier, the path is said to be so long and winding that nobody has ever found the exact location of Iitoi's house. The small figure standing at the entrance in the Man in the Maze baskets is Iitoi, or Siuku, who alone knows the safe path back to his home.

A unique and intriguing stone sphere engraved with a Man in the Maze design was found in the Superstition Mountains near Phoenix in 1933. It is impossible to date, but it has been suggested that it may be a Pima basket-weaver's model, though it might equally be a ceremonial artefact or even a child's toy.[13]

The labyrinth also appears in Hopi mythology in both circular and square forms. A circular variety of the seven-circuit classical labyrinth symbolizes the Sun Father, the giver of life. The lines and pathways represent the road of life and the four points where they end represent the cardinal points. The square form, known as Tápu'at (Mother and Child) is a variety of the true labyrinth symbol, where a subtle reconnection of the lines produces one labyrinth within another. This Mother Earth symbol depicts the unborn child within the womb and cradled in the mother's arms after birth.[14] The Hopi also refer to the labyrinth as a plan of the concentric boundaries of their traditional lands, which have secret underground shrines at key points around their circuits.

A number of labyrinth petroglyphs are to be found on the Hopi reservation among pueblos on the rugged mesas north of Flagstaff. A roughly circular labyrinth is carved on a rock south of Shipaulovi on Second Mesa and a collection of six – five square and one circular –

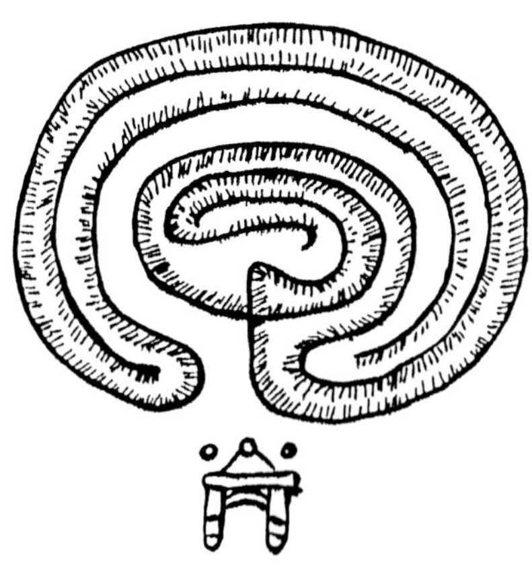

A small sketch of a labyrinth, drawn in the sand by a Piman, from Father Nentvig's *Rudo Ensayo*, an account of his travels in the Southwest during 1761–62.

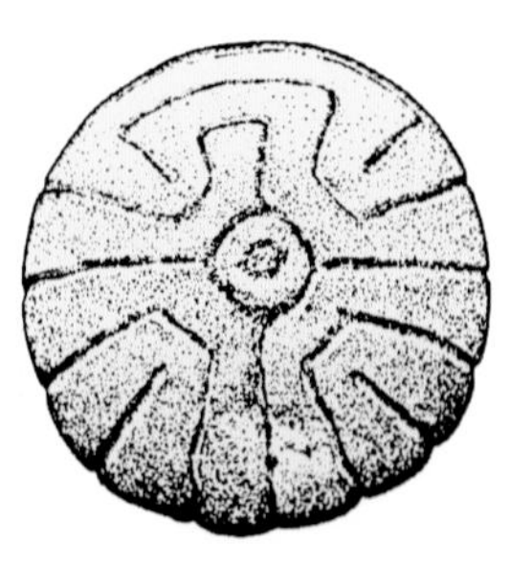

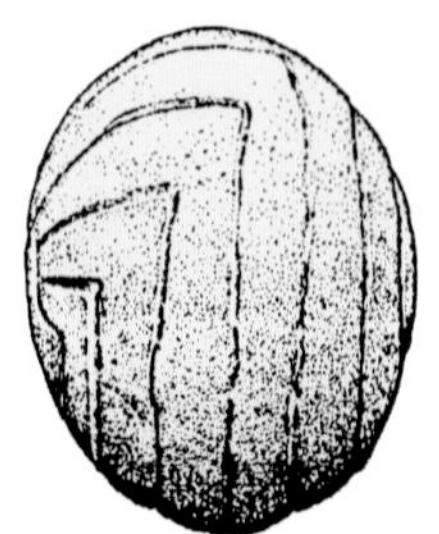

An engraved stone ball found in the Superstition Mountains near Phoenix in 1933. The labyrinth pattern completely surrounds the stone, although the purpose of this unique object is unclear, as is its age.

are located just south of the main road passing Old Oraibi on Third Mesa. The age of these carvings is difficult to ascertain, as they could date from any time since the twelfth century, when the Hopi settled this area. A small sandstone slab incised with a square labyrinth of the Tápu'at type was found built into a wall in Old Oraibi and another labyrinth is known from Walpi on First Mesa, carved on a ceremonial stick used at the ceremony of Wúwuchim, the first of three winter festivals. The labyrinth occasionally features in modern Hopi silverwork, but in the version traditionally used by the Pima and Tohono O'odham.

The Navajo, whose reservation covers much of northeastern Arizona and encircles the Hopi lands, have also used the labyrinth occasionally as a design for blanket weaving, borrowing it directly from the Hopi. A magnificent saddle blanket (*c.* 1930) in the Museum of Northern Arizona, Flagstaff, is woven from natural white and dark brown wool, and uses two labyrinths back to back. Modern Navajo silversmiths also produce numerous items of Man in the Maze jewellery, likewise influenced by Hopi use of the symbol.

There were once also labyrinths large enough to walk in this region, either drawn in the sand or laid out in stones. Records and photographs of small stone labyrinths on the Rio Yaqui in Sonora, and another from the early twentieth century on the south bank of Santa Cruz River, southwest of Casa Grande, attest to this.[15] These stone labyrinths were apparently not considered permanent and unfortunately we have no records of how they were used – whether for rituals or in children's games.

Labyrinth petroglyphs pecked out on rock faces and boulders are found occasionally among the extensive rock art throughout the southwest. Several have been recorded in southern Arizona near the Gillespie Dam on the north bank of the Gila river, and in New Mexico at Arroyo Hondo and Galisteo. A number of labyrinth petroglyphs in Arizona and northwest Mexico were recorded and photographed during the 1930s and '40s by William Coxon, a rock hound with extensive knowledge. Coxon claimed to have found about fifty different labyrinth designs in the southwest, but following a public disagreement with Harold Colton, a leading archaeologist who disparaged his work, refused to divulge the location of any of them.[16] Hopefully future fieldworkers will be able to rediscover some of these lost labyrinths for further study.

It is often difficult here, as in Europe, to determine the dividing line between labyrinths and labyrinthine spiralling designs. Meandering, maze-like patterns found in Californian rock art are unrelated forms with only passing resemblance to the labyrinth symbol. And as ever, the age of these labyrinth petroglyphs is very difficult to ascertain. Some appear alongside designs traditionally

The Hopi have two forms of the labyrinth – the classical style (above) and a square form known as Tapu'at (below), with two entrances that create two labyrinths, one within the other.

The Tapu'at labyrinth is engraved on this sandstone slab, found in the 1930s, built into a wall at Old Oraibi.

A large labyrinth petroglyph pecked on to the rockface of the canyon rim in Arroyo Hondo, near Taos, New Mexico. Probably carved around 300 years ago, the association with a rider on horseback suggests a Navajo or Apache origin.

attributed to the Anasazi, Mogollon, and Hohokam, which might date them to a time before European contact with this region. While association with other nearby designs can provide clues, and a number of chronologies for rock art in the region have been proposed, fitting the labyrinth into the pattern is not straightforward. The dating of rock art is a fledgling science, constantly under revision and not without controversy and contradiction.

Throughout the Americas the labyrinth symbol occurs in areas with a predominantly Spanish colonial history and this has lead to suggestions that Jesuit priests or Spanish soldiers, traders, or settlers introduced the design to the natives. In the southwest this could have happened at any stage from the mid-sixteenth century onwards, when Pedro de Tovar and the first of Francisco Coronado's Spanish conquistadors passed this way. Eusebio Kino, a Jesuit priest, visited the Casa Grande ruins (site of the labyrinth graffito) in 1694 and celebrated mass there. A long history of Jesuit, and later Catholic involvement in the spiritual welfare of the local populations has left a legacy of Christian practices mixed with more traditional observances and rituals. The Yaqui accepted Christianity at an early stage[17] but other groups, such as the Hopi, were always resistant to spiritual interference. While a Spanish origin for the labyrinth is plausible, some of the labyrinth petroglyphs found in New Mexico, southern Arizona, and Sonora could predate European contact. Besides, would a simple trick of drawing skill, demonstrated in the sand by a European priest or conqueror, become such a key figure in the creation mythology and symbolism of tribal groups?

The labyrinth symbol may have been discovered quite independently of the Spaniards. But so far, despite the wealth of excavated and documented material in the Americas, no labyrinth inscription or decoration has been found on a securely dateable object from pre-European times. This lack of evidence seems to speak strongly against a native tradition, though future discoveries could alter our perception. There might be objections to the suggestion that a design as complex as the labyrinth could arise more than once, at different times, in different continents. Other symbols, such as the swastika, double spirals, and meanders, are common among early rock art in the region and especially on the finely decorated pottery of the Anasazi and Hohokam. Any artist attempting to design decorative panels using double spirals and meanders on circular mediums such as pottery or basketry will eventually create the labyrinth (see page 23).

Further fieldwork and cataloguing of labyrinth petroglyphs is necessary, as well as new developments in dating techniques, before conclusions can be drawn as to exactly how and when the labyrinth first reached the New World.

Labyrinthine petroglyphs in the Southwest are difficult to date, as is deciding whether particular engravings should be classified as labyrinths, or merely labyrinthine. The top two petroglyphs from Arroyo Hondo and Cochiti Pueblo in New Mexico are certainly labyrinthine, the lower two, from near Casa Grande and Shipaulovi in Arizona, are more clearly labyrinths.

Labyrinths in the American Southwest

Destroyed examples marked in italics

Location	Type	Comments
Arizona		
Casa Grande	Labyrinth inscription	On inner wall of Hohokam tower house
Casa Grande	Labyrinthine petroglyph	Possibly a true labyrinth, petroglyph site 274
Gillespie Dam	Labyrinth petroglyph	1 mile downstream of dam, north bank of Gila River
Old Oraibi	Labyrinth petroglyphs	Five petroglyphs; four square, one circular
Old Oraibi	Labyrinth petroglyph	Tapu'at design, now in Heard Museum, Phoenix
Santa Cruz	Stone labyrinth	South bank of Santa Cruz river, now destroyed
Shipaulovi	Labyrinth petroglyphs	Two labyrinths reported
Superstition Mtns	Inscribed stone ball	Found in 1933, current whereabouts unknown
New Mexico		
Arroyo Hondo	Labyrinth petroglyph	Five-circuit labyrinth, Navajo origin?
Galisteo	Labyrinth petroglyph	On Bear Rock, Omero Mine Road, SE of Galisteo
Hidden Mountain	Labyrinthine petroglyph	Curious design based on a labyrinth?
Northern Mexico		
Rio Yaqui	Stone labyrinth	Photographed 1904, now destroyed
Rio Santiago	Petroglyph	Photographed by Coxon, location uncertain

The origin of the labyrinths in this region is one of the biggest mysteries of the labyrinth story. Included in this map and chart are the locations of documented petroglyphs, two former stone labyrinth sites, and several archaeological finds. Also marked are the reservation boundaries of the tribes that use the labyrinth in their craftwork and the location of the two sacred mountains that figure in the local labyrinth mythology. Baskets and craft items bearing labyrinths can be found for sale at trading posts on the reservations and are exhibited in a number of the major museums in Arizona and New Mexico.

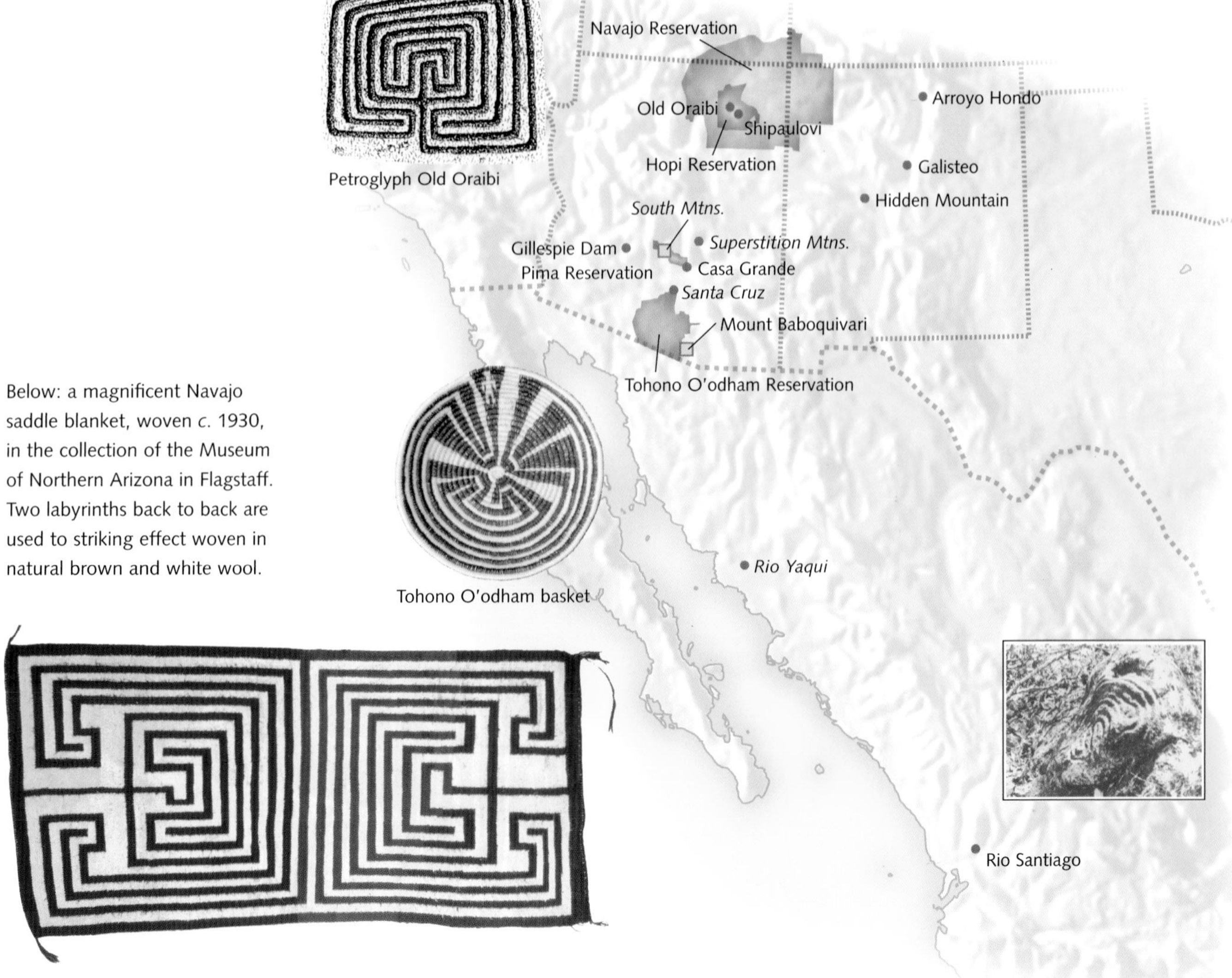

Below: a magnificent Navajo saddle blanket, woven *c.* 1930, in the collection of the Museum of Northern Arizona in Flagstaff. Two labyrinths back to back are used to striking effect woven in natural brown and white wool.

A Navajo Man in the Maze brooch.

A symbol of tribal identity

Evidence for the popularity of the labyrinth symbol amongst the Pima and Tohono O'odham peoples of southern Arizona can certainly be traced back at least 250 years and the use of the motif as a popular design element on their woven baskets is well known. The traditional basket weaving and pottery skills of these people have been handed down through successive generations and during the last century or so have become a valuable source of income as the increasing market for their work for the tourist and collector's market has developed. The Man in the Maze design is amongst the most distinctive of the design motifs used on their basketry and has become synonymous with their tribal identity. It appears on a wide variety of craft items produced in the American Southwest, especially in Arizona.

The distinctive overlay style of Hopi and Navajo silversmiths, created from two sheets of metal with the design in high relief cut with a fret saw and soldered to the backing plate, has been developed within the last 50 years. The pottery styles of the Southwest are more traditional and occasionally feature the labyrinth as a decorative element. Basketry is a skill inherited from the earliest inhabitants of this region, passed down through the generations. Weavers, young and old, are encouraged to enter their work in regional craftwork competitions, winning pieces are prized by their creators and sought by collectors. The development of innovative techniques combined with traditional motifs keeps this a vibrant craft.

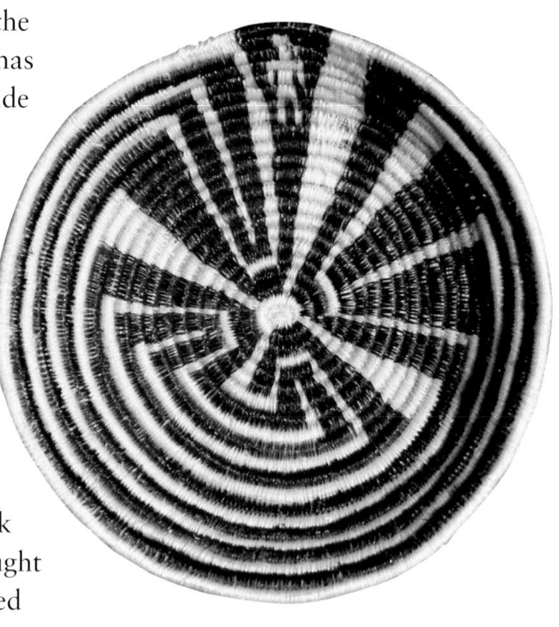

Above: Miniature Tohono O'odham basket woven from horsehair
Left: A proud Tohono grandmother displays her award-winning basket
Below: Tohono O'odham decorated bowl.

Above and left: labyrinths on the Pima-Maricopa reservation, Scottsdale, Arizona.

In recent years the Salt River Pima-Maricopa Community, situated on the edge of Scottsdale, have adopted the Man in the Maze as their the principle tribal symbol. Reflecting on the role of the labyrinth as a guidepost for determining life's journey, the tribal council have placed large labyrinth sculptures at entrances to their land and even use the symbol on the licence plates attached to official council vehicles.

To the south of Tucson, the Tohono O'odham also use the labyrinth to express their tribal identity. A bronze statue of a basket weaver installed at the centre of a painted pavement labyrinth, off Speedway in Tuscon (above and left), celebrates the heritage of the Tohono O'odham Nation. Official buildings on the tribal reservation are decorated with labyrinths (above right: on the court house in Sells) and local basket weavers have recently formed a co-operative to promote their work.

The Labyrinth in South America

The famously intriguing Nasca Lines cover 1,000 square kilometres of the arid Peruvian desert in the foothills of the Andes, north of the small town of Nasca. They were created during the first few centuries CE by moving the brownish oxidized stones that litter the flat pampas into lines and shapes that reveal the pale yellow sandy clay beneath. By far the largest collection of geoglyphs anywhere, they have rightly been called the eighth wonder of the world[18] and have formed the subject of many studies and theories since they were first reported by pilots flying over the area in the late 1930s.

A labyrinthine geoglyph marked during the first few centuries CE on the pampas north of Nasca in Peru. This design, and a similar example nearby, are not true classical labyrinths, but the pathway was probably walked as part of a ceremonial practice.

The purpose of these figures remains a topic of hot dispute, though more rational writers tend to agree that the lines and symbols were walked as part of processional ceremonies to ensure rainfall in the nearby mountains. Practically all of the animal and spiral patterns, and many of the other figures besides, are constructed from a single line that winds all the way through the design and back out again without crossing itself or producing a dead-end. Thus all these figures can be considered labyrinthine in a broad sense. Perhaps not surprisingly, this rich hunting ground contains several patterns that are also labyrinths in the strict sense. The first is found next to a major crossing point of lines and trapezoids with a low mound at their intersection. Unfortunately damaged by a track that cuts across it, the pattern is a serpentine line that winds its way back and forth into the centre. The second figure is certainly one of the labyrinth family, although the simple looping concentric pathway was almost certainly constructed without knowledge of the true labyrinth.

If these lines marked on the desert sands at Nasca were indeed created for ceremonial walking, then these simple figures offered a single, twisting pathway that ultimately reached a goal – a labyrinth. The design is not formalized as elsewhere, but the intention may well have been the same. Of course the similarity to other labyrinths worldwide could be ascribed to nothing more than coincidence. If it were the only evidence for an indigenous labyrinth in South America, we could dismiss it and move on, but other examples are known.

The labyrinth symbol has been recorded among the Caduveo native people of central Brazil, where the ethnographer Claude Lévi-Strauss collected a perfectly drawn classical labyrinth decorated with leaf-like appendages similar to tattoo designs from India. A similar Caduveo labyrinth was reported in 1948, collected from a woman who insisted that the design was indigenous and not introduced by Europeans, although she gave no explanation of its purpose. How the labyrinth could have reached this remote area, if not with colonial influences, is difficult to understand.

Considerable controversy surrounds the existence of labyrinths in Ecuador. Two engraved examples have been recorded in the

Collected by ethnographer Claude Lévi-Strauss in 1935, in the remote Gran Chaco region of Brazil, this drawing of a labyrinth by a Caduveo artist raises interesting questions concerning the occurrence of the labyrinth in South America.

collection of the late Father Carlo Crespi of the church of Maria Auxiliadora in Cuenca. This remarkable assortment of stone artefacts and plaques of gold, silver, and copper was widely celebrated during the 1970s by the writer Erich von Däniken for its depictions of pyramids, elephants, ancient unknown alphabets, and other "alien" symbols. Supposedly found in caves around Cuenca and given to Crespi for safekeeping, the collection may include genuine Inca objects, but it has been suggested that to satisfy the priest's requests for unusual antiquities, local artisans produced many of the items in nearby workshops.

Among this motley collection of curios, a square classical labyrinth with confused pathways engraved on a stone slab looks particularly freshly carved and suspicious. Likewise, a silver plaque with a crudely inscribed labyrinth surrounded by meander patterns is surely a forger's fantasy. The errors in the designs of both labyrinths could suggest that they were copied from a photograph of a labyrinth-decorated coin from Knossos.[19] Unconfirmed reports of labyrinth carvings on rock faces in the mountains around Cuenca must also be treated with suspicion. Following Crespi's death in 1982, his collection disappeared from view, although the labyrinth-engraved stone slab re-surfaced in 2001 in Vienna in an exhibition of "evidence" for lost prehistoric technologies and ancient astronauts.

An engraved stone slab with a poorly drawn labyrinth, formerly in the collection of Fr. Carlo Crespi in Cuenca, Ecuador. This and a silver plaque engraved with a blundered labyrinth in the same collection are of dubious origin.

Serious suspicion must also surround a labyrinth inscribed on the interior of an Olmec stone bowl from central Mexico, and another bowl inscribed with a spiralling labyrinthine design.[20] William Spratling, an antiquities dealer notorious for dubious objects and restorations, sold both items to the editors of an art journal in Mexico City during the 1940s or '50s. The bowls are definitely genuine, but the inscriptions were almost certainly added to both objects to ensure a good sale. Similar counterfeit objects surface from time to time in the art and antiquities market. A seal stone with a labyrinth on one face and supposedly of Minoan origin was probably manufactured in Beirut during the early 1960s. The current crop of replica Man in the Maze baskets, woven not in the American Southwest but in Pakistan, will undoubtedly cause confusion for collectors and researchers in the future.

While this Olmec bowl from central Mexico is genuine, the labyrinth inscribed inside the bowl was certainly added by an unscrupulous antiquities dealer, keen to secure a better price for the object from a credulous buyer.

So what are we to make of these South American labyrinths? While at least half of them appear to be modern forgeries produced for credulous collectors of antiquities, the labyrinths from central Brazil certainly deserve further investigation. The Nasca labyrinths, obviously a totally independent expression of the labyrinthine concept, suggest the design can appear independently of European influence. While the history of the labyrinth in Europe, and even in Asia, can be deduced fairly accurately, the labyrinths of the Americas continue to pose exciting challenges for future researchers.

Chapter 3

Christianity and the Medieval Mind

To visit the Cathedral of Notre Dame in Chartres is an awe-inspiring experience. Entering, it takes a moment for the eyes to adjust to the gloom; the hushed chatter of tour groups reverberates around the walls. As the tourists make their way to the high altar they pass between the chairs that line the nave, often oblivious of the pattern beneath their feet, but on certain days small expectant groups gather to await the removal of the chairs to reveal the floor in its full glory. Filling the nave is a complex circular labyrinth in lines of dark stone laid into honey coloured paving. It is an 800-year-old reminder of the fascination the labyrinth held for medieval architects, clerics, and pilgrims alike. This fascination continues to draw modern pilgrims to the cathedral today.

Lit by candles for a modern-day labyrinth walk, the beautifully preserved pavement labyrinth in Chartres Cathedral is without doubt the most famous of the medieval Christian labyrinths.

Of all the earlier forms of Christian labyrinths, the pavement labyrinths in the great Gothic cathedrals of France capture the imagination the most strongly. They are the leading inspiration for the modern revival of interest in labyrinths, with imitations and re-interpretations of the Chartres labyrinth now appearing in many settings. This round of revival and re-creation is not the first; we know of at least two similar episodes – during the Renaissance and in the late nineteenth century – since labyrinths were first brought into medieval cathedrals and laid out for walking.

Early Christian Labyrinths

The story of how labyrinths came to occupy the grand naves of the greatest Christian monuments of the Middle Ages and gain acceptance with the Church is long and tortuous. It took nearly a thousand years for this episode in the history of the labyrinth to unfold, during which it was transformed from an elemental pagan symbol into a configuration more suited to the medieval Christian mind. Imbued with further layers of symbolism, the labyrinth appears at this time not only in ecclesiastical settings but also in everyday locations throughout Europe. It became the root of the hedge maze puzzle, the most widely known labyrinth of all.

Many documented examples of labyrinth mosaics show how the symbol and mythology of the labyrinth spread throughout the Roman Empire during the first four centuries CE. Labyrinths appeared during this time in North Africa, the Near East, and across southern and western Europe. It seems likely that the legends of the labyrinth were popularized by the works of Greek and Roman authors, including Homer and Pliny. Despite its origins in pagan mythology, the labyrinth was absorbed into Christian symbolism, philosophy, and architecture.

The first example of this phase of labyrinth history is found in Algeria, North Africa, and provides illuminating insight into how the labyrinth may have been visualized in the early Christian mind. It is a mosaic pavement labyrinth of

The mosaic labyrinth from the basilica of Reparatus, now in Algiers Cathedral, Algeria. Only 8 ft (2.5 m) wide, it is too small to walk and clearly served a symbolic purpose. The word square at the centre spells out the words *Sancta Eclesia*.

typical Roman style laid in the floor of the Basilica of St Reparatus, founded in 324 CE in Al-Asnam, also called Orléansville, west of Algiers. A unique feature of this labyrinth is a word square comprised of the words SANCTA ECLESIA (Holy Church) filling the central compartment. Such letter labyrinths were popular with the Romans[1] and this example, enclosed within a labyrinth, has been interpreted by scholars as a depiction of the *Civitas Dei* (City of God, i.e. the Church) surrounded by the *Civitas Mundi* (City of the World) as outlined by St Augustine in his book *De Civitate Dei*. Here he derides "that beast the Minotaur, shut up in the labyrinth, from which men who entered its inextricable maze could find no exit".[2] Unlike the earlier Roman mosaic labyrinths, where Theseus and the Minotaur often appear in the central goal, here the fearsome fable has been replaced by sacred wording, offering the comfort of the Church. However, the old pagan story of the labyrinth is still hinted at in Ariadne's thread, picked out in tesserae, winding along the first section of pathway. Only 8 ft (2.5 m) wide, it is, like all other Roman mosaic labyrinths, too small to walk and intended only for visual contemplation – it was almost 900 years before a labyrinth designed for walking appeared in a Christian church.

The Hollywood Stone, moved in 1925 to the National Museum in Dublin, Ireland, is decorated with a classical labyrinth design carved on a large boulder, which was discovered by accident in 1908 at Lockstown, near Hollywood, County Wicklow. A group of men chasing a stoat turned over the boulder to reveal the carving. It stood beside a branch of St Kevin's Road, a pilgrim's track leading through the Wicklow Mountains to the monastery at Glendalough, founded in the mid-sixth century CE. While the age of the carving remains unproven, its sharpness and location indicate that it was a marker stone for the long and winding pilgrim's path through the rugged Wicklow Gap, suggesting that it probably dates from the early Christian medieval period, *c.* 550–1400 CE.[3] The choice of the labyrinth to decorate the stone was surely a commentary on the tortuous path that lay ahead for pilgrims. Had the stone been left where it was found, the connection would be apparent, but now lying isolated in a museum it has lost its context and stands silent.

The classical labyrinth carved on the Hollywood Stone, now housed in the National Museum in Dublin, Ireland, possibly once served as a marker for pilgrims following a rugged trackway leading to the monastery at Glendalough.

The labyrinth carved on a block of stone from the church of St Pantaleon in Arcera, Spain, still shows clear evidence of the seed pattern at the centre of its circuits. The age of this labyrinth is uncertain.

Another classical labyrinth, discovered in 1985 on a stone built into the wall of the ruined thirteenth-century church of St Pantaleon, in Arcera, northern Spain, may have been a tombstone from the earlier seventh- to twelfth-century church on the site.[4] Alternatively, it could be a considerably older carving that was later re-used as a building stone – labyrinth inscriptions on rocks from the early Bronze Age are well known in nearby Galicia and we can see the re-use of prehistoric carvings in later Christian buildings, for instance, in the steps of the cathedral in Santiago de Compostela.[5] Several experts have pointed out that the engraving of the central "cross" is deeper than the outer circuits. Whether this is a consequence of the initial marking or a deliberate attempt to Christianize the symbol before incorporating it into the fabric of the church, is debatable. The stone is currently on view in the Museum of Regional Archaeology in Santander, northern Spain.

A recently discovered labyrinth graffito on a piece of tumbled masonry among the ruins of the Roman town of Knidos in southwest Turkey,[6] provides another interesting example of an early Christian usage of the labyrinth. This labyrinth is of the classical type, but with an enlarged central goal, the consequence of the unusual construction technique from a series of concentric circles into which the traditional seed pattern has been inserted. The central goal is such a perfect circle that it must have been inscribed with a metal compass, possibly the first instance of the use of such a tool to draw a labyrinth. The labyrinth is accompanied by the inscription KYRIE BOETHIE ("Lord help [us]"). It is surrounded by a palm tree, a twining plant, and crosses, their style dating the carving to the sixth or seventh centuries CE. This combination of Christian imagery suggests that the labyrinth walls may have been looked to for protection.

A similar, though worn, inscription, abbreviated as KE BOETHIE, is found on a rock face in an old marble quarry at Dokimia, near modern Iscehisar, Turkey. It is situated above a number of broken concentric circles that have also been interpreted as a labyrinth.[7] Christian inscriptions and crosses datable to the sixth to eighth centuries have been found on adjacent rock faces.[8] Three further graffitos have been discovered in chapels dug into the Basarabi chalk cliffs at Dobruja, Romania. Although it is difficult to date these inscriptions, Viking raiders may have scratched them into the soft chalk during the tenth or eleventh centuries – a depiction of a shield alongside one of them certainly suggests early medieval origin. The shield labyrinth remains at the site; the two others on fallen masonry are now in Constantsa Museum.

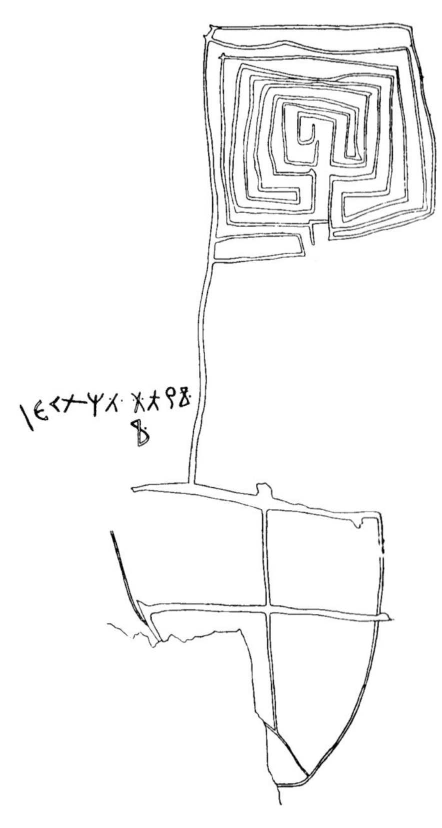

A blundered classical labyrinth scratched on the wall of a chapel cut into the chalk cliffs at Dobruja, Romania.

An important point about labyrinths in post-Roman Christian contexts is that all are modelled on the classical seven-path symbol. None displays the quartered Roman designs, for presumably these had long been lost to the Christian world, buried beneath centuries of decay and destruction. The classical labyrinth design, with its inherent simplicity, can be memorized and re-created. Our only examples from this period are carved on rocks that have survived the passage of time. Undoubtedly labyrinths were created in other media as well, but these were too fragile to survive. The labyrinth needed a new medium to allow its next developmental phase, one that could be replicated and hidden in times of trouble – the manuscripts that were circulating at this time in centres of learning in the European and Arabic worlds.

Early Christian Labyrinths

Destroyed examples marked in italics

Location	Type	Comments
Algeria		
Al-Asnam	Floor mosaic	Laid *c.* 324 CE, the earliest example
Tigzirt	Floor mosaic	Laid *c.* 450 CE, now destroyed
Spain		
Arcera	Stone carving	Age uncertain, in Santander Museum
Ireland		
Hollywood	Stone carving	Age uncertain, in Dublin Museum
Turkey		
Knidos	Inscription	6th–7th C., with Christian prayer
Dokimia	Inscription	6th–8th C., with Christian prayer
Romania		
Dobruja	Inscription	10th–11th C., with shield on chapel wall

Only a handful of the earliest Christian labyrinths survive. In floor mosaic, stone carving, and inscription, they leave behind a tantalizing legacy.

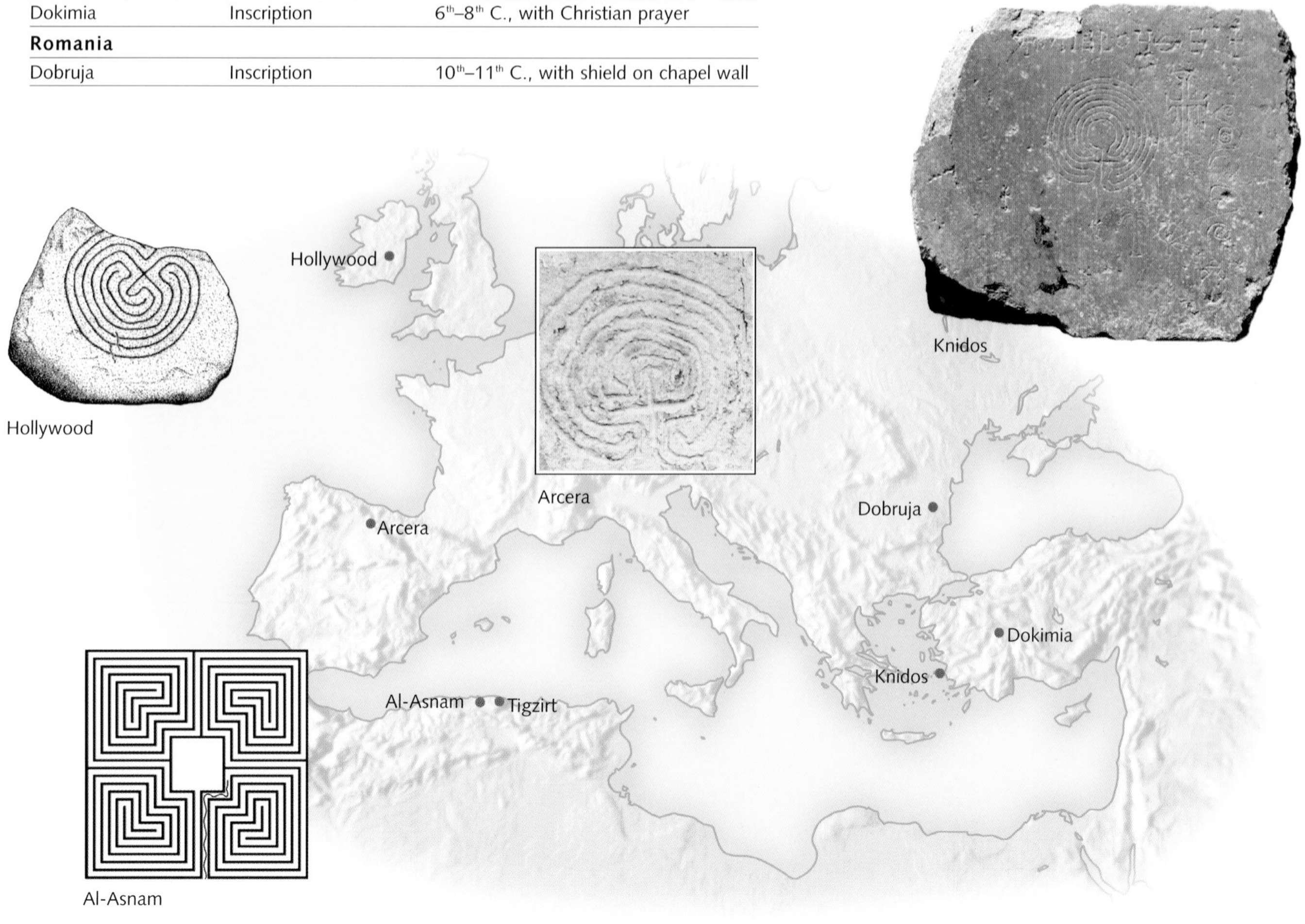

Knidos

Hollywood

Arcera

Al-Asnam

Manuscript Labyrinths

With such a scant and scattered selection among the ruins of early Christian settlements, it seems miraculous that the labyrinth survived and even proliferated during the second half of the first millennium CE. Though it was not incorporated into early church buildings, it survived in hand-copied texts that circulated Christian monasteries and the royal courts of Europe and transmitted classical learning to the medieval world. In the early sixth century, Boethius, in his influential *De Consolatione Philosophiae (Consolation of Philosophy)*, which was widely read throughout medieval Europe, referred to the "labyrinthine argument from which I cannot escape". Later copies of his work often include drawings of the labyrinth to illustrate philosophical complexities to the reader. The earliest copies of these texts are long destroyed, but from the early ninth century onwards, when the political stability of the Frankish Empire encouraged and protected the important monasteries and cathedrals where these texts were produced, more than seventy inscribed with the labyrinth symbol have been recorded.[9] Long before the advent of printing in Europe, scribes copied these manuscripts in the scriptoriums of monasteries and cathedral libraries. They would faithfully reproduce text, but were often at liberty to embellish illustrations, partly to bring the texts up to date, and partly no doubt to demonstrate their drafting skills. Most manuscript labyrinths were drawn with compasses on vellum and are based on a series of concentric circles with turns inserted at appropriate places, allowing a series of developments to the long-established labyrinth symbol.

A small classical labyrinth, labelled "*Uruem Jericho*" (city of Jericho) in a manuscript from Abruzzi. Drawn in the early ninth century, it is the earliest recorded manuscript labyrinth so far discovered.

Three such examples survive from the first half of the ninth century. One, in a manuscript produced in a monastery in the Abruzzi mountains in central Italy between 806 and 822 CE, is given as a plan of the city of Jericho. This was the fabled biblical city surrounded by seemingly impenetrable walls, which succumbed after being circled seven times by the Israelite legions (see Introduction). This oldest of all extant manuscript labyrinths is one of more than a dozen representing Jericho in manuscripts from Roman Catholic, Byzantine, and Jewish–Syrian sources. Nearly all depict classical or otherwise simple labyrinths.

The second specimen, in a chronicle compiled *c.* 830 CE in Aachen, Germany, has an inscription at its centre that reads "*domus dedali hac minotaurum conclusit*" ("House of Daedalus in which [is] imprisoned the Minotaur"), showing that the connection between the labyrinth and the Minotaur myth was still very much alive at this time. The third, from St Gall, Switzerland, is dated to *c.* 850 CE and accompanies a collection of poems about the planets, months, days of the year, and the stars. The labyrinth appears on the final page, following an illustration of the seven planets circling the earth. This

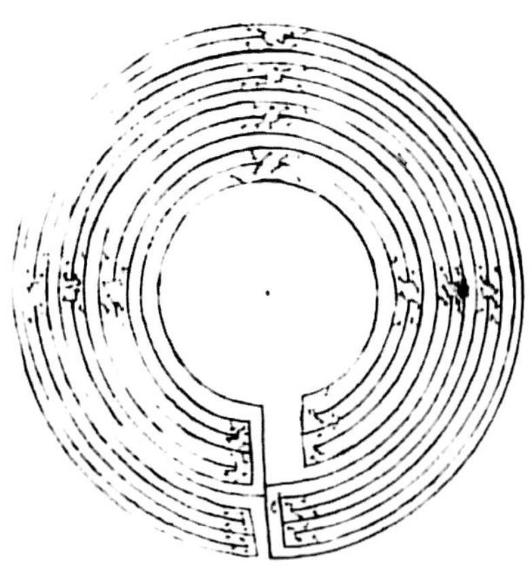

A curious labyrinth inscribed *c.*860–862 CE in a manuscript from Auxerre, France. A series of breaks and barriers depicted along the path of the labyrinth corresponds to the turn points of the later medieval design.

takes the labyrinth beyond the mythological and philosophical to a new symbolism of numbers and the workings of the universe.

By the mid-ninth century we come across a series of fresh developments in the labyrinth design. The first appears in a collection of historical and geographical texts compiled *c.* 860–62 CE at the monastery of St Germain in Auxerre, France. A curious eleven-path labyrinth, which superficially resembles a classical form, in fact displays a very different method of stacking the paths within the design. It also contains a series of breaks in its walls that effectively converts it into a multicursal maze. This labyrinth is certainly confusing; perhaps it was simply a draft, drawn by an uncertain hand. However, the positions of the breaks correspond precisely with those in a later form of labyrinth that within a few centuries was to dominate medieval manuscripts and cathedrals alike.

A parallel development can be observed in a Book of Gospels from Alsace, completed *c.* 871 CE by Otfrid of Weissenburg. Otfrid takes the classical labyrinth and adds four extra circuits to the outside edge, again bringing the number of paths to eleven. This kind of labyrinth, which is often referred to as the "Otfrid" type, is an important stepping stone between the classical and medieval labyrinth designs.

These two labyrinths are significant, for the number eleven was taken to symbolize sin in the medieval Christian mind. Being one greater than the number of commandments, the eleven paths of the labyrinth would have signified the passage through the sinful world to reach salvation at the goal. During the ninth and tenth centuries the conversion of a pagan symbol into a Christian icon was taken further by overlaying the cross on the circuits of the labyrinth, thus re-introducing the quadrant structure first seen in Roman mosaic labyrinths.

An especially elaborate example comes from an early eleventh-century copy of Boethius' *De Consolatione Philosophiae*,

This important labyrinth appears on the endpaper of the Book of Gospels written by Otfrid, at the Weissenburg monastery in Alsace, *c.*871 CE.

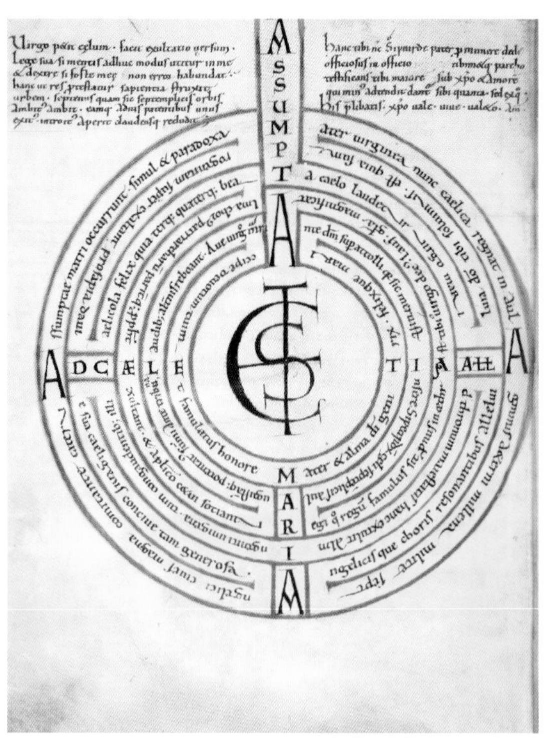

An unusual labyrinth with a prayer to the Virgin Mary inscribed along the pathway, produced at Abingdon, England, *c.*1000 CE.

produced in Abingdon, England. It contains an illustration of a six-path labyrinth, the paths of which are filled with a poem, "*Assumpta est Maria ad Caelestia, Alleluia!*" ("Mary is assumed into Heaven, Alleluia!"). The poem can be read either by following the path of the labyrinth, or by following the circles. One line in the verse prays for the acceptance of "Siweard into the hall of the sevenfold heaven". Siweard, the dedicatee of the poem, was probably the same individual who was appointed Abbot of Abingdon from 1030 to 1044 and who later acted as Archbishop of Canterbury.[10] The dedication of his prayer to Mary was apt because she was patron saint of Abingdon and protector of its inhabitants.

Above the labyrinth is an enigmatic inscription: "Wisdom has structured this city, which a seven-fold circle surrounds, and one and the same exit and entrance opens it with open approaches and closing, closes it again." The seven concentric circles of the labyrinth are obviously meant to reflect the sevenfold heaven mentioned in the prayer. Medieval scholars were forever debating the structure of heaven and reviewing and renewing their terminology, but most agreed that the earth, surrounded by the orbits of the sun and the planets, was encircled by the fixed stars in the firmament. Beyond this lay additional spheres representing the spiritual heavens, further sub-divided, where the saints and angels resided. While Siweard was hoping to find seven divisions of heaven, other medieval texts specified as many as fourteen. Complex illustrations of these medieval views of the universe, based on the Ptolemaic system, were popular in astronomical and calendrical manuscripts. The labyrinth symbol reflected the complex interplay of the scientific and the spiritual in medieval thought.

A refinement of the labyrinth design is seen on the flyleaf of a tenth-century computational manuscript from the monastery of St Germain-des-Prés in Paris. Once again, the labyrinth shows the central goal occupied by a particularly devilish looking Minotaur. The accompanying text records that the labyrinth was made by Daedalus and is so complex that once ensnared therein it is "impossible to progress from the darkness back to light".[11] This labyrinth is the first recorded example designed with an eye to both mathematical and visual symmetry. The eleven-path design has thirty-five moves between the entrance and the goal – the first seventeen exactly mirror the final seventeen, so that each part of the labyrinth path has its counterpart. Only the eighteenth move is unique and is the mirror line for the exquisite topographical symmetry of the plan. Comprised entirely of half and quarter turns, it also possesses very pleasing proportions. The pathway comprises seventy moves – the three score years and ten of a lifetime.

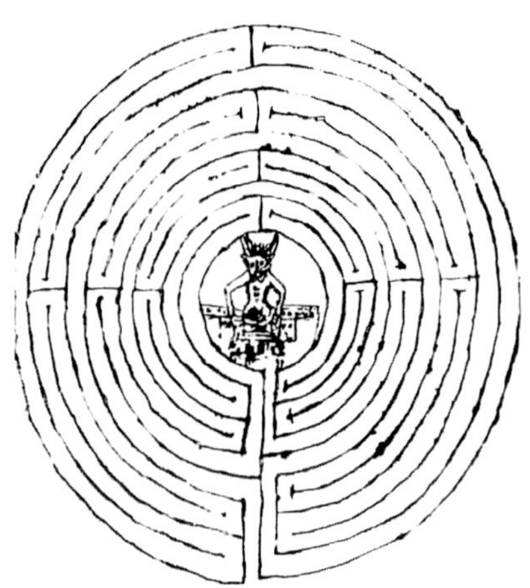

One of the first examples of the true medieval labyrinth design, seen in a tenth-century manuscript from St Germain-des-Prés in France.

Theseus battles with the Minotaur at the centre of the Otfrid-type labyrinth in this twelfth-century manuscript from Regensburg, Germany.

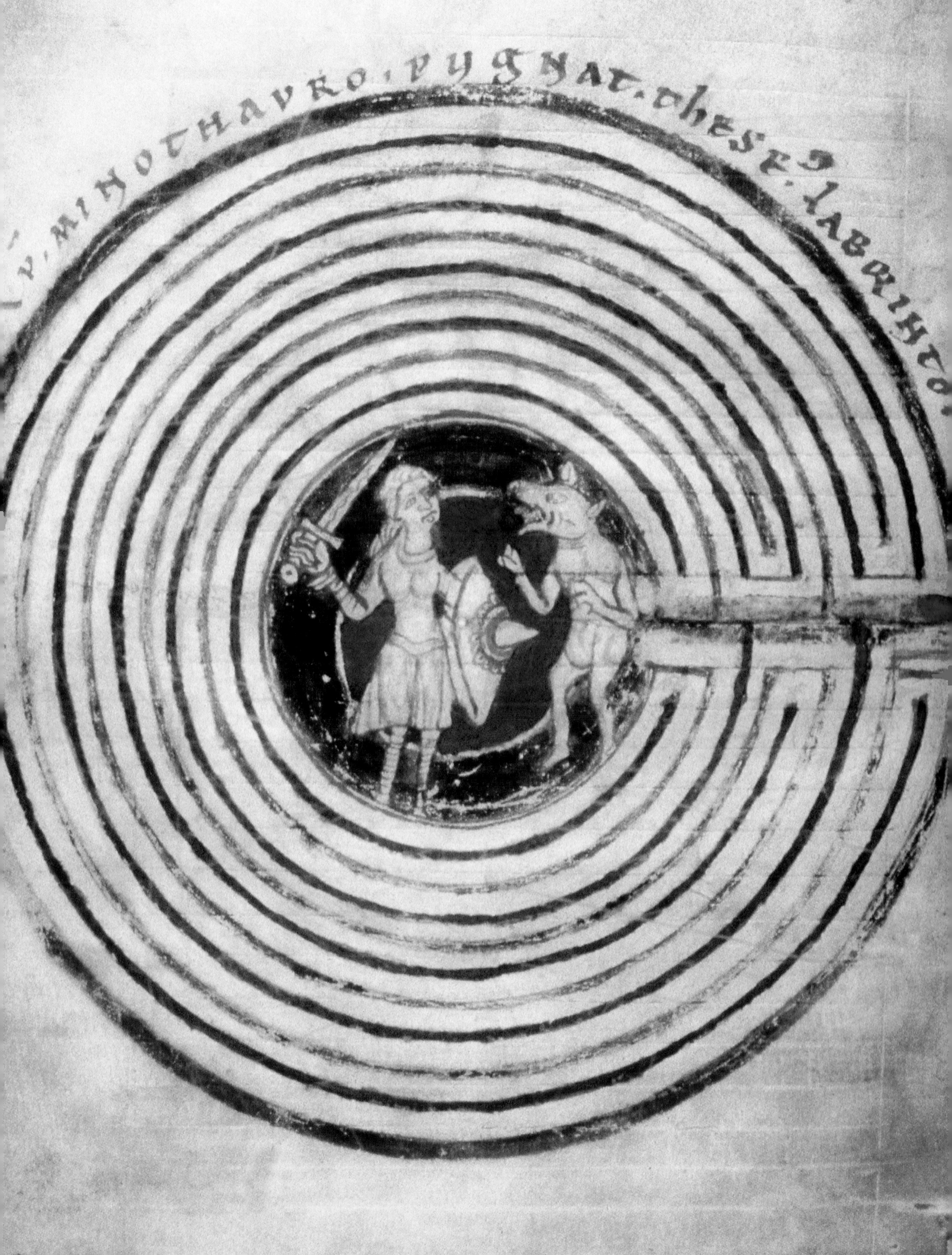
V. MINOTHAVRO. PVGNAT. THESE9. LABRINTO.

By the twelfth century the mathematically perfect eleven-path, four-axis labyrinth was the dominant design across Christian Europe, not only in manuscripts, but also in the fabric of churches and cathedrals. Often referred to as the "Chartres" labyrinth because it was employed on the floor of that cathedral several centuries after it first appeared in manuscripts, it should perhaps more accurately be called the "medieval" design. It is essentially the "perfect" labyrinth of its time. This same design appears constructed in many different materials on the village greens of England, in the formal gardens of Renaissance Europe, and even in the remoteness of Arctic Russia (see Chapters 4 and 5). It also features in the current revival of labyrinths in spiritual settings (see Chapter 6). The pagan labyrinth symbol had survived unchanged for over 2,000 years; its conversion to the Christianized form took little more than a few centuries. The next phase of labyrinth development was its transfer from the pages of a codex to the fabric of a church.

To understand how this transition took place, it is important to appreciate fully the context in which manuscript labyrinths are found. While some of them appear in philosophical texts to illustrate the complexity of the subject matter and others are presented as Christian symbols, a fair number accompany calendrical texts important to the Church for calculating the date of Easter, the principal Christian festival, and other movable holy days. In the early sixth century the Christian Church in Europe adopted the canon established by Dionysius Exiguus for determining the date of Easter. According to the Dionysian canon, it fell on the first Sunday following the first full moon on or after the spring equinox, 21 March. Tables for determining lunar cycles to establish the date of Easter are often accompanied by depictions of labyrinths, their twisting pathways providing a visual link with the cycles of time and Pythagorean teachings on the Harmony of the Spheres.

The *"Domus Dedali"* (house of Daedalus) is clearly identified with the labyrinth on the island of Crete in this section of the Mappa Mundi, created *c.*1280 CE, and on display in Hereford Cathedral, England.

Most of these unique manuscripts are safely stored in national and regional libraries, and few are available for public inspection, except by special arrangement. For further study of this important and diverse group of labyrinths, the fully illustrated catalogue provided in Hermann Kern's *Through the Labyrinth* remains the best source. However, one such labyrinth is kept on permanent display – the tiny labyrinth labelled "*Laborintus id est domus dedali*" ("Labyrinth, the house of Daedalus") that occupies the island of Crete on the Mappa Mundi in Hereford Cathedral, England. Created *c.* 1280 by Richard de Bello, it was taken to Hereford in 1305. This map of the then-known world is centred on Jerusalem and depicts a plan of the world that seems strange to modern eyes. The major cities and rivers of Europe are faithfully depicted, but outlandish beasts and monsters inhabit the far reaches of Africa and Asia.

A labyrinth labelled "*Urbs Jericho lune fuit assimilata figure*" (the city of Jericho was shaped like the Moon), produced at Regensburg during the late twelth century, is preserved in a manuscript in the Bayerische Staatsbibliothek in Munich.

Important Christian Labyrinth Manuscripts

Many of the Christian manuscripts containing labyrinths produced between the ninth and fourteenth centuries are now stored in national archives and museums. The monasteries where many of them were originally produced (named on the map below) are scattered across Europe. Their distribution is not dissimilar to the later locations of labyrinths in churches and cathedrals.

Hereford
St Omer
Aachen
Corbie
Paris
Weissenburg
Regensburg
Freising
Admont early 12th C.
Auxerre
Reicheneau
St Gall
San Sebastián *c.* 1072
Piacenza
Bobbio
Abruzzi
Monte Cassino

Labyrinth Symmetry and Structure

The adoption of the labyrinth as a Christian symbol during the early medieval period was the spur for a series of important developments to its design. Within the space of just a few centuries, the classical labyrinth, almost universal during prehistory and found on a number of early Christian inscriptions and manuscripts, was all but replaced by a series of much more complex designs with more obvious Christian symbolism and application. However, the variety of shapes and decoration that adorn many of these later medieval labyrinths often makes it difficult to understand their evolution and relationship to each other.

We have already seen how the double meander, also known as the Greek key, or fret pattern, can be expanded to create a classical labyrinth (shown opposite). Applying this process in reverse provides a valuable means of examining the key parts of a labyrinth, those crucial sections where the pathways turn to enter a new circuit. These condensed versions of labyrinth designs – known as compression diagrams – show the skeleton of the design free from the confusion of lengthy pathways and the distraction of differing overall shapes and additional decorative elements.

Meander becomes labyrinth.

Classical and Otfrid Compared

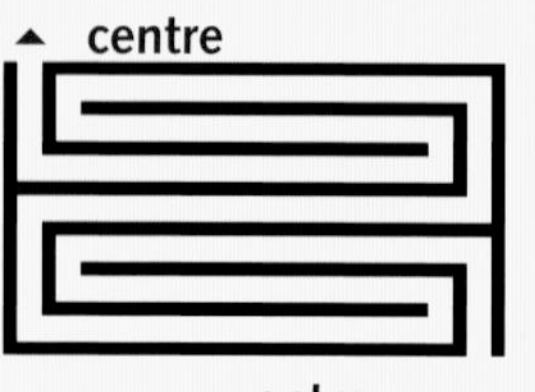

The classical labyrinth (left), the original and simplest of labyrinth designs, can be condensed to produce a compression diagram (below left), with the entrance lower right and the goal at top left. This reveals the double meander that represents the overall movement through the labyrinth. Compare this with the Otfrid labyrinth design (right), which was developed in the ninth century. Its compression diagram (below right) reveals it to be based on a triple meander. This simple development increased the number of circuits from seven to eleven, the number that represented sin in the medieval mind. The labyrinth can be seen as symbolic of the one true path through the sinful world, leading to salvation at its goal.

Medieval Symmetry

The visual and topographical symmetry of the medieval labyrinth (below left) is quite striking. The compression diagram for this labyrinth (below right) shows how the path through the labyrinth progresses. Completing the innermost circuits (in light grey) first, the pathway then meanders its course back out (in white), heading for the outermost circuits and then back towards the centre (dark grey). Notice how one half of the labyrinth mirrors the other half. Of the thirty-five separate sections of pathway traversed before reaching the centre, the first seventeen moves are the exact counterparts of the last seventeen, only move eighteen is unique and provides a hidden axis of symmetry for the pathway.

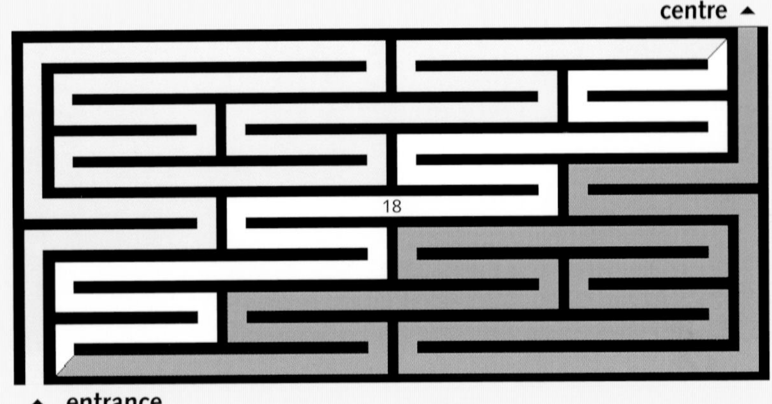

Medieval and Reims Compared

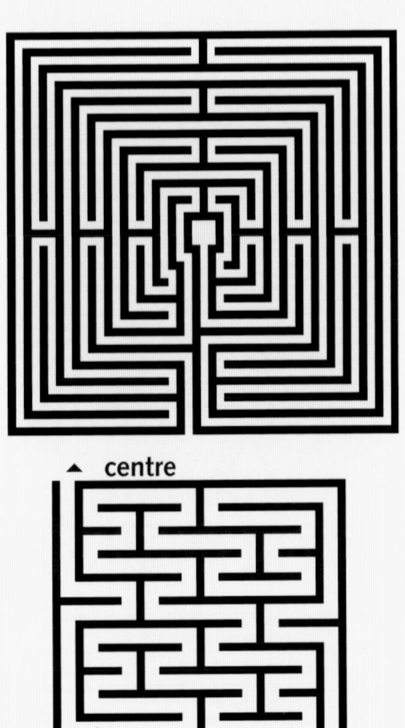

The medieval labyrinth design (left), which became widespread from the tenth century onwards, keeps the eleven paths of the Otfrid design, but introduces three further axes along its cardinal directions around which the paths turn. The compression diagram for this design (below left) reveals the elegance of the path sequence travelled to reach the goal and the striking symmetry of the design. Stacking the pathways to create a labyrinth of this type is surprisingly complex and only a limited number of solutions that maintain such symmetry are possible. Compare with the design and compression diagram of the labyrinth at Reims (right). Notice how this labyrinth travels the outer three circuits first, then the middle five and the inner three, a very different progression indeed.

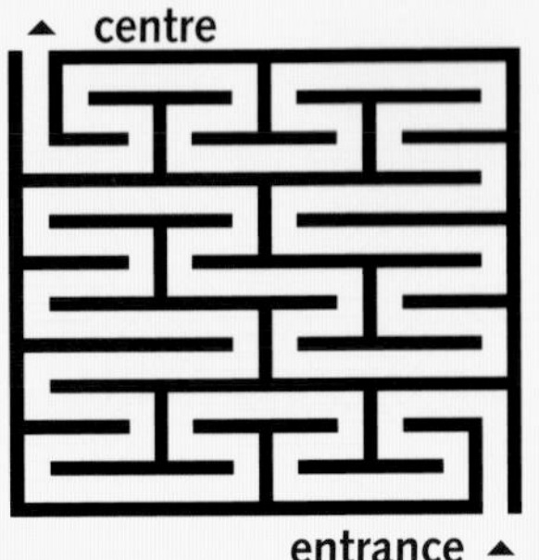

Labyrinths in Churches and Cathedrals

Pavement labyrinths constructed in coloured stone or tiles and other decorative materials are a striking feature of a number of medieval churches and cathedrals across Europe. Occurring from Ireland in the west to Poland in the east, they probably originated in northern Italy, where a number of small pavement labyrinths were laid in the floors of churches during the twelfth century.

Most notable among these is the mosaic labyrinth at Pavia. Constructed *c.* 1100 on the floor in the choir of the San Michele Maggiore basilica, it is only 10 ft (3.3 m) in diameter. Just a small section survives, the upper third of the design that was covered until 1972, preserved beneath an altarpiece installed in 1592. Fortunately a drawing of the labyrinth from the late sixteenth century records the larger part of the labyrinth mosaic now missing, allowing the full design to be reconstructed. The labyrinth was of the eleven-path medieval type that became widespread in the manuscripts of the late tenth and eleventh centuries. Theseus battling the Minotaur occupies the centre, but surrounding it are additional mythical figures. The side panels show an ocean swimming with fish and the confrontation between David and Goliath, an Old Testament parallel for the myth of Theseus and the Minotaur. A passage in a sermon by St Augustine makes the symbolism clear: "On the one side is the devil in the form of Goliath, on the other is Christ typified by David." The fight between good and evil is implicit in the symbolism of the labyrinth. The more obvious imagery of the Devil pitted in battle against Jesus would never have been placed on the floor to be trampled underfoot.

The preserved section (above), and a reconstruction of the complete labyrinth pavement (below), in the San Michele Maggiore basilica in Pavia, Italy.

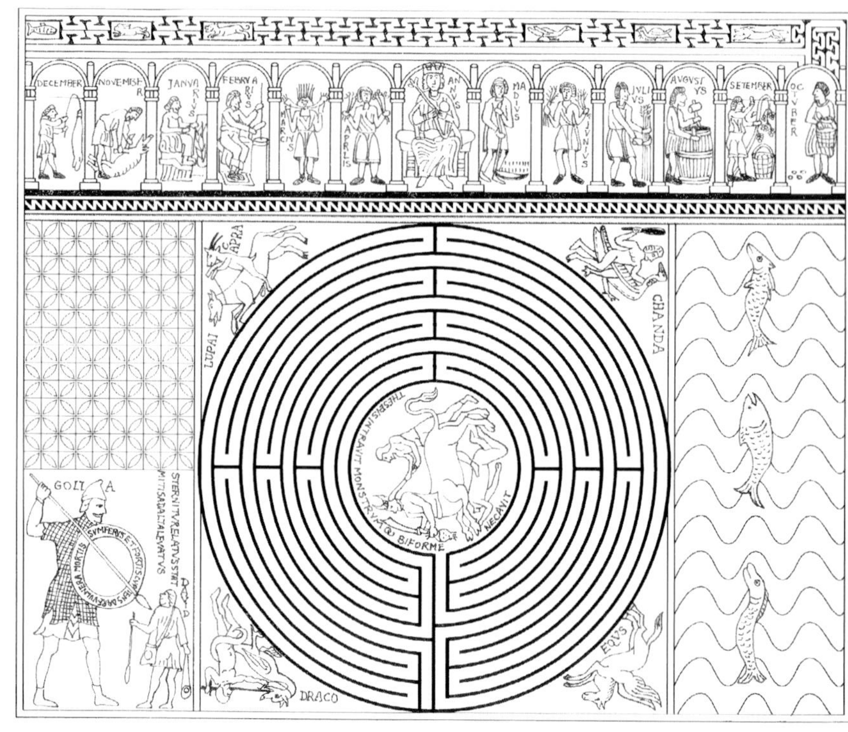

What takes us by surprise is the frieze along the top of the panel depicting the twelve months of the year and an enthroned Annus – symbolizing the passage of the year. This has clear parallels with the use of the labyrinth to illustrate computational tables and calendars in earlier manuscripts. Indeed, it may explain how the labyrinth found its way into cathedrals as a floor decoration at this time. While

The small labyrinth formerly set into the floor of Santa Maria in Aquiro in Rome.

the manuscripts would have been familiar to the learned clergy, floor mosaics would have been on show to the laity. Like wall decorations in churches and cathedrals across Europe, they would have been both educational and decorative, although all the early examples are too small to walk.

A similar labyrinth, constructed *c.* 1107, once existed in the Church of San Savino in Piacenza, but all trace of it has now been lost. It was accompanied by an inscription, possibly inspired by Matthew 7:14 "This labyrinth typifies the present world, broad at the entrance, but altogether narrow at the return. In this way ensnared by this world, weighed down by sin, one can only return to the doctrine of life with difficulty." It too featured Theseus and the Minotaur at the centre and was situated near a mosaic, still preserved, that features the months of the year.

Although a little worn from centuries of tracing by visitors' fingers, the labyrinth at Lucca Cathedral is otherwise well preserved.

The labyrinth in the Church of Santa Maria in Aquiro in Rome, only 4 ft (1.5 m) in diameter and laid in yellow marble with green and red porphyry, was unfortunately destroyed in the late nineteenth century. A plan made in 1847 has survived, showing it to have been of the same medieval design as the labyrinth in Pavia. Since the church was dedicated in 1189 it seems likely that this example dates back to the end of the twelfth century. A similar labyrinth once existed on the floor in front of the sacristy in the Santa Maria in Trastevere basilica, also in Rome. Also built in the mid-twelfth century, it is said to have resembled the labyrinth at Pavia, but was incorrectly restored as a series of concentric circles during the early eighteenth century.

In addition to the pavement labyrinths, three carved Italian labyrinths from this period have survived. The well known late twelfth-century depiction of a labyrinth carved on the north side of the bell tower of Lucca Cathedral is accompanied by an inscription: "Here is the labyrinth that Daedalus from Crete built, which no one can exit once inside; only Theseus was able to do so thanks to Ariadne's thread." Another relief from the convent church of San Pietro de Conflentu in Pontremoli has survived both the collapse of the original church and the final destruction of the rebuilt church by bombing in 1945. Carved in relief on a sandstone slab, it depicts the medieval labyrinth design surmounted by two riders on horseback. Whether these figures are involved in a tournament or are engaged in a medieval version of the Roman *Ludus Troia* game is unclear, although the inscription around the labyrinth "*Sic currite ut comprehendatis*" ("so run, that you may obtain") is a quote from I Cor. 9:24. In this case the inscription of the "JHS" monogram of Christ, at the centre of the labyrinth, makes it clear that the prize is redemption through Christ. This stone is currently preserved in the Castello Pignaro-Pontremoli.

A similar labyrinth carved on a sandstone slab formerly located in the church of San Pietro de Conflentu in Pontremoli, Italy.

An unusual example of a classical labyrinth in a medieval ecclesiastical setting, at the top of a pillar in the cloister of San Benedetto monastery in Conversano, Italy.

A final example at the top of a pillar in the cloister of the San Benedetto monastery in Conversano is quite unusual, for it is of the classical design, almost unique in a medieval ecclesiastical setting. All three of these examples are (or were) at about eye level and were meant to be used for contemplation. The Lucca labyrinth has been considerably worn over the centuries by people tracing the paths with their fingers. A depiction of Theseus fighting the Minotaur that once stood at the centre has been rubbed completely away.

The true flowering of the labyrinth during the medieval period took place in northern France. The wave of cathedral construction and the quest for ever-grander monuments and wider spaces in which to worship provided the space for the labyrinth to be laid full size across the nave. For the first time in Christian history, the design was now large enough to walk; the labyrinth had changed from being contemplative to interactive. The reasons for this transformation have been the subject for much scholarly debate; clues lie in the detailed study of individual labyrinths.

By far the best known example is the pavement labyrinth in Chartres Cathedral, which was laid *c.* 1202 as part of the extensive rebuilding of the cathedral after the disastrous fire of 1194. Measuring 42 ft 4 in (12.89 m) in diameter, it is the largest single design ornament in the whole cathedral – a striking object to greet the medieval pilgrim entering the building. Unfortunately, due to regular services and crowds of tourists, it is usually covered in chairs. The centre of the Chartres labyrinth was formerly occupied by an engraved brass plate bearing a representation of Theseus and the Minotaur. The plate was torn up in 1792 and melted down for making cannons for the army of the Republic, but the rivets that held it in place are still present, polished by the continuing passage of feet. The elaborate design has a rosette at the centre, echoing the tracery of the famous rose windows of the cathedral, and 113 "teeth" enclosing 112 "cups", or "lunations", arranged around the circumference, like a huge cog wheel.

Much has been written by modern authors on the meaning of this ornamentation – one interpretation is that it is a device for determining the date of Easter, though this is based on faulty understanding of medieval lunar calendars. Direct parallels can be found in the crenellations surrounding the exterior walls of earlier Roman mosaic labyrinths and in the depictions of Jerusalem on medieval maps. The labyrinth has always been employed as a metaphor for the holy city and Jerusalem needed defences as much as Troy or Rome.

However, frequently quoted references naming the labyrinths of this region as *Chemins de Jérusalem* (Roads to Jerusalem) date back to only the late eighteenth century. According to this tradition, pavement labyrinths were walked as a substitute for the long, arduous pilgrimage to Jerusalem during the troubled times of the Crusades. The recapture of Jerusalem in 1099 and its subsequent fall to Saladin in 1187 made the city a dangerous and sometimes unattainable destination. Although it was briefly recovered between 1229 and 1244, a pilgrimage to Jerusalem was not realistic for most people at that time. Chartres itself was a well-established pilgrims' destination and many of the other cathedrals and churches where labyrinths have been recorded, each with its own collection of holy relics, were on

The engraved brass plate (above) at the centre of the labyrinth in Chartres Cathedral, France (below), was removed in 1792, but the labyrinth is otherwise beautifully preserved. It was laid during the first few years of the thirteenth century.

established pilgrimage routes, especially on the road to Santiago de Compostela in Galicia, northwest Spain, one of the most popular destinations for the devout.

The oft-repeated story of medieval monks or pilgrims traversing labyrinths on their knees as atonement for their sins is probably no more than a romantic antiquarian fantasy. It is known that during the eighteenth century people would make their way around the labyrinths at Reims and Arras on bended knees while reciting their prayers,[12] but there is no evidence that this display of Catholic piety had roots in earlier times. A popular myth that the pathways of the labyrinth at Chartres was once carved with words from the Psalms is based on a seventeenth-century engraving of the labyrinth overlaid with penitential prayers to be recited whilst following the path.

A seventeenth-century engraving showing people walking the Chartres Cathedral labyrinth.

The careful placement of pavement labyrinths within the geometric layout of cathedrals has been taken by some modern writers to indicate that they contain a wealth of coded information. The illustrated notebook of the architect Villard de Honnecourt, who would have seen the labyrinth when he visited Chartres around 1230, contains an interesting sketch of a circular labyrinth, a mirror image of the design at Chartres.

A sketch of a circular labyrinth in the illustrated notebook of the architect Villard de Honnecourt.

Unfortunately the builders of the labyrinths have left no manuscripts to tell us of their intentions. The numerical relationship and symbolism of the dimensions of the labyrinth at Chartres, as well as its placement and relationship to other structural features of the cathedral, has been extensively discussed.[13] The architects of the cathedral would certainly have been familiar with these mathematical and geometric principles, but it is difficult to assess what, if any, significance they held for the cathedral's clergy or pilgrims.

Chartres is situated in the archdiocese of Sens and the cathedral at Sens also possessed a labyrinth. Although it was circular and of a similar size to Chartres, the connection of the paths up the central axis of the labyrinth was different. It was destroyed in 1768 when the numerous tombstones that formed the floor of the cathedral were lifted and the floor was repaved to make it level again.

Another notable example in the Sens archdiocese, also sadly lost, was situated in the cathedral at Auxerre. It was destroyed *c.* 1690 when the floor was repaved and no record of its design has survived, although it is said to have been similar to Sens. Auxerre is of considerable interest because the documents that have survived relating to its former use are crucial to understanding the meaning and purpose of these remarkable monuments.

The labyrinth in Sens Cathedral, France. This plan, based on a manuscript (MS 215, fol. 33V) preserved in Auxerre Bibliothèque, is different from the commonly published design, but is more likely to be correct.

They record the use of the pavement labyrinth at Auxerre as the scene of a symbolic game and dance at Easter, the high point of the annual round of Christian festivities in the medieval Church. A ball game known as "pilota" was played on the labyrinth in the cathedral and is first recorded in 1396. Similar festivities are alluded to in documents relating to the labyrinths at Chartres and Sens. The documents mostly recount attempts to outlaw the game and the efforts of the clergy at Auxerre to continue to observe the ritual, a battle that was finally lost in 1538. They also provide tantalizing details of the game and the dance. In the early afternoon of Easter Sunday the canons and chaplains of the cathedral would gather around the labyrinth and, joining hands, form a ring-dance. Accompanied by the organ, they chanted the *Victimae Paschali Laudes* (Praises to the Easter Victim) and danced around the labyrinth while the dean stood at the centre and threw a leather ball back and forth to the circling clergy. When the music died down and the singing and dancing had ceased, everyone repaired to the chapter house for a sumptuous meal provided by the most recently appointed canon. Ironically, the various attempts by the canons to escape the considerable expenses of hosting the event have provided us with these delightful details of the ritual.

The central plaque of the labyrinth in Amiens Cathedral commemorates Bishop Evrard de Fouilloy, who commissioned the building of the cathedral in 1220 CE, and the architects who built the cathedral. The original plaque, preserved in the Musée de Picardie in Amiens, is all that survives of the labyrinth laid in 1288.

Many theories have tried to explain the use of medieval pavement labyrinths, especially in light of the records from Auxerre. The dance here is a joyous celebration of the mysteries of Easter, but the labyrinth also clearly symbolized the pattern of Christ's preordained life and inevitable fate. As well as representing the tortuous path the good Christian followed towards redemption, both in everyday life and on pilgrimage, labyrinths would have served a contemplative purpose as an allegory of medieval Christian life.

A plan of the labyrinth installed in Amiens Cathedral in the mid-1890s as an exact replica of the original, which was destroyed in the 1820s.

Another group of pavement labyrinths is to be found to the north of Paris, in the archdiocese of Reims. Unlike the circular labyrinths to the south of Paris in the archdiocese of Sens, most of these are octagonal. A pair of surviving examples is found in Amiens Cathedral and nearby in the basilica at St Quentin. Octagonal, but otherwise similar to Chartres in basic design, Amiens was laid in 1288, but destroyed in the late 1820s. Complaints from local historians eventually led to the re-laying of a copy in the mid-1890s. This replica gives an idea of the splendour of the original labyrinth. A fourteenth-century manuscript plan preserved in the cathedral library names the labyrinth as *Maison de Dédalus* (House of Daedalus).

The Gothic cathedrals of France were the pinnacle of medieval architecture and contained within their structure and decoration a multitude of references to the medieval understanding of astronomy, mathematics, and geometry. Much of this knowledge was based directly on the works of Pythagoras, Plato, and other classical scholars. The reference to Daedalus is yet another reminder of the pagan roots of the medieval ecclesastical labyrinth. The cathedral at Amiens was the tallest building of its time and the masons working high in the roof were surely reminded of Daedalus, not only the creator of the Cretan labyrinth, but the first man to fly, with his wings of wax and feathers. Little wonder, then, that they should build the *Domus Daedali* (House of Daedalus) within the *Domus Dei* (House of God).

The labyrinth at St Quentin, constructed in 1495, is a copy of the Amiens labyrinth. It is slightly smaller and lacks the decorative plaque at the centre, but is itself a worthy example and one of the few from the period that can be walked by visitors today. A similar labyrinth at Arras, laid in yellow and blue-black stones, was sadly destroyed in 1795. A plan of the labyrinth, found in 1916 among the ruins of Arras, caught the attention of pioneering researcher W.H. Matthews. He was stationed at Arras, St Omer, and Amiens while serving during World War I, and on returning from France, he produced his influential book *Mazes & Labyrinths –Their History and Development*.[14]

The labyrinth in Reims Cathedral, east of Paris, was unique. Destroyed in 1779 at the request of Canon Jacquemart because noisy children playing on it were constantly disturbing divine office, it was constructed between 1287 and 1311. This labyrinth was also octagonal, although of a design quite different to other examples in France, and further embellished with four bastions arranged around the outer circumference. Each one contained a depiction of one of the architects employed on the construction of the cathedral, holding a tool of his trade.

Not all of these ecclesiastical labyrinths were designed for the public to see. The labyrinth in the chapter house of Bayeux Cathedral in Normandy would have been exclusive to the clergy and was too small to walk. Composed of patterned tiles, now sadly worn and lacking their original coloured glazes, it otherwise survives in good condition. Set into a brick floor, it was clearly intended for decoration or contemplation and probably dates from the late fourteenth or early fifteenth century. A similar small labyrinth, destroyed in 1802, was formed of tiles on the floor of the guard chamber of St Etienne Abbey in Caen and was no doubt influenced by the one at Bayeux. The labyrinth once found in the Abbey of St Bertin in St Omer is the only other known example of a pavement labyrinth in an interior monastic setting. Constructed *c.* 1350, its design was unique, with a meandering pathway set in a square frame. Despite the apparently random nature of the pathway, it can be demonstrated that the pattern was developed directly from the widespread medieval design found in cathedrals.[15] The labyrinth comprised 2,401 stones in total, set as a square that occupied the full width of the south transept. Although destroyed when the Abbey was closed in 1789 following the French Revolution, a half-size replica, still surviving, was subsequently constructed in St Omer Cathedral.

The pavement labyrinth formerly situated in Reims Cathedral was destroyed in 1779 because noisy children playing on the labyrinth were disturbing services in the cathedral. Constructed during the late thirteenth or early fourteenth century, it was approximately 33 ft (10.2 m) wide.

Formed from 2,401 square paving stones, the labyrinth formerly occupying the south transept of the Abbey of St Bertin in St Omer was of a unique design and nearly 36 ft (10.85 m) wide.

The preserved labyrinth at St Quentin was not constructed until 1495. Its design was almost certainly based on the labyrinth in nearby Amiens; which, unusually, also had a black pathway bordered by white walls.

Decorative Labyrinths

Although the majority of pavement labyrinths are in France and Italy, their popularity in the Middle Ages was widespread. A labyrinth in the Church of St Severin in Cologne, Germany, was destroyed *c.* 1840 and only a small central slab beautifully inlaid with coloured marble and porphyry depicting Theseus fighting the Minotaur survives. Another in Włocławek Cathedral, Poland, appears to have been carved on a sandstone slab set into the floor, possibly during the fourteenth century. A portion of this slab was sketched *c.* 1877; by this time it had been moved to the doorway of the cathedral. Regrettably the stone was broken up during renovations carried out in 1891–93 and incorporated into a wall of the nearby seminary.

A number of other small labyrinths are found in churches, cathedrals, and abbeys across western Europe, including two notable examples in the British Isles. A beautiful gilded roof-boss in the form of a medieval labyrinth in St Mary Redcliffe Church, Bristol, is unique. Dating from the 1390s, it is one of nearly 1,200 bosses that decorate the roof of this fine Gothic church and is located on the ceiling of the north aisle. A stone carved with the medieval labyrinth design was found in 1931 among rubble in the ruined mid-fifteenth-century church of St Lawrence at Rathmore, County Meath, Ireland,

Set into the south wall of the church tower at Hern St Hubert, Belgium, the block on which this unusual classical labyrinth is carved probably dates from medieval times.

A labyrinth formed from nine glazed tiles preserved in Mirepoix Cathedral, France.

This gilded roof boss in St Mary Redcliffe Church, Bristol, England, dates from the 1390s. It was possibly an architect's signet.

Now sadly lost, the labyrinth floor tiles from Toussaints Abbey in Châlons-sur-Marne, France, were decorated with eleven-path classical labyrinths.

and is now set into the church wall. Its original purpose and position in the church are not known. Two similar carved slabs are still to be seen in the parish churches of Hern St Hubert, Belgium, and Genainville, France. The latter has an unusual design – a medieval pattern rendered in the style of the Reims labyrinth, with bastions at the four corners.

A remarkable wooden lectern dating from between 1388 and 1404 and still preserved in the museum of the cathedral at Volterra, Italy, has one side inlaid with a square marquetry labyrinth formed of coloured woods. Labyrinths embossed on encaustic or glazed floor tiles in Mirepoix Cathedral (with a Minotaur at the centre), the Chapelle de la Prévute in Toulouse, and in Toussaints Abbey in Châlons-sur-Marne, all in France, represent a final category of small decorative labyrinths.

The labyrinths of the medieval cathedrals and churches of Europe are certainly one of the most diverse and exciting groups known. Despite their placement in some of the most public of buildings from the period, they remain in many ways the most enigmatic. Modern research and scholarship is gradually piecing together the story of their origins and meaning, something that was obvious to the original creators and so intimately bound up in the thinking of the time that it needed no explanation.

A unique labyrinth formed of coloured wooden inlay is preserved on the lectern in Volterra Cathedral, Italy, and dates from the late fourteenth century. A small lion or centaur stands at the centre.

The Sixteenth-Century Revival

The St Omer labyrinth was the inspiration for the exaple still preserved in beautiful condition in the Town Hall in Gent, Belgium. Located in the Pacification Room, so called because it was here that a peace treaty was negotiated in 1576 between the Protestants and Catholics of Flanders, the room itself was built in 1528 and served as the courtroom for the town magistrates, although nowadays it is used for weddings and civic functions. The floor, laid in blue-black and white stone tiles, was completed in 1533 and is dominated by a large rectangular labyrinth similar to that once in the Abbey of St Bertin. Both are notable for the incorporation of a large cross into the upper portions of the design, which serves as a reminder of the devotional nature of the labyrinth even in the judicial setting at Gent.

The beautifully preserved labyrinth in the Town Hall in Gent, Belgium. The design is based on the labyrinth at St Omer, and is 43 x 36 ft (13.27 x 11.05 m), one of the largest examples of its type.

The simple square labyrinth design that appears in the influential *Il quarto libro* design book by Serlio, published in 1537.

The Gent labyrinth has two sixteenth-century counterparts in Italy. A labyrinth among the famous floor decorations in the basilica of San Vitale, Ravenna, is often assumed to be sixth century, but its design dates it to the restoration of the floors after severe flood damage in 1538–39. An identical design appears in the influential *Il quarto libro* design book of Serlio, published in Venice in 1537. Another labyrinth with this design, laid in red and yellow bricks, decorates the floor of the treasury in the Castel Sant' Angelo in Rome. The labyrinth motif was chosen for symbolic protection of the revenues and archives stored in this room from the time of its construction for Pope Paul III until the late eighteenth century. Remarkably, we know precisely when this labyrinth was constructed, as archives record that the mason, Gerolamo de Milano, was paid for paving the treasury on 31 December 1546.

While the labyrinth at Ravenna remains in a Christian setting, the Castel Sant' Angelo labyrinth, much like the one at Gent, was chosen to symbolize the business conducted there. This marks the start of a gradual drift of labyrinths away from spiritual use in the Christian Church to their employment for new patrons in secular settings. Gent, Ravenna, and Sant' Angelo are part of an important revival of interest in labyrinths in the sixteenth century that was to have far-reaching effects on their subsequent history – their spread into gardens and the development of puzzle mazes (see Chapter 5).

The labyrinth laid with yellow and red bricks in the floor of the treasury of the Castel Sant' Angelo in 1546. It has recently been uncovered after many years hidden from view beneath linoleum.

The marble labyrinth in the floor of the San Vitale basilica in Ravenna was probably created during the 1540s. The design is notable for indicating the direction of movement through the labyrinth – from the centre outwards – although the labyrinth is too small to walk and serves a decorative and contemplative purpose.

Medieval Church and Cathedral Labyrinths

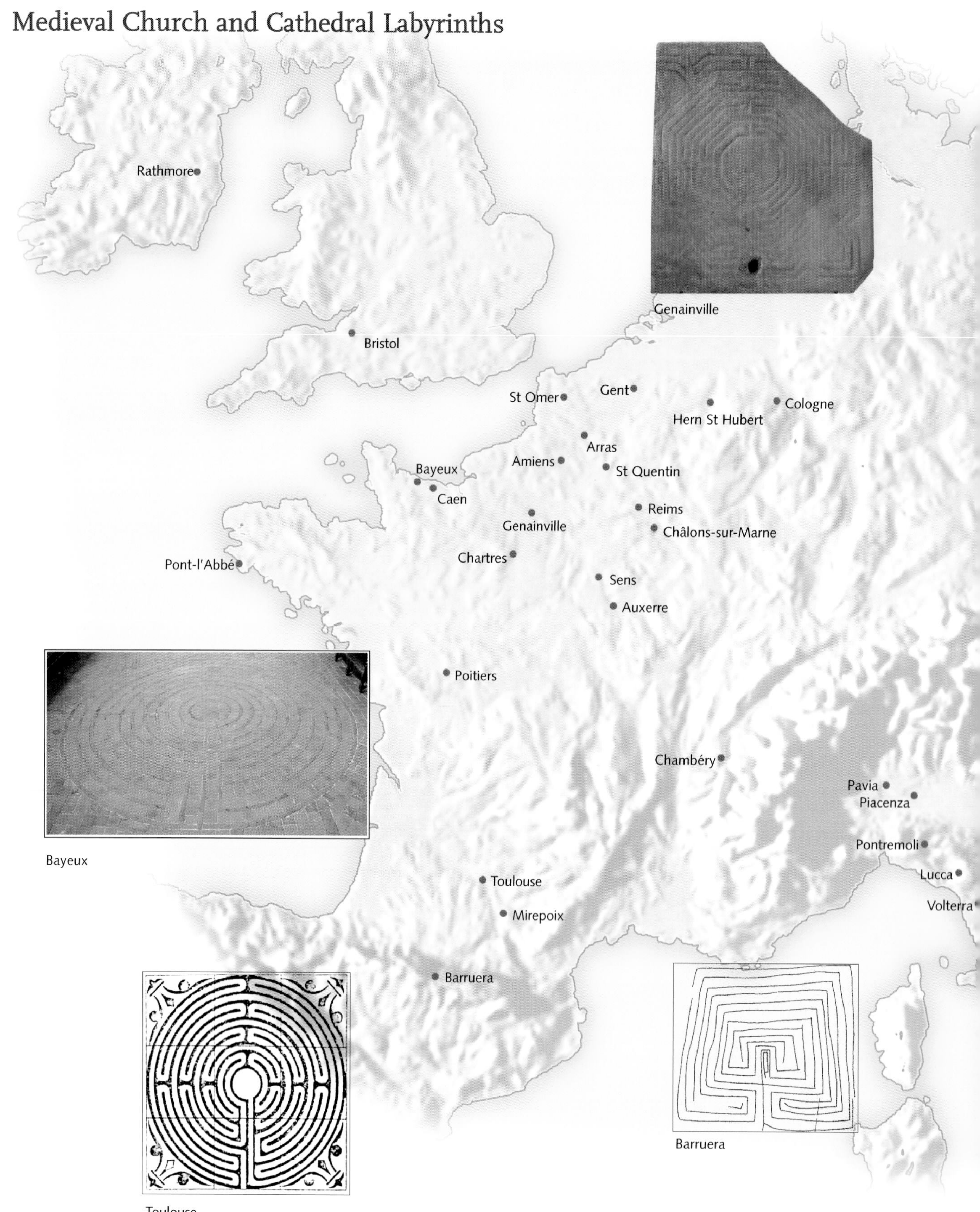

Bayeux

Barruera

Toulouse

The most impressive of all church and cathedral pavement labyrinths are found in France and Italy, and first appear in the twelfth century. The ecclesiastical labyrinths of the late Middle Ages occur in a variety of forms. A few classical types are found as decorative features or simple engravings, but the medieval design is far more common. Outlying examples in the British Isles and Poland are from the late fourteenth century onwards. The recently discovered graffito on a pillar in the church of Santa María de Taüll in Barrurera is the only example so far recorded in Spain; it is unusual also for its classical design and twelfth-century date.

Destroyed examples marked in italics

Location	Type	Comments
Italy		
Conversano	Stone carving	Age uncertain, on cloister colonnade
Lucca	Carved on wall	Late 12th C., with inscription
Ravenna	Pavement	Laid *c.*1538, survives in good condition
Rome	Brick pavement	Laid 1546, surviving in Castle S.Angelo
Rome	Pavement	Laid *c.*1189, St M. in Aquiro, destroyed late 19th C.
Rome	Pavement	Mid 12th C., St M. in Trastevere, ruined early 18th C.
Pavia	Mosaic pavement	*c.*1100, only upper section survives
Piacenza	Mosaic pavement	*c.*1107, described in 1650, now destroyed
Pontremoli	Stone carving	12th C.? surmounted by horseriders
Volterra	Wooden lectern	*c.*1390s, inlaid on lectern in coloured marquetry
Spain		
Barruera	Graffito	12th C., classical labyrinth on church pillar
France		
Amiens	Pavement	Laid 1288, destroyed *c.*1825, restored *c.*1894
Arras	Pavement	Octagonal, destroyed 1793
Auxerre	Pavement	Constructed *c.*1334, destroyed 1690
Bayeux	Tiled pavement	Late 14th– early15th C., located in chapter house
Caen	Tiled pavement	Destroyed 1802, similar to Bayeux?
Chartres	Pavement	Surviving, but often covered with chairs
Châlons-sur-Marne	Floor tiles	Mid-16th C., decorative tiles, now lost
Chambéry	Pavement	Supposedly 1625, elliptical, destroyed; unproven
Genainville	Stone carving	14th C., octagonal with bastions
Mirepoix	Floor tiles	*c.*1530, 9 tiles form labyrinth, copied from Toulouse
Poitiers	Graffito	Surviving graffito of supposed pavement labyrinth
Pont l'Abbé	Floor tiles	Late 15th– early 16th C., recorded, but unproven
Rheims	Pavement	Late 13th C. destroyed 1779, octagonal with bastions
St Omer	Pavement	Late 13th century, destroyed *c.*1789
St Quentin	Pavement	1495 copy of Amiens, well preserved
Sens	Pavement	Late 12th– early 13th C., destroyed 1769
Toulouse	Floor tiles	Mid-15th C., model for tiles at Mirepoix
Belgium		
Gent	Pavement	Laid 1533, rectangular, based on St Omer
Hern-St.Hubert	Stone carving	Age uncertain, set into wall, possibly re-used
Germany		
Cologne	Pavement	Late 13th C.? destroyed 1840, central panel preserved
Poland		
Włocławek	Stone carving	Mid-14th C.? pavement slab, now destroyed
England		
Bristol	Roof-boss	*c.*1390s, in St Mary Redcliffe Church
Ireland		
Rathmore	Stone carving	Mid-15th C., architectural decoration

This medieval church ceiling in Denmark is decorated with vibrant frescos applied to fresh wet plaster. Typical decorations across southern Scandinavia included scenes from the Bible and from traditional stories; a number of labyrinths have been discovered among them.

Scandinavian Church Labyrinths

The splendid medieval wall and ceiling frescos found in churches throughout southern Scandinavia are truly a surprise for anyone accustomed to the often faded and defaced examples elsewhere in Europe. Painted in bright colours they feature a myriad of subjects from biblical stories to scenes from local folklore and everyday life. Not surprisingly, the labyrinth often appears among this rich iconographic collection. Over thirty labyrinth depictions have been recorded scattered across the southern provinces of Norway, Sweden, and Finland, with the largest concentration in Denmark.[16] A number of new examples have been found in recent years as church restoration projects remove centuries of limewash to reveal original medieval paintings perfectly preserved beneath.

This process occasionally uncovers medieval labyrinth graffitos. These are mostly confined to the island of Gotland, perhaps on account of the numerous unaltered medieval churches on the island, or the high density of stone labyrinths found there. A labyrinth graffito on the wall of the tower of Lye Church is accompanied by a short runic inscription: "I am a poor, sinful man" – a sentence from the Lutheran confession of sins, introduced into Swedish liturgy *c.* 1540. Another example, in Hablingbo Church, is adjacent to a fresco of a curious labyrinth design with nineteen walls, with a figure that may be dancing along the pathways. The graffito is unfinished as only the central seed pattern has been drawn; perhaps the "artist" was disturbed before finishing his handiwork.

Unlike the pavement labyrinths in churches and cathedrals to the south, the frescos in Scandinavia are nearly all of the classical design, or developments from it. The one exception, at Grinstad in Sweden, although only partly preserved, is of a curious medieval design, with a number of errors apparent in the connection of the paths. This labyrinth could have been copied from a poor sketch of a labyrinth in a French cathedral, or from an old manuscript. It seems that the painter was not familiar with the correct form of the design, and was simply "doing his job".

A labyrinth graffito on the wall of the tower of Lye church, Gotland, is accompanied by a runic inscription: "I am a poor, sinful man."

The technique of fresco-painting demands a quick hand and a keen eye, with little chance to correct mistakes, so it should not surprise us to find that some fresco labyrinths display errors. The labyrinth at Roerslev, Denmark, is rendered in red and black pigments – the central seed pattern and the first half of the circuits in red, the outer circuits in black. Did the artist run out of red paint halfway through the job, or is this meant to demonstrate the construction method? One of the labyrinths among a collection of four at Maaria church in Turku, Finland, has no entrance because of a mistake the artist made in joining up the lines. The labyrinths from Seljord, Norway, and Hablingbo, Gotland, show how interesting alternative forms of the classical design are created when the connection of the seed pattern is altered, by error or with intent.

Classical labyrinth designs built in stone (see Chapter 4) were widespread in Scandinavia in the Middle Ages and it is difficult to say to what extent church labyrinths are modelled on stone labyrinths, or vice versa. As with other fresco sequences in their churches, preachers would no doubt have used labyrinth designs to illustrate their sermons, but the exact role they played is unclear. Labyrinths often appear alongside depictions of similar geometric figures such as the widespread "Solomon's Knot", as well as ships, noblemen, and

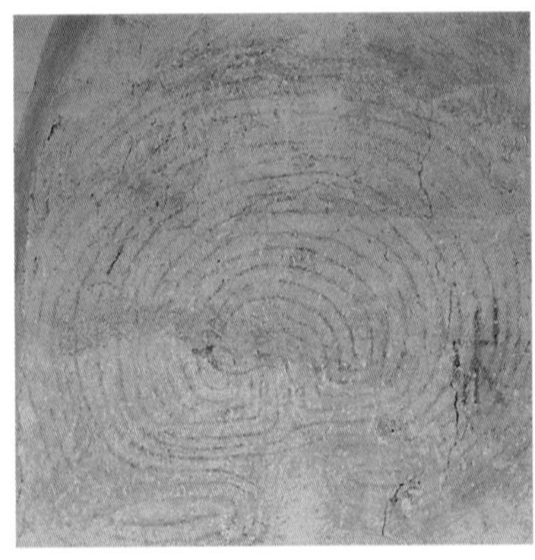

Four fresco labyrinths that show a variety of designs, all clearly created from different seed patterns or unusual methods of connecting the points. Top row: Hablingbo, Gotland; Tåning, Denmark, and Seljord, Norway; below: Hesselager, Denmark.

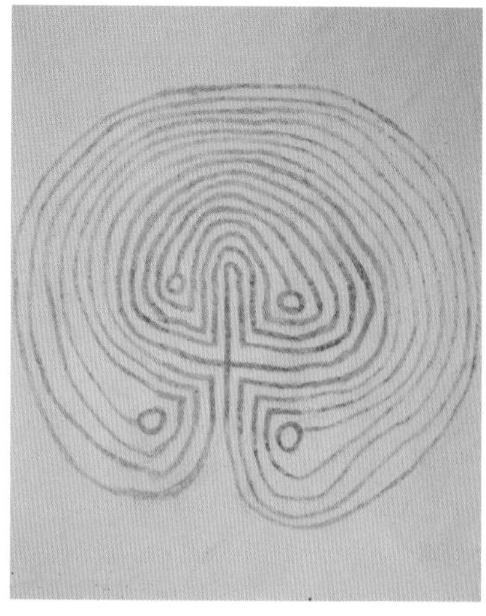

The large labyrinth recently discovered in Roerslev church, Denmark, is rendered in red and black pigments – the central seed pattern and the first half of the circuits were clearly completed before the artist decided to change colours.

figures from local folklore. Many biblical stories are also illustrated, providing a picture book for the common people at a time when the invention of movable type for printing books was only just appearing in Europe.

Many of these Scandinavian labyrinths are difficult to see or only partially preserved; some were discovered then covered again for protection. Among the finest are the examples at Vestre Slidre and Seljord in Norway; Hablingbo and Grinstad in Sweden; Hesselager and Roerslev in Denmark; and Korpo and Maaria Kyrka in Turku, Finland. All date from between the late fourteenth and early sixteenth centuries, with the possible exception of the unique example at Grinstad, which may belong to the early thirteenth century, the period when pavement labyrinths were first appearing in the cathedrals of France.

Labyrinths in Scandinavian Churches

Destroyed and hidden examples marked in italics

Location	Type	Comments
Denmark		
Bryrup	Wall painting	Not currently visible
Gevninge	Wall paintings	Two faded examples, above vault line
Gylling	Wall painting	Traces found, not currently visible
Hesselager	Vault painting	Dated 1487, good condition
Nim	Wall painting	Traces found, not currently visible
Roerslev	Vault painting	Recently uncovered, splendid
Skive	Wall painting	Recently restored, fine but obscured
Skørring	Wall paintings	Traces of 2nd example also found
Tåning	Vault painting	Covered and not currently visible
Vissenbjerg	Wall painting	Covered for protection
Sweden		
Båstad	Vault painting	Poorly preserved
Ganthem	Graffito on pillar	Large, but difficult to see
Grinstad	Wall painting	Unique design, early 1200s?
Hablingbo	Wall painting	Unique design, unfinished graffito nearby
Horred	Inscription	Inscription on church bell
Levide	Inscription on cross	Moved to Julskov, Denmark, now destroyed
Lye	Graffito on wall	Accompanied by Runic inscription
Östra Karup	Wall painting	Only partially preserved
Sorunda	Vault sculpture	*c.*1500, blundered design on sculpted shield
Norway		
Seljord	Wall painting	Unusual design
Vestre Slidre	Painted by doorway	Well preserved on exterior wall
Finland		
Korpo	Wall paintings	2nd partial example alongside
Pernå	Wall painting	Faded but preserved
Sibbo	Wall painting	Faded, central figure of woman?
Turku	Vault paintings	Four labyrinths, splendid

The labyrinths in southern Scandinavian churches include several graffitos and inscriptions. The majority date between the late fourteenth and early sixteenth centuries and are all of the classical type, except the example of medieval design preserved at Grinstad, Sweden.

The Maaria Kyrka on the outskirts of Turku, Finland, contains an incredible selection of traditional scenes and symbols, including four labyrinths.

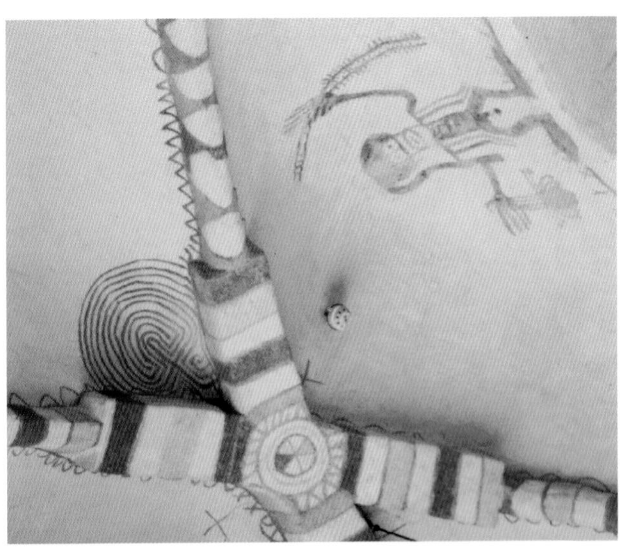

The two examples shown here are both accompanied by curious grotesque figures, presumably characters from local medieval folklore.

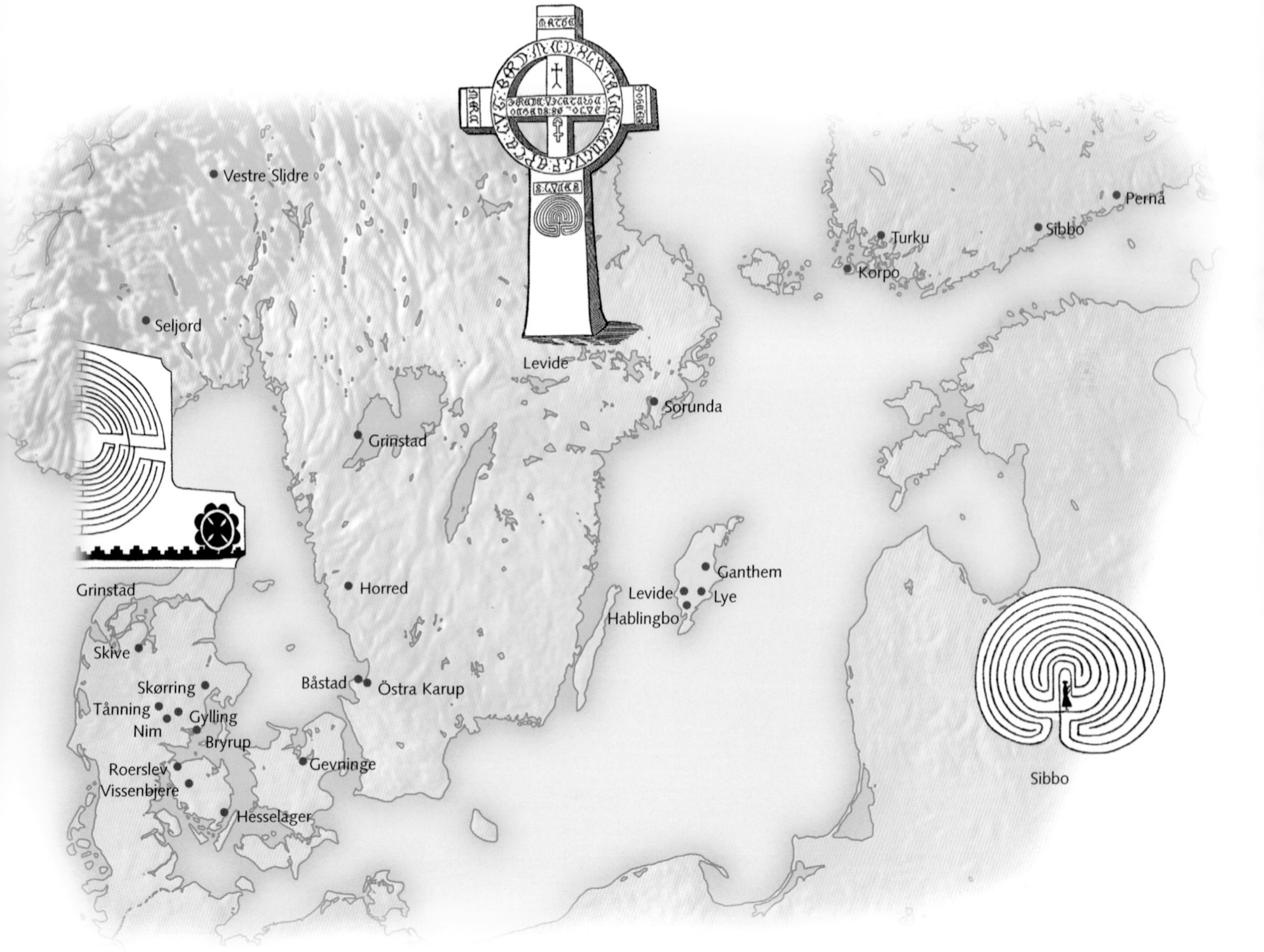

Vestre Slidre
Seljord
Levide
Sorunda
Grinstad
Turku
Korpo
Sibbo
Pernå
Grinstad
Horred
Ganthem
Levide
Lye
Hablingbo
Skive
Skørring
Tånning
Gylling
Nim
Bryrup
Båstad
Östra Karup
Roerslev
Vissenbjere
Gevninge
Hesselager
Sibbo

The Nineteenth-Century Revival

Popular interest in history and architecture during the mid-nineteenth century and especially the fascination for the Gothic spurred on by John Ruskin, Augustus Pugin, and others, had profound effects on the building and restoration of churches and cathedrals. The construction of the railways allowed cheap, efficient transportation of building materials and enabled architects to travel widely in search of inspiration. This was an age of great optimism and major public works. The building of new churches and chapels for a rapidly expanding population and new religious movements went hand in hand with the restoration of churches and cathedrals that had suffered years of damage and neglect.

New artistic movements were also afoot. The short-lived Pre-Raphaelite Brotherhood, a group of dissident artists founded in London in 1848, rejected the conventional artistic opinions of the time and sought their inspiration from the arts and crafts of the medieval era. The Arts and Crafts movement, influential across Europe from the 1850s, brought the appreciation of the purity of medieval art forms to a new audience. William Morris, Ford Maddox-Brown, Edward Burne-Jones, and Dante Gabriel Rossetti were leaders of the movement and all four collaborated in the creation of an oak wood cabinet with two inlaid labyrinths, designed by J.P. Seddon in 1861 and now in the Victoria and Albert Museum.

Pioneering studies of labyrinths in the cathedrals of France were written by Emanuel Wallet (1843), Jules Gailhabaurd (1858), and Emile Amé (1859), and in English by the Reverend Edward Trollope.

In St Omer Cathedral, France, laid as floor decoration in front of the altar, is a half size replica of the labyrinth that was formerly in the Abbey of St Bertin, also in St Omer. It was probably created in 1843.

Artists and architects were familiar with labyrinths at a time when the general public was also witnessing a revival of traditional hedge mazes in public parks and pleasure gardens across Europe (see Chapter 5).

The majority of labyrinths seen in churches and cathedrals in Europe today were constructed during the late nineteenth century. They are found mostly in England, France, and the Netherlands and many draw their influence from the medieval labyrinths in the cathedrals of Chartres, Amiens, or St Omer, or from published plans of these. The designs of these nineteenth-century copies often reproduce the errors found in contemporary engravings quite precisely.

Some of the earliest pieces of evidence for this labyrinth revival can still be seen in France. In St Omer Cathedral, laid as the central part of the pattern on the floor in front of the high altar, is a half-size replica of the labyrinth once in the Abbey of St Bertin. The origin of this labyrinth is something of a mystery. Some writers claim a sixteenth-century date, although the communion table and the marble plinth on which it rests, installed in 1843, stands firmly on the paving scheme containing the labyrinth design. It seems reasonable to assume that plinth and pavement belong to the same time.

The small labyrinth in the north porch of the church at Guingamp in Brittany dates from the late 1850s and is overlooked by a much revered Black Madonna statue. The inlaid stone at the centre is inscribed "Ave Maria".

Another fine example in the north porch of the Notre Dame Church in the town of Guingamp in Brittany appears to date from the late 1850s. The design is simple, with only five paths surrounding the centre; the setting in front of a much-revered statue of the Virgin is quite beautiful. In 1856 the London architects Clutton and Burges won a competition to design the church of Notre-Dame-de-la-Treille in Lille. Their design included a small octagonal labyrinth to be laid in the floor of the nave, though sadly it was never built.

Further examples from France include a replica of the St Quentin labyrinth in the parish church of St Foy in Sélestat, Alsace. The labyrinth was installed during extensive renovations between 1875 and 1893 and is surrounded by representations of the four biblical rivers of paradise: Pison (Ganges), Gihon, Hiddekel (Tigris), and Euphrates (Gen. 2:10–14). Another, based on the St Omer labyrinth, in the church of St Euverte in Orléans, was probably laid

during a restoration of the church between 1855 and 1858. The building is now a school and the labyrinth may no longer exist. The cathedral at Chambéry may once have had an elliptical labyrinth, supposedly laid in 1625, but all that remains today is a curious elongated adaptation of the St Omer design laid during the 1860s and usually hidden beneath chairs. A final example from as late as 1927 is once again loosely based on the St Omer design, but with a number of dead ends, and this time fills the complete floor of the church in Mailly-Maillet.

A fascinating selection of labyrinths was built in England. A small tiled replica of the Chartres labyrinth was laid in the church of St Mary in Itchen Stoke, Hampshire, in 1866, when the old church was demolished and the architect, Henry Conybeare, built a new church, modelled on the then-recently restored Sainte-Chapelle in Paris. Formed from hundreds of specially manufactured dark green and russet brown tiles, it is a beautiful example of Victorian craftsmanship. The restoration of Ely Cathedral by Sir George Gilbert Scott in 1870 included the construction of another labyrinth, the only example in an English cathedral. Just inside the west portal, the labyrinth effectively guards the entrance to the cathedral and has already acquired a local folk saying that it stops the Devil from entering the building. It was carefully designed to have a path length equal to the height of the west tower, under which it is laid out. The angular design is unique and bears only passing resemblance to the labyrinths of northern France. Although it is known that Scott visited Amiens Cathedral for inspiration, no labyrinth was on display there at that time. A small labyrinth – actually a maze based on a

The curious labyrinth in Chambéry Cathedral dates from the 1860s, but is usually hidden beneath chairs.

The church of St Mary, in Itchen Stoke, England, built in 1866, possesses a unique labyrinth modelled on the Chartres design, made from specially moulded glazed tiles.

The pavement in Ely Cathedral, designed by Sir George Gilbert Scott in 1870, is the only labyrinth in an English cathedral.

rectangular version of the design of the famous hedge maze at Hampton Court – was laid *c.* 1875 on the floor under the west tower of the church of St Helena and St Mary in the village of Bourn, southwest of Ely. It is not difficult to imagine that the influence came directly from the recently completed labyrinth in Ely Cathedral.

The parish church in the village of Alkborough, Lincolnshire, contains several labyrinths. The first, 6 ft (2 m) in diameter, was made in 1887 in coloured cement in the porch and is a plan of the design of the ancient Julian's Bower turf labyrinth southwest of the church. Created in 1887 by J. Goulton-Constable, lord of the manor, it was intended to ensure that the design of the turf labyrinth would be preserved should it become overgrown. A memorial window to Goulton-Constable in the church also includes a small stained-glass replica, and his tombstone, erected in 1922 in the village cemetery, is also marked with an inlaid labyrinth.

Our final example from nineteenth-century England is without doubt the most remarkable of all. Mary Watts, the wife of George Frederick Watts, the well-known artist and sculptor, erected the Watts Mortuary Chapel between 1895 and 1898, with the help of local artisans. The chapel is located on the edge of the small village of Compton in Surrey, where Watts lived and worked, and was for many years considered little more than an indulgent folly. However, it is now rightly recognized as one of the finest buildings of the Arts and Crafts movement. The exterior is sumptuously decorated with flamboyant terracotta panels, a mixture of Celtic and Art Nouveau design elements. The interior is a riot of foliage, angels, and cherubs, created in painted and gilded gesso. In the midst of all this are five separate labyrinths: four as shields held by a series of hand-carved terracotta angels, inscribed "The Way, the Truth, and the Life", surrounding

Two labyrinths preserved in Alkborough Church. The design in the porch is modelled on the ancient Julian's Bower turf labyrinth, also situated in the village, and the stained glass labyrinth is a memorial to a former lord of the manor.

Above and below: Mary Watts' angels holding labyrinths adorn both the outside walls and the gilded altar of the Watts Chapel in Compton, England.

the outer walls, and another of richly gilded gesso on the triptych altarpiece. The designs of these labyrinths are based on the example in Ravenna – those on the exterior of the building are identical, while the one on the altar has four additional pathways.

The fashion for labyrinths in churches during the late nineteenth century evidently spread to the Netherlands, where four examples have been discovered to date.[17] Two are in the church of St Servaas in Maastricht, in the Bergportaal and the choir. The Bergportaal labyrinth is based on the medieval design, but with the outer two paths removed. It features silhouettes of the cities of Maastricht at the start, Jerusalem at the centre, and Rome, Constantinople, Cologne, and Aix-la-Chapelle at the four corners – cities of great secular and religious importance to the people of Maastricht. The choir labyrinth – now covered over – is based on the St Omer design, with an additional decorative border. The architect, Pierre Cuypers, installed both of these labyrinths during restoration work in 1886. A simple five-path labyrinth in the church of St Nicolaas in Nieuwegein is dated from between 1875 and 1905. In its centre is an inscription: "*Per crucem ad coronam*" ("Via the cross to the crowning"). The labyrinth in the entrance of the St Martinuskerk in Oud-Zevenaar is actually a maze, an example of the blurring of categories between maze and labyrinth.

A few labyrinths from this period can be found in museums and public buildings. One modelled on a typical Roman mosaic design, laid in the 1870s in dark red and white tiles, fills the floor of a room in the Thorvaldsens Museum in Copenhagen, Denmark. Another, laid *c.* 1875 in multicoloured tiles on the floor of the Chaucer Room of Cardiff Castle, Wales, by William Burges, is an enlarged version of the octagonal labyrinth he planned for Lille Cathedral.

As this selection shows, the nineteenth century was a period of dramatic revival of interest in medieval labyrinth forms and their use within the symbolic structure of the church. While many designs were purely decorative, intended to create an authentic "Gothic" atmosphere for new churches, a few were of deeper spiritual or symbolic significance. However, the eclectic architecture of the nineteenth century also enabled the labyrinth to be freed from the trappings of the medieval liturgical setting in which it originated, and appropriated for use in secular buildings for educational as well as decorative purposes.

The nineteenth century offers a fascinating group of labyrinths for study, with well documented points of origin. Appreciation of the art and architecture of this period is a relatively new field and, without doubt, there are further exciting nineteenth-century labyrinths awaiting discovery and documentation.

Below: the decorative tiled labyrinth laid in the 1870s in the Chaucer Room of Cardiff Castle, Wales.

Gothic Labyrinths in Churches and Civic Building

Destroyed and hidden examples marked in italics

Location	Type	Design Style	Comments
Denmark			
Copenhagen	Pavement	Roman labyrinth	In Thorvaldsens Museum, 1870s
Copenhagen	Pavement	6-path simple maze	1903 floor mosaic in Rådhus (town hall)
France			
Chambéry	Pavement	Meandering St Omer	1860s, design based loosely on St Omer
Guingamp	Pavement	6-path, unique design	Late 1850s in north porch
Mailly-Maillet	Pavement	Adapted St Omer type	1927 paved floor of parish church
Orléans	Pavement	Adapted St Omer type	Probably 1850's, poorly preserved
St.Omer	Pavement	Copy of St Omer	Probably *c.*1843, half sized replica
Sélestat	Pavement	Amiens octagonal type	1880s copy of Amiens
Germany			
Munich	Pavement	Amiens octagonal type	1906, courtyard in Neues Rathaus
Netherlands			
Maastricht	Pavement	9-path medieval type	1886 labyrinth in entrance doorway
Maastricht	Pavement	St Omer type	1886 labyrinth in choir, now covered
Nieuwegin	Pavement	5-path unique design	Late 19th C., tiled labyrinth
Oud-Zevenaar	Pavement	Simple maze	Late 19th C., tiled maze
United Kingdom			
Alkborough	Pavement	Copy of turf labyrinth	1887 porch labyrinth and stained glass
Bourn	Pavement	Hampton Court maze	1875 tiled maze in parish church.
Cardiff Castle	Floor tiling	Amiens octagonal type	*c.*1875, tiled floor in Chaucer Room
Compton	Corbels & altar	Ravenna types	*c.*1895–98, 5 labyrinths in Watts Chapel
Ely	Pavement	5-path, unique design	1870 pavement labyrinth in Cathedral
Hadlow Down	Memorial cross	5-path, unique design	1911 memorial for 4th Viscount Hood
Itchen Stoke	Pavement	Chartres replica	1866, small copy of Chartres in tiles

Often modelled on examples from the medieval cathedrals of France, the labyrinths created during the Gothic Revival are a curious mixture of grand installations and local interpretations. Mostly created during the late nineteenth century, the majority of these labyrinths still survive.

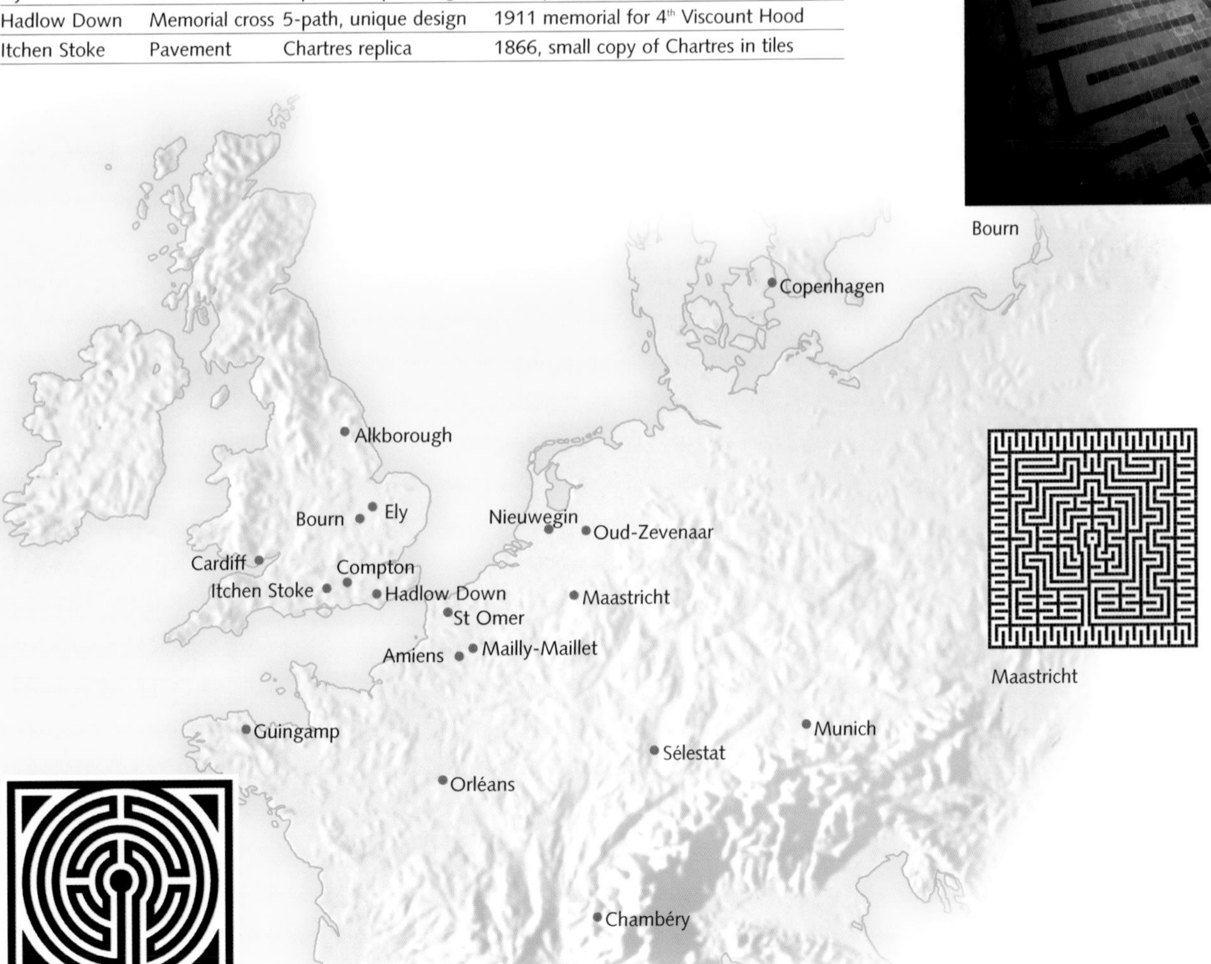

Bourn

Maastricht

Guingamp

Chapter 4

Labyrinths of Turf and Stone

On fair days and holidays, all over the British Isles and Germany, crowds would once gather to take part in ceremonies and dance on labyrinths cut into the turf of village greens and hilltops. An ancient pagan ritual, or simply a celebration of springtime and the joyfulness of youth? These turf labyrinths were arenas for rustic entertainment for many centuries, but easily became overgrown and lost, and all but a handful have disappeared. Their northern counterparts, formed of stones and boulders, are found across Scandinavia and Arctic Europe. Many are the work of hunters and fishermen, superstitious folk always at the mercy of the sea and the weather. Their labyrinths have left us a wealth of evidence, but hardly any documentation to tell us how they were used.

Measuring 132 ft (40.2 m) from corner to corner, the turf labyrinth on Saffron Walden Common, England, was created in 1699 and is the largest surviving example in Europe.

European labyrinths formed of turf and stone occur in a surprising variety of designs and locations. The turf labyrinths of Britian and Germany are often situated on village greens or hilltops. Those in Scandinavia, created from stones and boulders, are usually found on remote headlands or islands. Many date from the Middle Ages; a few may be considerably older.

Turf Labyrinths

A turf labyrinth is formed by cutting away the ground to leave ridges of turf and shallow trenches, so that the pattern produces a single pathway leading to the centre. In most the turf ridge forms the path; occasionally the trench is the course to follow. Some are surrounded by embankments; in others a small mound stands at the goal. Most were circular and between 30 and 80 ft (9 and 25 m) in diameter, although square and other examples are known. Classical designs are found throughout the area, medieval types exclusively in England, and Baltic types principally in northern Germany.

Because they are living, turf labyrinths are soon overgrown and lost if not repaired. At many locations this was done regularly, often in connection with fairs or religious festivals, and records of these responsibilities often provide the earliest accounts of their existence. It is little short of miraculous that any have survived and the few that have are now protected monuments.

The origin of European turf labyrinths remains unclear. In his *Itinerarium Curiosum* (1724), William Stukeley theorized that the turf labyrinths in Britain were a relic of Roman occupation, citing Pliny the Elder (first century CE), who alludes to the existence of turf-cut labyrinths as a playground for children in the Roman world. However, the first documentary evidence for turf labyrinths in northern Europe does not appear until the fourteenth century. Many are found on village greens and commons, and folklore and local records suggest that they were a popular feature of village fairs and festivities, particularly at Easter, Mayday, and Whitsuntide. The double spiral that replaces the central area of the classical labyrinth in several examples in northern Germany and Poland confirms this, as it produces a quick exit, ideal for processional dances.

Names and Traditions

Turf labyrinths are often given the name Troy: City of Troy, Walls of Troy, and Trojaborg are common local variants, and occur throughout northern Europe. This may be due to the popularity of the Troy legend in the Middle Ages[1] rather than to the continuation of ancient practices of forming labyrinths on the ground. Several turf labyrinth sites in England and Germany are named Jerusalem, presumably in recognition of the long, tortuous route that led to the ultimate holy city of the medieval period. Another name, often presented as evidence for a Roman origin for these labyrinths and encountered particularly in the north and east of England, is Julian's Bower (often Gelyan in early documents). Early writers[2] linked this name with Julius, the favoured son of Aeneas, who was credited with introducing the *Ludus Trojae* (Trojan game) to the Romans. However, a recent study[3] identifies the name as a medieval allusion to a lovers' retreat or bower, which is connected with the game in which a girl stood at the centre of the maze while young men raced around the pathway for a wager. A number of reputed turf labyrinth sites with the name Maiden Bower are obviously related.

Turf labyrinths with names such as Shepherd's Maze, Robin Hood's Race, and Shoemakers' Race credit their creators, whether factual or traditional. Shepherds are often cited as the creators of turf labyrinths on hilltops in England, Wales, and Germany. Supposedly this is how they whiled away the hours when watching their flocks. Several turf labyrinths in central Germany are known as Schwedenring or Schwedenhieb (Swede's Ring or Cut) and are attributed to invading Swedish soldiers stationed in the area in the early seventeenth century during the Thirty Years War.

Another group, encountered primarily in southern England, are the mizmazes, derived from the medieval English word maze, referring to a state of confusion, amazement, or muddle. In Germany a number of turf labyrinths were known as Windelbahn (Winding Path) or Zauberkreis (Magic Circle). Schlangengang and Schlangenweg (Snake's Path) compare the pattern to the coils of a snake. The widespread Wunderburg and Wunderkreis (Magic Castle or Circle) may refer to the city of Jerusalem, which was also known as a Wunderburg in medieval German literature.[4]

Turf Labyrinths in the British Isles

Over forty turf labyrinth sites are known in the British Isles, with all but four of them in England. The eight surviving examples provide a fascinating selection of sizes, styles, and designs.

One of the finest surviving turf labyrinths in England, the Julian's Bower in Alkborough, North Lincolnshire, is southwest of the church, where several copies of the labyrinth are also to be found (see p.115). Of the familiar eleven-circuit medieval design, it is on high ground overlooking the confluence of the River Trent and the Humber. An interesting tradition tells of a river spirit known as Gur, who took exception to the cutting of the labyrinth and the visiting Christian pilgrims. To frighten visitors, he sent a great wave up the river in an attempt to wash the maze and pilgrims away, but the wave failed to do any damage. He continues to try each spring tide, when the Trent Bore races past Alkborough.

Set in a deep hollow, the Julian's Bower at Alkborough is first documented in the late seventeenth century, but is commonly held to be much older. The design is of the medieval type with eleven circuits.

Much speculation has centred on the age and origin of this Julian's Bower. A local tradition asserts that it was cut as a penance by a knight involved in the murder of Thomas á Becket in 1170. Other sources point to the existence of a Benedictine cell founded at Alkborough during the twelfth century. However, the design is modelled on the labyrinths that first started to appear in French cathedrals in the early thirteenth century. The labyrinth is deeply sunk into a hollow, the result of years of weed-pulling and removal of soil from the trenches gradually lowering the paths. A precise dating is impossible, especially as regular re-cutting is likely to have removed objects that might provide an answer.

Several other turf labyrinths are recorded in Lincolnshire, but alas are now all destroyed, including a pair at Appleby, an example at Louth first recorded in 1544, and an interesting dodecagonal (twelve-sided) example at Holderness on the north shore of the Humber estuary. It appears that this labyrinth was cut in the late eighteenth century and was a popular place of entertainment for the youth of Hull. It had disappeared by 1850, but a replica was made in the pleasure garden of a hotel at nearby Withernsea shortly after.

The Walls of Troy labyrinth at Holderness had an unusual dodecagonal outline and an additional inner circuit.

The splendid Mizmaze at Breamore in Hampshire is set on a remote hilltop surrounded by trees. The turf pathway and trenches, cut to reveal underlying chalk, is of the eleven-circuit medieval design with a central mound. The earliest record of it is an order to restore it in 1783 and folklore has filled the gaps in historical knowledge. Local tradition records that it was cut either by a shepherd boy or by monks from Breamore Priory (now destroyed) who would traverse it on their knees to absolve their sins. The suspicion that this turf labyrinth is of truly medieval origin is considerably boosted by the discovery of a quantity of twelfth- to fourteenth-century pottery among trees by the site. Perhaps villagers gathered here on feast days or holidays.

The Mizmaze located on a remote hilltop at Breamore is surely one of the most evocatively situated turf labyrinths.

Another mizmaze, in a field south of Leigh in Dorset, is now sadly overgrown and all that remains is a hexagonal earth bank that formerly surrounded the circular labyrinth, and traces of a central mound. Local traditions record that it was the venue for gatherings. It was the custom for the young men of the village to scour out the trenches and pare the banks once in six or seven years, and the day appointed for the purpose was passed in rustic merriment and festivity. It was also alleged to be the meeting place for local witches. Indeed the last witch to be apprehended in Dorset and tried at Wincanton, in 1664, was caught at Leigh Common performing her rites. Although the labyrinth became overgrown some 200 years ago, this site is of particular interest, as its appearance on a map from *c.* 1570 provides one of the earliest pieces of evidence for the existence of turf labyrinths in England.[5]

Situated within the private garden of Troy Farm, near Somerton, Oxfordshire, Troy Town is one of the best preserved turf labyrinths and has a fifteen-circuit classical design that is unique in Britain but widespread in Scandinavia. Little is known of its history, but it is believed to date from the mid-sixteenth century, when the turf labyrinth was a popular garden feature. It is in keeping with garden styles of the time and faces away from the road, so was intended for the owner's enjoyment rather than that of the passing public.

The Troy Town labyrinth situated in a private garden near Somerton, Oxfordshire, undergoing re-turfing and restoration during 1997.

Similar turf labyrinths in private gardens are by no means unknown. One at Chequers in Buckinghamshire, now an official residence of the British Prime Minister, is first depicted on an estate map from 1629. Of the familiar medieval design, it stood next to the bowling green. Named on another map from 1739 as The Maze, by the nineteenth century it had acquired the fanciful name of the Druid Maze, but by the 1920s had become overgrown.

To the north of Nottingham, the site of the Sneinton Shepherd's Race turf labyrinth has now been swallowed up by the city.[6] It was also known as Robin Hood's Race, from the association with the local hero. The earliest description by Dr Charles Deering dates to the 1740s: "...east of St Anne's Well there is a kind of a labyrinth cut out of a flat turf, which the people call Shepherd's Race: this seems to be a name of no old standing, probably occasion'd by its being observed that those who look after the sheep on this common often run it for an airing." After some discussion of the design, Deering goes on to conjecture that: "I should think this open maze was made by some of the priests belonging to St Anne's Chapel, who being confined so far as not to venture out of sight or hearing, contrived this to give themselves a breathing for want of other exercise." This statement may be the source of later theories regarding the use of turf labyrinths as penitential circuits, culminating in a fanciful drawing by Mrs Miles, a local artist, of monks traversing the labyrinth on their knees. The proximity of the labyrinth to the chapel and well of St Anne may be significant, but there is no evidence to connect them.

An imaginative depiction of monks on their knees carrying out penitential circuits of the Shepherd's Race at Sneinton, first published in 1858, has popularized the unfounded notion that turf labyrinths were constructed specifically for this purpose.

A plan of the Sneinton labyrinth from the 1740s shows a design derived from the medieval type, with four "lobes" containing curious dagger-like crosses around its perimeter and confused pathways at the centre. In 1778 the Shepherd's Race was restored, and further changes made to the design. This configuration survived until February 1797, when the labyrinth was ploughed up. One month after this crime, a local printer, J.Wigley, published a souvenir pamphlet accurately recording its final layout.

Ordinarily this would have been the end of the road for an ephemeral object such as a turf labyrinth, but at Sneinton the tradition was revived in the 1820s, when a tea garden opened adjacent to St Anne's Well. A copy of the Shepherd's Race was constructed in the garden, and this seems to have survived until *c.* 1860. Another copy of the Shepherd's Race, but formed of box hedges with a gravel path, existed at the same time in Poynter's Tea Garden above St Anne's Well, not far from the site of the original labyrinth. The owners of the garden had a large poodle that would run the labyrinth in return for a halfpenny, which it would then exchange for a biscuit at the tea house.

The turf labyrinth in the village of Asenby, North Yorkshire, was on the top of a large mound surrounded by earthworks, the remains of a Norman motte and bailey, which presumably dates from the eleventh or twelfth centuries. The mound, known locally as the Fairy Hill, is topped with a worn hollow; all that remains of the labyrinth. It was still in good condition during the late nineteenth century[7] when local children would run the paths and then press their ear to the ground at the centre "to hear the fairies singing". Perhaps this was an allusion to the euphoric condition often reported after running a labyrinth.

This plan of the Sneinton Shepherd's Race was published by a local printer shortly after the labyrinth was destroyed in 1797.

The Shepherd's Race on Boughton Green in Northamptonshire was of a curious devolved medieval design. Like the labyrinth at Asenby and a now-disapppeared Maiden's Bower at Ripon it had a spiral replacing the central circuits. An intriguing tradition recounts that attempting to run the labyrinth three times would result in certain death. The labyrinth was on a triangular piece of land next to a medieval chapel and a holy well famous for its ability to petrify bones and wooden objects. The green was long famous as the site of a three-day fair held around the feast day of St John (23 June). The fair was granted a charter by King Edward III in 1351 and seems to have grown from devotional pilgrimages to the chapel and the holy well. After mass and the drinking of consecrated waters, games were played, which may have involved the labyrinth on the green. The fair was noted for unruly "country sports" and livestock trading, and during the eighteenth and early nineteenth centuries was a regular port of call for travelling menageries. However, by the early twentieth century it had dwindled and was finally wound up in 1915. During 1917 the army, using the green for trench warfare exercises, dug

The Shepherd's Race on Boughton Green, destroyed in 1917, was of a curious devolved medieval design.

The beautifully tended labyrinth on the village green at Hilton was cut in 1660. It now has nine circuits surrounding the central pillar, but was originally of the eleven-circuit medieval form.

through the Shepherd's Race and destroyed it: a sad end for this fascinating relic.

Charmingly situated on the village green at Hilton in Cambridgeshire, is a turf labyrinth with a memorial pillar at its centre. The design is a curious nine-circuit adaptation of the medieval type that has occurred as a result of mis-cutting and tidying-up the circuits during many restorations. This has caused the level of the labyrinth to drop a foot or more below ground level. The pillar that stands on the central mound states (in Latin): "William Sparrow, born 1641, died at the age of 88, formed these circuits in 1660." 1660 was the year of the restoration of the monarchy under Charles II, following the collapse of the Puritan-dominated Commonwealth (1649–59), during which many traditional customs and dances had been outlawed. Turf labyrinths would surely have fallen into disrepair, and the Sparrow family, staunch Royalists, would certainly have wanted to celebrate the restoration of the monarchy. Their cutting of a labyrinth on the village green is consistent with the erection of maypoles and the restoration of other old traditions at this time.[8]

The village of Comberton near Hilton also had a turf labyrinth with a connection to the Sparrow family. Known as the Mazles, it was probably of the medieval design[9] and may have been constructed shortly after 1660 as a copy of the example at Hilton. It stood on Comberton village green, next to land owned by a man who in 1654 married Martha Sparrow of Hilton, presumed to be William's sister. The Mazles became an integral part of the village Easter fair and feast, and was re-cut every third Easter, but it fell into disrepair and was finally destroyed in 1929.

Situated on the crown of St Catherine's Hill, overlooking the city of Winchester, the Mizmaze has an unusual design with nine paths deeply cut through the turf to expose the underlying chalk.

The Mizmaze, a large rectangular turf labyrinth of an unusual nine-circuit design, is situated on the crown of St Catherine's Hill on the south edge of Winchester. The hilltop is encircled by the ditches and ramparts of an Iron Age hill fort and the summit is crowned by a clump of beeches. They conceal amid their roots the remains of St Catherine's Chapel, which stood here from *c.* 1080 until it was destroyed *c.* 1539. St Catherine's Hill was for many years the traditional playground of the pupils at the Winchester colleges, who probably cut the labyrinth in the late seventeenth century. It might seem unlikely that schoolboys should have created the mizmaze, but they had access to books containing designs for garden labyrinths, and this example is not without parallels. In Chaldon Mine, Surrey, five labyrinths, all of classical design, and a number of other geometric figures chalked on the walls of an abandoned underground mine system are accompanied by names, initials, and dates, the majority from the 1720s. It seems that the graffitos were the work of boys from a local school who used the mine system as a secret meeting place;[10] the labyrinth was evidently used as a drawing game as well as a symbol for the boy's secluded underground den.

Known simply as The Old Maze, the turf labyrinth in Wing, Rutland, is of the eleven-circuit medieval type, with the innermost circuits straightened out to flank the central goal. Nineteenth-century plans show a curious loop at the centre, presumably to return the runner to the outside again. If this ever existed it has now been restored to the correct layout. The labyrinth is regularly tended and is always a pleasure to visit. Next to it stands a large flat-topped mound, the site of a former windmill, from which it is claimed spectators watched the sport of running the maze.

Among the graffiti chalked during the 1720s, deep underground in the stone mine at Chaldon, are five labyrinths. This one is accompanied by a fylfot swastika – another ancient design often employed as a test of drawing skill.

The turf labyrinth at Wing with a light dusting of snow picking out the course of the pathway.

A plan for a garden labyrinth published by Guillaume de la Perrière in 1539 (above) is almost identical to the layout of the turf labyrinth at Saffron Walden (below), which was probably created in 1699.

The Maze on Saffron Walden Common in Essex is the largest surviving turf labyrinth in Europe. The design, a seventeen-circuit adaptation of the medieval type, is circular, but as the Reverend George Tyack put it in the 1890s: "at four equal distances along the circumference the pathway sweeps out into a horse-shoe projection." A raised mound marks the goal. Local tradition asserts that this labyrinth was originally cut by a wandering soldier or shoemaker. The first reference to a turf labyrinth in Saffron Walden is the often-quoted entry from the 1699 accounts of the Guild of the Holy Trinity, which records that 15 shillings was paid for "cutting the maze at the end of the common". An ash tree formerly occupied the central mound, but burnt down during a riotous Guy Fawkes night in November 1823. The embankment that surrounds the labyrinth was created in the 1820s to stop cattle damaging it and was not part of the original construction.

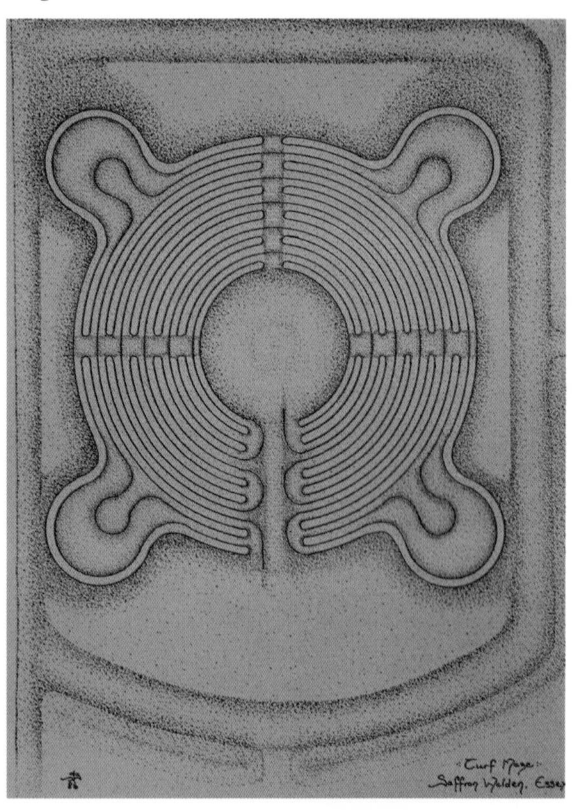

The Common has long been a fair site, and the labyrinth would have been a part of the festivities. A nineteenth-century document[11] records that: "The Maze at Saffron Walden is the gathering place of the young men of the district who have a system of rules connected with walking the maze, and wagers in gallons of beer are frequently won or lost. For a time it was used by the beaux and belles of the town, a young maiden standing in the centre, known as home, while the boy tried to get to her in record time without stumbling."

Some have compared the design of the Saffron Walden labyrinth to the one formerly in Reims Cathedral, France, but in fact it comes from an influential book of the period, Thomas Hill's *The Proffitable Arte of Gardening*, the first gardening book in English. The design in Hill's book was by no means original; it had been copied in turn from Guillaume de la Perrière's *Le Théatre des bons engines, auquel sont contenuz cent Emblemes morauix*, published in Paris in 1539.

There were formerly three turf labyrinths at Temple Cowley, near Oxford. The first was situated on land that belonged in the Middle Ages to the Knights Templar. Adjacent to it were several nine-men's morris pitches, famously mentioned by William Shakespeare in his *A Midsummers Night Dream* (Act II, Scene I):

The nine men's morris is fill'd up with mud,
And the quaint mazes in the wanton green,
For lack of tread, are indistinguishable.

These lines, written in the 1590s, have been taken to indicate the decline of turf labyrinths at this time, but in fact Titania was bemoaning the floods that ruined the crops as a consequence of an

The Tarry Town labyrinth at Temple Cowley.

The Troy-Town at Pimperne was of a singularly unusual design.

enchantment placed on the realm. Shakespeare must have been familiar with turf labyrinths to have described them so casually, but whether this dates the Temple Cowley labyrinths is debatable.

The Troy-Town at Pimperne, Dorset was both the largest and the most curiously designed of all the turf labyrinths in the British Isles. The groove pathway between turf ridges was little more than a meandering track occupying a roughly triangular area 250 ft (76 m) across. John Aubrey, writing in 1686, said that it was "much used by the young people on Holydaies and by ye School-boies". Destroyed by ploughing in 1730, its site is now a cemetery, although for many years after its demise the field was known as Troy-Town and latterly as Miz-Maze (1814) and Maze Field (1861).

The only surviving turf labyrinth in Yorkshire, and the smallest historic example in Europe, is the charming City of Troy on a remote roadside verge high on the Howardian Hills between Brandsby and Dalby. Of classical design, the seven paths that encircle the central goal are banked towards the centre to allow easy running, although the total exercise takes less than a minute. The location of this labyrinth was moved *c.* 1900, when the original was destroyed by wagons, and its exact age remains a mystery. Despite suggestions of a Viking origin,[12] the Dalby labyrinth may date to only 1860, when it was supposedly cut by workmen repairing the adjacent road. Apparently the design was copied from a drawing in a newspaper, but an alternative version of the story states that it was modelled on a carving on a local barn door. Either way, this was the period when labyrinths first received serious attention from historians[13] and were beginning to reappear in churches and cathedrals.

Surrounded by a low wooden fence for protection, the City of Troy labyrinth near Dalby may have been first cut as recently as the 1860s. The current location dates to *c.* 1900.

Despite the abundance of turf labyrinths throughout England, to date only two sites have been identified in Scotland. The first was at Stewartfield, a ruined dower house built on a

The only known plan of the Walls of Troy at Stuartfield, destroyed in 1869.

remote hillside near Dalguise in Perthshire. Traces were still visible during the late nineteenth century;[14] the fact that the house was constructed in 1821 suggests that this labyrinth was created during the early nineteenth century.

The second example was at Stuartfield in Aberdeenshire. Also cut during the early nineteenth century, this small labyrinth was known locally as The Walls of Troy and was of the classical design. It was destroyed in 1869 by a local ploughman who boasted that he had "demolished the Walls of Troy and laid the ceety in ruins". A Walls of Troy place-name near Aberdeen is also recorded, the only other clue to a possible turf labyrinth site in Scotland, although the Rev. Trollope, writing in 1858, mentions labyrinths to be seen in the vicinity of Strathmore. Moreover, it is known that during the mid-nineteenth century children would draw the Walls of Troy design on school slates or trace it in wet sand.

Temporary turf-cut labyrinths, created by shepherds and known as Caerdroia, were formerly cut into the turf of Welsh hillsides.

In 1740 a Welsh history book, *Drych y Prif Oesoedd*, records a custom formerly prevalent among shepherds, of cutting labyrinths into the turf whilst watching their flocks. These were known as Caerdroia, from *caer y troiau* – literally "the city of Troy", which can also be translated as "the city of turnings". P. Roberts depicts the Caerdroia layout in his *Cambrian Popular Antiquities* in 1815, a typical classical design with a squared-up base. He goes on to record that it was still cut by shepherd boys, and often employed as a drawing exercise by schoolboys. These accounts suggest that turf labyrinths, although widespread in Wales, were considered a temporary affair and were not maintained as they were in England. This may account for the apparent dearth of turf labyrinths in Wales, though sites are recorded in neighbouring Shropshire, and at a huge Iron Age hill-fort on the summit of the Herefordshire Beacon.

Only two turf labyrinth sites have been recorded in Ireland, both in County Londonderry during the mid-nineteenth century, but their exact locations are unknown. That the design was known there is evident from the relief of a labyrinth in the chapel at Rathmore in County Meath (see page 102) and a fascinating cobblestone pavement in a farmhouse at Castletownroche in County Cork. This was created by a workman during the 1790s to replace the wooden floor, which had collapsed during a wedding party. The use of the labyrinth in the pattern may have been as a good luck charm or even as a way of commemorating the unforgettably disastrous dance.

A unique cobblestone labyrinth set into the kitchen floor of Bridgetown House in Castletownroche. The floor was covered over in 1964, but the labyrinth is still preserved in situ, beneath a modern concrete floor.

Turf Labyrinths in Germany

The documented history of turf labyrinths in Germany in many ways parallels the story in the British Isles. With hazy origins in the late medieval period, their popularity peaked during the sixteenth and seventeenth centuries, followed by a decline and a subsequent, if surprising, revival during the early and middle nineteenth century.

The earliest evidence comes from the former Germanic territory of Prussia, in what is now Poland. The Teutonic Knights of Germany, who colonized this region in the 1220s, surely introduced these labyrinths. Indeed all of the documented labyrinth locations in regions that now belong to Poland and the Czech Republic are to be found in areas colonized by German peoples during the Middle Ages. Stanislaus Sarnicius, writing in the 1330s, records that all over Prussia it was the custom to cut labyrinthine figures known as Jerusalem in the turf on hilltops next to castles. People would run these labyrinths after a good meal for exercise and supposedly the knights regarded walking them as symbolic of their duty to defend the real Jerusalem.[15] Unfortunately we have no record of the plans of any of these early turf labyrinths from Prussia.

There was certainly a turf labyrinth to the south of Stolp, now Slupsk, in neighbouring Pomerania, also in present-day Poland. This was the largest such labyrinth recorded anywhere in Europe, 148 ft (45 m) in diameter. It was surrounded by a low embankment planted with trees and another tree stood in the centre. The design was an unusual variation on the classical, with a central spiral and eighteen circuits surrounding the central mound. Designs of this type are found throughout northern Germany and have parallels with designs of stone labyrinths along the Baltic shorelines of Scandinavia.

Several informative descriptions of the Stolp labyrinth[16] record its name variously as Windelbahn, Windelburg, and Wandelburg, and describe the festival that was held at the labyrinth at Whitsun every third year by the journeymen of the shoemakers' guild. A Maigraf (May King) was elected on the morning of the festival and the guild apprentices collected contributions from house to house. In the afternoon the procession of the shoemakers' guild moved from their lodge to the Windelbahn, with their banner and the Maigraf at the head, the apprentices carrying two fools on barrows decorated with spring leaves. At the festival the Maigraf walked to the centre of the Windelbahn and made a comic speech, ending with cheers for the Emperor, the town, the elders,

The huge Windelbahn labyrinth at Stolp was surrounded by trees, and another tree stood on the mound at the centre.

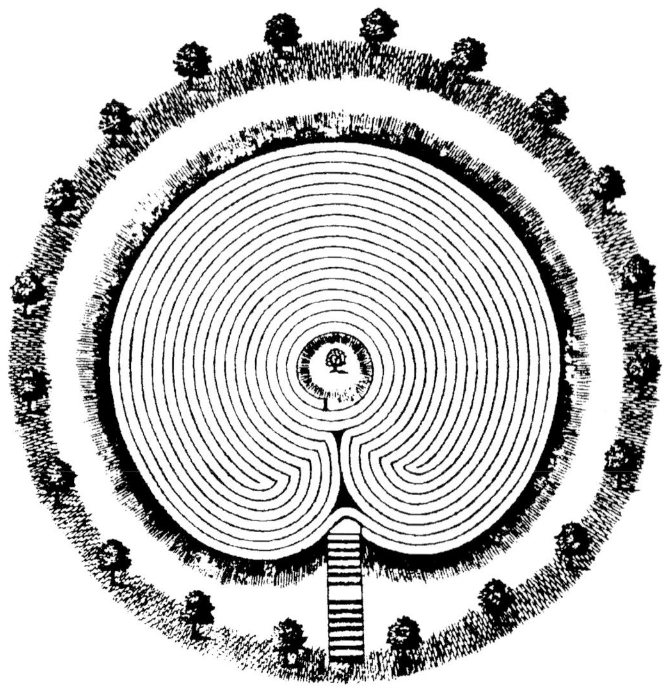

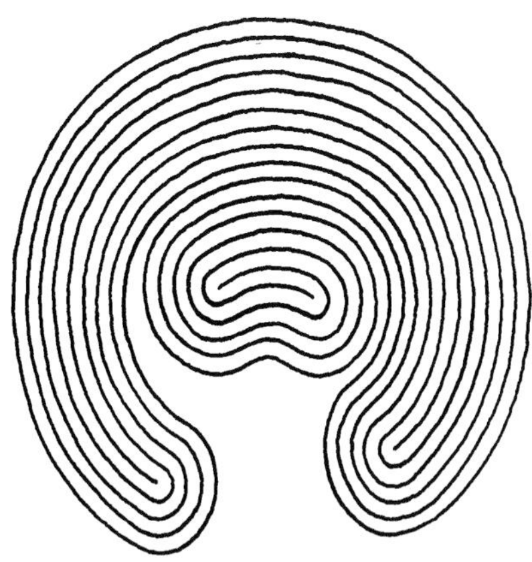

The Wunderkeis at Eberswalde was of a type common in Germany, with a separate entrance and exit and a double spiral at the centre – a design known as the Baltic type.

the guild master, and the women. The music began, the Maigraf danced out of the Windelbahn and there followed a series of speeches and toasts, with drinks offered from a special cup to the officers as they danced around the labyrinth. After the dance, children ran on to the Windelbahn to collect strewn flowers. With the official part of the festival over, the people continued the entertainment in planted bowers, one for dancing and the other for those who preferred to drink and smoke. At nine o'clock in the evening the procession danced its way back to the town accompanied by music.

The origin of this remarkable festival is unlikely to predate the founding of the town in 1310. According to one popular tale, the Duke of Pomerania was caught in an ambush outside the town, but was saved by journeymen of the shoemakers' guild. In gratitude, he donated the piece of land where the Windelbahn was subsequently built, and granted them the privilege of holding the festival every third year. Whatever its origin, early in the twentieth century the traditional games on the labyrinth were sadly discontinued.

The Wunderkreis (magic circle) labyrinth on the Hausberg hill at Eberswalde in Brandenburg was supposedly built in 1609 by the local headmaster. It was repaired by the school children every year on the Monday before Ascension Day and had two entrances to allow two children to start running simultaneously in opposite directions. Those who managed to find their way without a mistake were given an egg as a prize. The site of the labyrinth was partly destroyed by 1786, when the townspeople began to use it as a gravel pit, and a replacement labyrinth was built at the nearby sports ground *c.* 1850. It had an oak tree at its centre, but had all but disappeared by the 1890s. Another small hill in the town of Rosswein in Saxony was once the site of a turf labyrinth documented in 1721. Known as Wunderburg, it was formed according to local tradition by the dance of a monk skilled in witchcraft.

One of the largest and most remarkable German turf labyrinths, 105 ft (32 m) in diameter, with a fully grown lime tree at its centre, the Rad (Wheel) still survives in a clearing in the Eilenriede forest just outside Hanover. The design is Baltic, with a separate entrance and exit. It was first documented in 1642, when Duke Friedrich of Holstein and his bride the Duchess Sophia Amalia visited their brother-in-law in Hanover. The host brought his guests to the Eilenriede forest, where they spent two days living in tents, hunting and playing

The Rad is a Baltic type labyrinth situated in a clearing deep in the Eilenriede forest. It survives in good condition and has a fully grown lime tree at its centre.

The Trujaborg on the Dransberg hill at Dransfeld was regrettably destroyed by quarrying as recently as 1957.

games, including running the labyrinth. In 1649 it was recorded that young men and women used to enjoy running the paths of the Rad; one partner would start at the centre while the other began at the entrance. It is also recorded that the city magistrate was responsible for the repair of the labyrinth, carried out by gardeners at Whitsun.

A turf labyrinth of similar design to the Hanover example was formerly situated on the summit of the Dransberg hill at Dransfeld near Göttingen, and known locally as the Trujaborg. It was regrettably destroyed in 1957 by quarrying. Little is known of its history, but one source[17] records a procession up the Dransberg hill on Ascension Day 1614. Then known as the Kreis (Circle), or Kreuz (Cross), it was said to have a circumference of seventy-three paces, and was composed of fifteen Schlangenwegen (Snake Paths). Local tradition ascribed the construction of the labyrinth to a shepherd who is said to have marked out the design with his staff prior to cutting it, and who was eventually buried at the centre.

The region of Thuringia, around the city of Leipzig, was formerly home to a number of turf labyrinths. Two fascinating examples survive, both are of classical design and linked to Swedish soldiers who invaded in the early seventeenth century.

The well preserved Schwedenring in the village of Steigra. A spring festival with traditional dancing is now held annually at the labyrinth .

The well-preserved turf labyrinth found on the northern edge of Steigra is variously known as the Schwedengang (Swede's Path), Schwedenring (Swede's Ring), and Schlangengang (Snake's Path). The labyrinth is situated next to an earthen mound ringed with kerbstones known as the Schwedengrab (Swede's Grave), although excavation has revealed nothing. Local folklore explains that Swedish soldiers cut the labyrinth during the Thirty Years War (1618–48). It was once the responsibility of youths just confirmed into the Church to repair the labyrinth on the third day of Whitsun each year. In recent years its upkeep has become a matter of pride in the village and a regular spring festival is held with dancing on the labyrinth.

In the village of Graitschen auf der Höhe, the Schwedenhieb still survives on the summit of a hillock near the church. Its upkeep has been the responsibility of the villagers for some centuries.

The other labyrinth, known as Schwedenhieb (Swede's Cut) or Schwedenhügel (Swede's Hill) is to be found on a small conical mound near the chapel in Graitschen auf der Höhe. Just southwest of the labyrinth, there used to be a dancing ground surrounded by seven chestnut trees, which was used particularly at Whitsuntide. In recent years interest in the labyrinth has increased, and its design has been adopted as the official village seal. Swedish soldiers are said to have built it during the Thirty Years War, perhaps in memory of one of their officers, who is supposedly buried beneath it.

The apparent connection between these classical-style labyrinths in Thuringia and the Swedish soldiers based in the region during the early seventeenth century seems to provide a tidy solution for their origin. The victory of the Protestants under King Gustavus Adolphus over the Catholics at the battle of Lützen in 1632 was marred by the

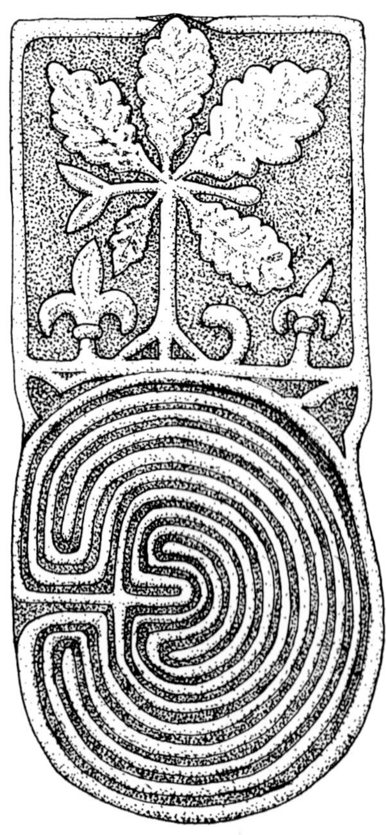

death of the Swedish king, and it is easy to imagine that the labyrinths were cut as a memorial to him or his officers. There were turf labyrinths in southern Scandinavia to provide a model, and the stone labyrinths, widespread around the Baltic Sea, would surely have been familiar to the soldiery. However, Schweden- names are freely applied to any ancient earthworks in the region of Thuringia, and it is possible that they could predate this Swedish influence.

There are no records of turf labyrinths in Austria or Switzerland, though the design must have been known. A sixteenth-century stone relief of an eleven-circuit classical labyrinth surmounted by an oak tree is set into the wall of a house known as Zum Irrgang (Tortuous Path) on Augustinergasse in Zurich. There is an eighteenth century record of a turf labyrinth in Prague, Czech Republic, likewise a former territory of the Austro-Hungarian Empire. The Labyrinth of Libussa was near the Alte Zeughaus, the market place in the centre of the old town. It is said to have been the dancing ground of the arch-magician Libussa, the legendary foundress of the city – where her feet had touched the ground the grass would not grow.

A carved plaque depicting a labyrinth is set into the wall of the house known as Zum Irrgang in Zurich, Switzerland.

Another group of turf labyrinths in Germany deserves our attention. Friedrich Ludwig Jahn, considered by many to be founding father of the German gymnastic movement, was also a keen labyrinth enthusiast and through his influence a number of turf labyrinths were incorporated into the layout of exercise grounds built in Germany during the early nineteenth century. The first, a slightly modified version of the labyrinth at Eberswalde, was built at Hasenheide in Berlin in 1816, and another was installed in Munich in 1828. Two more are recorded in Berlin in 1842 and 1844.[18] One of the copies of the Eberswalde labyrinth survived for almost a century and became an important local festival site. Built in 1846 or '47, the Wunderkreis at Kaufbeuren in southern Bavaria had a gravel pathway that ran between serpentine turf ridges to a double spiral at the centre, and was ideally suited for processional walking. Film footage survives of crowds gathered round the labyrinth as children in costumes and carrying garlands skip their way around. Regrettably, the labyrinth was destroyed during World War II, when a barracks was built over the site – a sad close to this chapter of German labyrinth history.

The Wunderkreis at Kaufbeuren, formerly the location of an annual dance festival, was destroyed *c.*1937, but fortunately photographs and film footage of the labyrinth and festivities survive.

Turf Labyrinths in Scandinavia

The presence of some thirty Trojeborg place names in Denmark has long been a mystery. While some of these refer to specific castles, farm buildings, or sites of former farms and were possibly applied to convey the owners' pride and pretensions, a number refer to empty fields. While no documentary evidence for turf labyrinths exists in Denmark, the presence of labyrinth frescos in churches has led scholars to suggest that these Danish Trojaborg names may refer to turf labyrinths,[19] long since lost to the plough or to neglect.

A few reports point to the existence of turf labyrinths in southern Scandinavia, but only one, from southern Sweden, can be proven. This comes from the parish of Asige in Halland, Sweden[20] and mentions a labyrinth formed from turf ridges with a hollow path that the people of the parish used to repair every Midsummer's Eve, until it was destroyed by ploughing *c.* 1853. A local woman's sketch of the labyrinth survives and seems to confirm that it was made of turf, rather than stone.

Despite this paucity of turf examples, Scandinavia has probably the highest concentration of labyrinths anywhere in the world. Alongside the frescos already covered in Chapter 3, there are in excess of 600 labyrinths formed of stones and boulders, extending from the southern shores of the Baltic Sea, up to the high Arctic regions – the topic of our next study.

The only positively documented turf labyrinth in Scandinavia was situated at Asige in southern Sweden. A sketch made in the 1850s records the design as classical.

Found principally in the British Isles and Germany, the turf labyrinths of northern Europe are surprisingly well recorded. All positively documented examples are included on this map and accompanying chart. However, they are easily overgrown and destroyed and only eleven examples survive, eight in England and three in Germany. Numbers on the map identify lost sites in the British Isles.

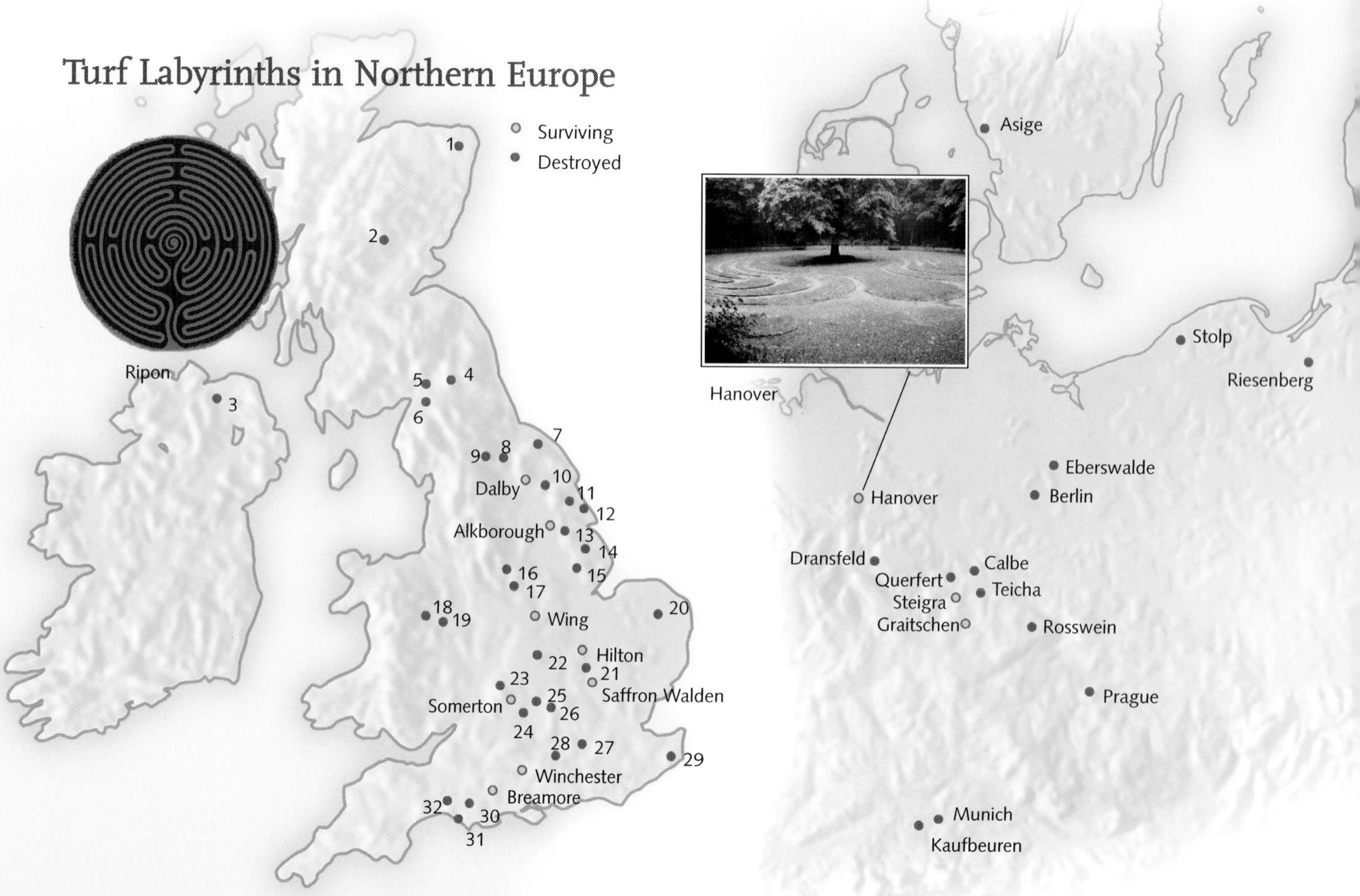

Turf Labyrinths in Northern Europe

Surviving
Destroyed

1 2 3 4 5 6 7 8 9 10 11 12 13 14 15 16 17 18 19 20 21 22 23 24 25 26 27 28 29 30 31 32

Ripon
Dalby
Alkborough
Wing
Hilton
Saffron Walden
Somerton
Winchester
Breamore
Hanover
Asige
Stolp
Riesenberg
Eberswalde
Berlin
Hanover
Dransfeld
Querfert
Calbe
Teicha
Steigra
Graitschen
Rosswein
Prague
Munich
Kaufbeuren

Map numbers given for British Isles. Destroyed and overgrown examples marked in italics

No.	Location	Name	Size (m)	Design style	Comments
	British Isles				
	Alkborough	Julian's Bower	13.4	11-path medieval	Second example now lost
13	*Appleby*	Troy's Walls	?	?	Two with different designs
8	*Asenby*	Fairy Hill	15.5	Medieval and spiral	Now very overgrown
22	*Boughton Green*	Shepherd's Race	11.3	Medieval and spiral	Destroyed 1917 by Army
	Breamore	Mizmaze	25.3	11-path medieval	Splendid hilltop location
5	*Burgh*	?	? small	?	Two recorded 1815
4	*Carvoran*	Julian's Bower	?	?	Recorded 1725
25	*Chequers*	Druid Maze	? large	11-path medieval	Recorded 1629, traces 1921
16	*Clifton*	?	*c.* 12	Ravenna-type	Recorded *c.* 1800
21	*Comberton*	Mazles	15.2	11-path medieval	Destroyed *c.* 1928
3	*Co. Londonderry*	Walls of Troy	?	?	Two recorded late 1800s
	Dalby	City of Troy	7.9 x 6.7	7-path classical	Cut mid-1800s?
7	*Egton*	?	?	?	Traces visible 1872
27	*Greenwich*	The Maze	?	?	Recorded 1697 estate map
26	*Heath*	Shepherd's Maze	? square	?	Traces recorded *c.* 1920
28	*Hillbury*	Troy Town	?	?	Site uncertain
	Hilton	The Maze	16.8	9-path medieval	Cut 1660, on village green
11	*Holderness*	Walls of Troy	12.2	12-path medieval	Dodecagonal, recorded 1815
15	*Horncastle*	Julian's Bower	?	?	Site uncertain
32	*Leigh*	Mizmaze	19.8	Medieval type?	Recorded 1570, overgrown
14	*Louth*	Gelyan Bower	?	?	Recorded 1544, destroyed
19	*Nesscliffe*	?	?	?	Traces still visible 1897
10	*North Grimston*	?	*c.* 25	7-path classical?	Overgrown, on hilltop
20	*Norwich*	?	?	?	Recorded 1662, near chapel
30	*Pimperne*	Troy Town	*c.* 75	Meandering path	Destroyed 1730
31	*Puddletown*	Troy Town	? circular	?	Site still visible
9	*Ripon Common*	Maiden's Bower	18.3	Medieval and spiral	Destroyed 1827
6	*Rockcliffe*	Walls of Troy	7.9 x 7.3	Classical type	Visible 1885
	Saffron Walden	The Maze	40.2	17-path medieval	Cut 1699, the largest survivor
18	*Shrewsbury*	Shoemakers' Race	? large	Octagonal?	Destroyed 1796
17	*Sneinton*	Robin Hood Race	*c.* 30.5	Medieval type	Destroyed 1797, two later copies
	Somerton	Troy Town	18.3 x 15.8	15-path classical	Cut 16th century? Private
2	*Stewartfield*	?	?	?	19th century antiquarian folly?
1	*Stuartfield*	Walls of Troy	*c.* 12	7-path classical	Destroyed 1869
23	*Tadmarton Heath*	?	?	?	Recorded 1861
24	*Temple Cowley*	Tarry Town	5.1	Simple classical	Three different examples
29	*Walmer*	Troy Town	?	?	Traces still visible 1893
	Winchester	Mizmaze	27.4 x 26.2	9-path Reims-type	Cut late 1600s? on hilltop
	Wing	The Old Maze	15.2	11-path medieval	Beside village green
12	*Withernsea*	?	?	?	*c.* 1860, copy of Holderness?
	Sweden				
	Asige	?	?	11-path classical	Destroyed *c.* 1853
	Germany				
	Berlin	Wunderkreis	?	Baltic types	Three cut, 1816, 1841, and 1844
	Calbe	Schlangenweg	?	?	Also called Wunderburg
	Dransfeld	Trujaborg	*c.* 17.5	7-path Baltic	Destroyed 1950s
	Eberswalde	Wunderkreis	*c.* 20	15-path Baltic	First cut 1609?
	Graitschen	Schwedenhieb	9.75	11-path classical	On hillock near church
	Hanover	Rad	32	9-path Baltic	In Eilenriede forest
	Kaufbeuren	Wunderkreis	? large	15-path Baltic	Cut 1846, destroyed 1942
	Munich	?	?	?	Cut 1828
	Querfert	Wunderburg	?	?	Recorded 1531
	Rosswein	Wunderburg	?	?	Recorded 1561 and 1721
	Steigra	Schwedenring	12 x 10.8	11-path classical	On north edge of village
	Teicha	Wunderburg	?	?	Recorded 1750
	Poland				
	Riesenberg	Jerusalem	?	?	Cut 13th/14th century?
	Stolp	Windelbahn	46	18-path Baltic	Destroyed 1908
	Czech Republic				
	Prague	Das Labyrinth	?	?	Libussa's dancing ground

Inspiration for Modern Replicas

The traditional turf and stone labyrinths of northwestern Europe have provided inspiration for a number of modern replicas and interpretations. The adaptability of the basic labyrinth design, contrasting with the complexity of its symbolism, appeals to both the spiritual and secular aesthetic of artist, patron, and public alike, whatever the setting. Easily formed, often with little or no material costs, labyrinths have proved as popular during the current revival of interest as they were at the time of their original construction. The sinuous twists and turns of turf labyrinths have provided the stimulus for a number of modern replicas in public parks and gardens. Especially in Europe and the Americas, holidaymakers and enthusiasts have enjoyed creating simple labyrinths built of stone, often on remote beaches and rugged headlands. These labyrinths are often formed with little or no fanfare and sometimes no record of the builder is left. As with examples from the past, many are pre-destined for long-term survival and will surely cause confusion for future researchers.

Three modern turf labyrinths. Situated on the crown of Solsbury Hill, overlooking Batheaston, England (left), the turf labyrinth created during the early 1990s is kept in good condition by the constant passage of feet of visitors and dog walkers. An egg-shaped turf labyrinth (below left) within the jaws of a 300 ft (91 m.) replica of the Ohio Serpent Mount, was installed at the Norton Museum of Art in West Palm Beach, Florida, by Adrian Fisher to accompany an exhibition of his work in 1997. An unusual five-circuit labyrinth with five-fold symmetry (below), installed by the Rolawn turf company at the Gateshead National Garden Festival in 1990, was an effective and unusual display piece.

Two seaside labyrinths. Overlooking the shoreline, the example at Nyhamn on the island of Gotland (above left), was built by holidaymakers in the 1960s and continues a long established tradition. The labyrinth at Port na Curaich on Iona in the Western Isles of Scotland (above) is a recent addition to the collection of monuments on this sacred island.

The ancient stone labyrinths preserved in Scandinavia have provided inspiration for copyists in the past. During the late nineteenth century, schoolmasters on the island of Gotland constructed a number of replicas as lessons for their children, and this tradition has recently been revived in Scandinavia and elsewhere. Often situated on seashores or other locations where stone is plentiful, many of these modern labyrinths combine traditional designs with innovative ideas.

Three modern stone labyrinths. The labyrinth in Valbypark on the outskirts of Copenhagen (right) was built by Jørgen Thordrup in 1995 with help from a local school class. Situated in a playground next to a café, it is a popular meeting place for children and families. An innovative stone labyrinth installed by designer Marty Kermeen in a private garden in Plano, Illinois, (below left) is lit with electric lanterns. The labyrinth created in 1976 at Tulstrup in Denmark (below right) was the venue for local school reunions where classes would dance around a maypole.

Stone Labyrinths

Stone labyrinths are more abundant in Scandinavia than anywhere else in the world. Throughout the Nordic countries of Sweden, Norway, and Finland, beyond the Arctic Circle, and particularly around the shorelines of the Baltic Sea, stones and boulders were used to mark out the walls of labyrinths. Over 500 examples have been recorded, and cataloguing continues. Stone labyrinths are also known from Iceland, Arctic Russia, and Estonia. All these outlying groups originated from Nordic settlers or trading contacts, though a single stone labyrinth in southwest England is more difficult to explain. Stone labyrinths in India and the American Southwest (see Chapter 2) are remarkably similar, but they are not culturally connected; they simply express the desire to produce a walkable form of the labyrinth symbol in local construction materials.

Early writers have proposed dates as far back as the Bronze Age for some Scandinavian stone labyrinths. However, study of post-glacial land uplift rates proves that some locations must be of more recent origin, and probably date from the medieval period. Stone labyrinths have always been difficult to date, but during the late 1980s a major breakthrough was pioneered by Dr Noel Broadbent of the Centre for Arctic Cultural Research at Umeå, Sweden. Noting that geologists in Arctic regions had for some time measured lichen growth on rocks to judge the length of time that surfaces had been exposed, Broadbent developed this technique – called lichenometry – to fit the needs of archaeology. The growth rate of the common and widely distributed lichen *Rhizocarpon geographicum* has been correlated around the shores of the Baltic Sea, using stone structures of known age, to provide a growth rate curve with standard deviations of ±35 to 50 years, depending on the area. Measurement of the largest lichen found encrusting the boulders of a labyrinth provides a useful means of dating its construction.

The results reveal that labyrinths were constructed from the end of the thirteenth century, with a notable peak in the sixteenth and seventeenth centuries. Earlier examples were sometimes accompanied by later copies nearby.[21] The sixteenth and seventeenth centuries were a period of extensive colonization of the Baltic by Swedish settlers. Many of the labyrinths are near natural harbours and the remains of seasonal fishing dwellings, where fish were dried and salted during the arctic summer. One can easily imagine children playing in these labyrinths while the fishing parties worked. During the same period labyrinths were also painted in churches in southern Scandinavia.

Unlike the turf labyrinths to the south, which show remarkable diversity of design, Scandinavian stone labyrinths are predominantly of the classical type. Baltic types, with double spirals at the centre to produce separate entrances and exits, are also widespread and appear to be connected with traditional folk customs and dances. The medieval type is practically unknown, although it is recorded once as a church fresco, at Grinstad in Sweden (see page 108), and is also found, surprisingly, in the remote landscape of Arctic Russia.

Names and Traditions

Throughout the region Troy names for labyrinths, such as Trojeborg (Troy Fortress), Trojenborg, and Tröborg, are by far the most common. This may represent an ancient knowledge of the original Troy labyrinth symbol, or the popular Troy legends of the Middle Ages. Sometimes the names of other famous cities are used. Viborg, Trondheim, Ninive (Nineveh), Jeruusalem, and Konstantinopel are all recorded. Jerusalem names are particularly widespread in Finland and Estonia, which also has the curious Türgi Linn (Turkish City), presumably a reference to Constantinople. Some of these names, deriving from glorious or lost cities of the past, can be surprisingly recent. In Finland a labyrinth known as Lissabon can only date to sometime after the destruction of Lisbon by the earthquake of 1755.

Many of the names given to Scandinavian labyrinths reflect attempts to convert the concept of "Troy" into similar-sounding words in local dialects.[22] Thus we find labyrinths named Trelleborg (Round Fortress), Trolleborg (troll = goblin), Trädenborg (träde = walk), and Trilleborg (trill = wheel). Related to these are names that refer to the shape and nature of the labyrinth: Rundgårdar (Round Court), Ringboslott (Ring Castle), and Gångborg (Walk Fortress).

A third group of names is especially interesting, recording traditional practices associated with labyrinths. In Sweden and Finland, where most labyrinths occur in areas with predominantly Swedish-speaking populations, many are known as Jungfraudans (Young Girl's, or Virgin's, Dance). This game where a young maiden stood at the centre while the boys ran the paths to reach her, is common wherever labyrinths occur in Europe. It can be traced back to the Homeric legends of Troy, where the abducted Helen was centre stage.[23] Labyrinths of the Baltic type, with double spirals at the centre and two entrances, are especially suited for this tradition, as two boys could race against each other. The Jungfruringen (Virgin Ring) labyrinth on the island of Köpmanholm in the Stockholm archipelago was still danced this way during the late nineteenth century.

Finland also has Pietarinleikki (St Peter's Game) names. These refer to a medieval game in which St Peter, on board a sinking boat with thirty people, needs to devise a seemingly random process to select fifteen to jump overboard without including any of his fifteen friends. The codes for successful selection were recorded in Latin verse and carved on wooden calendar sticks. The discovery of one of these patterns alongside a labyrinth engraved on a rock face at Skarv, in the Stockholm archipelago, revealed how the tracing of the correct labyrinth path also contained this same code, explaining the link between the two games.[24]

Several characters from Scandinavian legend have also become associated with the labyrinth. The hero Grimborg has to fight his way through iron fences to reach the castle containing the king's daughter. The king sends 12,000 soldiers to defend her; Grimborg has to kill them all before escaping with his bride. This story was ritually re-enacted at Otterstad in Västergötland as recently as the 1930s. The local people would make a labyrinth of snow on a frozen lake and skate the paths to reach the girl at the centre, dodging the enemy "guards" and singing the "Song of Grimborg".[25]

Labyrinths in Iceland were generally referred to as Volundarhús (Wayland's House). The handful of stone labyrinths and labyrinth graffitos in Iceland are probably all from the seventeenth century or later, but two fourteenth-century manuscripts decorated with labyrinths labelled "Volundar Hüs" show that the labyrinth was already well known in Icelandic culture.[26] Volundar or Wayland was recognized in Nordic mythology as the master smith. Humiliated and imprisoned by his king, he escapes by fashioning wings of eagle feathers and flying away – an obvious parallel to Daedalus. One of the manuscript labyrinths from Iceland is accompanied by a corrupted version of the familiar Theseus and the Minotaur legend, where the hero, Egeas, builds a labyrinthine trap for a creature known as the Honocentaurus. With a lure of meat smeared with honey, he dispatches the beast and claims his bride.

In Finland there are a number of labyrinths named Jätinkatu (Giant's Street), Jatulintarha (Giant Fence), and Kivitarha (Stone Fence). The origin of this group of names may lie with the legends of the hero Kullervo, as recorded in the Finnish *Kalevala* epic. Kullervo is ordered to clear some land in a forest and build a fence around it by his uncle Untamo, his father's killer. On the way to avenging the crime, Kullervo mischievously fells the trees with a magic charm that ensures that nothing will grow in the clearing, and uses the timber to build a fence around it with no entry or exit. Perhaps the mysterious labyrinths were also considered to be the work of Kullervo.[27]

Folklore records a number of fascinating traditional uses for Scandinavian stone labyrinths.[28] In Finland and southwest Sweden hunters, herders, and shepherds walked the labyrinths as a spell to protect themselves and their flocks from wolves, who were magically confused by the winding paths. Until the early twentieth century fishing folk walked the labyrinths before putting to sea to ensure good catches and bring favourable winds – contrary winds would be lured into the labyrinth behind them and trapped. A particular example from Nederkalix in Sweden records that as fishermen walked the labyrinth there the smågubbar (little people or trolls) would follow them inside. The fishermen ran to their boats and put to sea, leaving the trolls confused and unable to find the way out to follow them and cause bad luck. This notion that the circuitous walls of a labyrinth could magically confuse or contain spirits and protect people occurs wherever the labyrinth is found.

All around the Baltic coastline stone labyrinths have been found near to "compass roses" – cross- or star-shaped arrangements of boulders aligned on the cardinal points. It has been suggested that some of the earlier labyrinths in this region may have served as a symbol to advertise the availability of pilots, essential for safe navigation through the labyrinthine archipelagos of the Baltic coastline[29]. A number of labyrinths and compasses are near harbours and fishing dwellings where such knowledge and services would have been available. They are found particularly along established sailing routes that linked trading stations and transit points for pilgrims en route to the shrine of St Olav in Trondheim.

Stone Labyrinths on the Scilly Isles

The surviving early eighteenth century Troytown on the island of St Agnes in the Scilly Islands, off the tip of Cornwall in England, is the only historic stone labyrinth in the British Isles. Local tradition records that it was constructed by the son of the island's lighthouse keeper in 1729.[30] Originally classical in formation, the central section had devolved into a double spiral by the early 1980s, but was restored to its original pattern in 1988. It is difficult to know whether this labyrinth should be considered a local adaptation in stone of the well established tradition of turf labyrinths in England, or whether the influence came from Scandinavia. Ships from the Baltic would have taken on pilots and supplies at the Scillies, and the islands are notorious for their dreadful history of shipwrecks. In recent years many more labyrinths have appeared in the archipelago. This trend appears to have started during World War II, when bored aircrew stationed on St Martin's created several simple mazes of boulders on the northernmost headland. The location is now home to more than a dozen such stone mazes and labyrinths, which come and go as tourists plunder stones from old examples to create new specimens. The collection has grown over sixty years or more to cover the entire foreshore. Further stone labyrinths have appeared on other islands. This isolated group of relatively recent examples illustrates well the process by which one "ancient" labyrinth can become the spur for a series of replicas.

The Troytown on the island of St Agnes, after its controversial restoration in 1988.

A number of the stone labyrinths and mazes are found on the foreshore at the north end of St Martin's. All have been built since the 1940s.

Stone Labyrinths in Sweden

The complex character and history of the stone labyrinths found throughout Sweden are well demonstrated by the examples on the Swedish island of Gotland. Formed from boulders, the earliest stand on headlands or sites commanding wide views over the sea. The famous Trojaborg just outside Visby is situated on a former shoreline (now inland due to tectonic coastal uplift) below a rocky crag, where the town gallows were. Its eleven paths are deeply worn and the boulders are now perched on turf ridges. First documented in 1740, it was formerly a popular gathering place on May Day Eve. A similar example is in a churchyard at Fröjel, where the location suggests that the medieval church was built next to an already well established sacred site. Fröjel is the "Sanctuary of Freja", the fertility goddess of pre-Christian Sweden. Another labyrinth found near the farmstead of Ottes, at the southernmost point of the island, is now overgrown, but stands next to three ancient stone cairns.

The Trojaborg at Visby, Gotland, measuring nearly 60 ft (18 m) in diameter, is arguably the best known of all stone labyrinths in Scandinavia.

The labyrinth at Fröjel, Gotland, is situated within the churchyard, a unusual location that poses interesting questions concerning its origin.

Located on a headland overlooking the Baltic Sea, the labyrinth at Hallshuks, Gotland, may appear to be of ancient origin, but was actually constructed during the late nineteenth century.

Created by visitors during the 1960s, the small labyrinth at Nyham, situated just above the shoreline, is a more recent addition to the collection on Gotland.

Elsewhere on the island are labyrinths painted during the fifteenth century on church walls. It has been suggested[31] that they were modelled on the stone labyrinths at Visby or Fröjel, which certainly provided the inspiration for several stone labyrinths in villages or next to schools that were built by schoolmasters for their pupils at the end of the nineteenth or early twentieth centuries. Surviving examples in Bunge and Othems are both from this period, as are the two on headlands next to lighthouses at Hallshuks and Holmuddens. This curious mix of labyrinths is complemented by several recently constructed by holidaymakers at seaside locations. A pair at Tofta Södra and Nyhamn are on the shoreline adjacent to holiday cottages. Those that prove popular receive regular attention, ensuring their survival in the collection of thirty or more recorded on this one island. This assortment of devotional, educational, and recreational labyrinths provides one of the most fascinating examples of the enduring appeal of the genre.

A group of some seventeen or more labyrinths on the west coast of Sweden extends from Grebbestad in Bohuslän northwards as far as Oslofjord in the south of Norway. Most are found next to fishing settlements along the coast or on offshore islands. In this region the rapid rise of land since the Ice Age has caused dramatic changes to the landscape – the early Bronze Age shoreline is now some 50 ft (15 m) above sea level, so any labyrinths near the current foreshore must be medieval or later. There are also two examples on high ground next to grave fields in Bohuslän, an area that is littered with prehistoric monuments and extensive rock art panels. The overgrown labyrinth at Björnemyren, south of Tanum, is situated next to a megalithic tomb dated to *c.* 3500 BCE and a grave field with burials from the Bronze and Iron Ages. The Trinneborgs Slott labyrinth at

The Trinneborgs Slott at Ulmekärr in Bohuslän, Sweden, stands amid an ancient grave field, a location that also suggests considerable antiquity for the labyrinth.

nearby Ulmekärr is situated in a small grave field. A number of standing stones were removed from the field in the 1800s to build a bridge, but the labyrinth survives in excellent condition.

Unfortunately, lichonometry, useful for dating coastal labyrinths, does not work on inland boulders amongst dense vegetation, but archaeologists have tentatively ascribed these examples to the late Iron Age, *c.* 0–500 CE.[32] A similar group of ten labyrinths on the islands around Gothenburg has one supposedly ancient labyrinth in its midst, alongside a grave field on a hilltop at Storeberg.

A fascinating group of twenty or so stone labyrinths is found far inland in southern Sweden, high in the hills among grave fields dating from the Bronze Age to the Viking period. John Kraft has recently demonstrated that the majority are distributed in a pattern coinciding with Iron Age land ownership boundaries. There was one labyrinth within each tribal boundary, nearly always near to an important grave field. Although associated with these monuments to the dead, the age of the labyrinths cannot be determined by current technology, and the mounds of boulders would have provided suitable material to plunder for building the labyrinths at any time. It is possible that they are medieval, perhaps placed next to the grave fields for superstitious reasons, but their specific locations strongly suggest that they date from pagan times. Perhaps the labyrinth symbolized the pathway to the spirit world or served as a spirit trap, either as a place for safe containment of souls or as an interface with them.

Although some of these labyrinths have been destroyed, several important examples survive. The Trelleborg at Vittaryd in Småland stands beside the road opposite a grave field with fifty cairns from the late Iron Age. The labyrinth at Lindbacke, on the edge of Nyköping, is likewise near to an ancient grave field and a spring dedicated to the late Iron Age god Frey. The best known example of these labyrinths is situated at Tibble in Badelunde, close to Västerås. This Trojeborgen labyrinth is first documented on a map from 1764 and is perched on top of an esker, which provided the stones for the labyrinth and the surrounding Iron Age cairn field, now destroyed by quarrying. North of the labyrinth, the Anundshög mound and a complex of Viking Age runestones and burial settings mark this as a sacred site with a long history. But without question, the most fascinating of these grave field labyrinths comes from Låssa in Uppland. A rather overgrown stone labyrinth, known as the Rösaring, is situated alongside a grave field of Bronze, Iron, and Viking Age stone cairns, at the southern end of an embanked straight track. Excavation of the track provided a radiocarbon dating of 815±80 CE and revealed traces of a wooden structure at the northern end of the road. It is thought this track was a "Death Road", along which bodies would be taken from the hut, on horse- or oxen-drawn carts, for burial in the cairns at the far end.

Adjacent to an extensive grave field at Vittaryd in Småland, Sweden, the Trelleborg labyrinth is rather overgrown but survives on a roadside embankment.

The labyrinth at Lindbacke, near Nyköping, Sweden, is situated adjacent to a sacred grove and spring.

The Trojeborgen at Tibble in Badelunde, Sweden, is situated in an area rich with prehistoric monuments.

Some twenty or more labyrinths have been recorded on islands in the Stockholm Archipelago near the capital of Sweden. Most of this group is situated on the outermost islands, concentrated in the north. The labyrinth on Björkskär, overgrown for many years, was recently restored and the boulders affixed to the rock face with a special synthetic rubber adhesive.[33] The two labyrinths on Norsten have recently evolved into puzzle mazes[34] due to visitors rearranging the boulders. The examples on the islands of Svenska Högarna and Borgen are among the best preserved, their original classical form marked out with large water-rolled boulders laid on the bare rock. These labyrinths are the work of fishing communities during the Middle Ages. Nearby, visitors are still creating simple boulder labyrinths and mazes to this day.

By far the largest group of labyrinths in Scandinavia is the 250 or more examples that line the Gulf of Bothnia in northern Sweden and Finland. Around 100 of these are found in the Swedish province of Norrbotten alone. They are nearly all at low levels, near the current coastline or on offshore islands, and are clearly associated with seasonal fishing settlements. A number of the labyrinths in the Swedish half of this region have been dated by lichonometry to between 1500 and 1650 CE, the peak of the herring fishing industry. The oldest labyrinth so far in this region, at Jävre in Norrbotten, is dated to the end of the thirteenth century. On a hilltop next to a Bronze Age burial cairn, it was constructed from stones plundered from the cairn.

Laid on the bare rock of an offshore island, the labyrinth at Borgen in the Stockholm archipelago is clearly the work of the communities that visited these remote islands for seasonal fishing.

A labyrinth-inscribed wooden box used as a cheese press from Vestergötland, Sweden, is clearly dated 1701.

Labyrinths in Finland and Estonia

The Åland archipelago, a group of islands in the Baltic midway between Finland and Sweden, has long been a staging post for trade across this often stormy, and in winter, frozen land-locked sea. The remoteness of these islands has ensured the survival of many of the thirty-five labyrinths documented in the archepelago, although only a few survive on the main islands. The example at Gregersö, close to Mariehamn, is well preserved and not difficult to find. The splendid examples on the uninhabited islands of Ådskar, Nyhamn Storlandet, and Emskär are also well preserved. Many of these labyrinths are medieval, or later, but the one on Granhamnsholmen, standing next to a large stone cairn on the summit has been dated to the Iron Age,[35] the only example of a pagan labyrinth in the Baltic archipelagos.

A total of over 140 stone labyrinth sites have been documented in Finland.[36] The majority on the mainland have long since perished, while those on islands in the Turku and Helsinki archipelagos have fared better. Some thirty examples are recorded on islands between Helsinki and Tallinn in Estonia, all in regions colonized in the late Middle Ages by Swedish-speaking farmers and fishing communities. At least five labyrinths are known in Estonia. Two are preserved on the island of Aksi. One was built in 1849 by a Swedish soldier; the other was constructed as recently as 1915. Another at Kootsaare, on the island of Dagö, was excavated in 1986. Also in Estonia, a carved labyrinth has been recorded on the wall of a windmill, now in the grounds of the Rocca al Mare Museum near Tallinn. Labyrinth carvings are by no means uncommon in Scandinavia and several appear on wash boards and wooden boxes, mostly from the late eighteenth or nineteenth centuries, which are preserved in museums.

A labyrinth carved on the wooden wall of an Estonian windmill, originally built in 1748 on the island of Ormsö, is now preserved in an open-air museum near Tallinn.

Situated amongst trees at Gregersö, in the beautiful Åland archipelago, this small labyrinth formed from boulders originally stood on the shore, but is now well inland.

Labyrinths in Iceland

On one of the westernmost headlands in northwest Iceland, the Völudarhúsið (Wayland's House) labyrinth at Dritvik is surely one of the most remote in Europe. Formed of jagged blocks of lava on the flanks of the Snæfellsjökull volcano, the labyrinth is situated near a fishing station that operated between the seventeenth and nineteenth centuries. The Baltic design may have reached Iceland with the Norwegian and German fishing crews that worked these remote coastlines. Three more labyrinths have been recorded in northwest Iceland, but all have now perished.[37]

Although only one stone labyrinth in Iceland has survived, carved labyrinths can be seen preserved on wooden bed-boards in the National Museum of Iceland in Reykjavik. These boards, slotted into the front edge of box beds at night, were used as chairs by day in the cramped wooden houses of seventeenth- to nineteenth-century Iceland. The board fronts are carved with traditional patterns and motifs; three have labyrinths on the back. One of these is flanked by an inscription: "*Vølundarhus mannsævinnar*" – "Wayland's House: man's life is like this."

Located at 64° 45′N and 23° 25′W, on one of the westernmost headlands in Northwest Iceland, the Völudarhúsið (Wayland's House) labyrinth at Dritvik is surely one of the most remote in Europe.

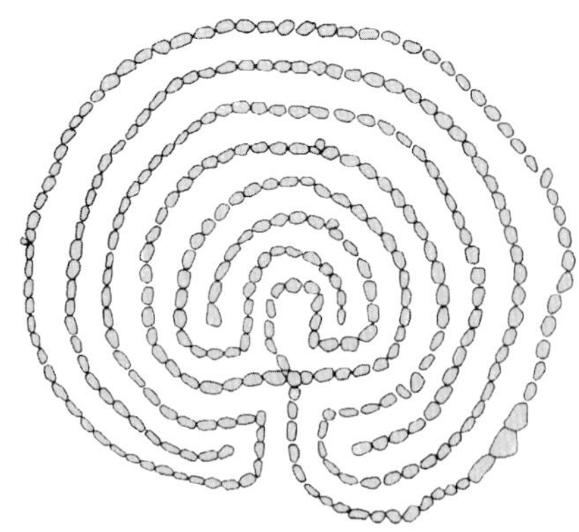

The labyrinth at Holmengrå, north of Kirkenes in eastern Finnmark, Norway, is one of eight preserved in this remote Arctic region. It is dated to 1000 –1600 CE.

Labyrinths in Norway

Apart from a few stone labyrinths in the far south of the country and two frescos in southern churches, labyrinths are rare in Norway. One, at Myklebust, is known as Julianske Borg, a name surely borrowed from the east coast of England (see page 121); the other is on the summit of the Vartdals mountain; local folklore tells that walking it would absolve wrong-doers of their sins. The northern coastline of Finnmark in Arctic Norway is home to a group of eight preserved stone labyrinths, mostly of the classical design. They are on small offshore islands or headlands near Saami burial grounds, dating from *c.* 1200–1700.[38] Several are at low elevation above sea level, precluding any dates prior to the Middle Ages. The proximity to burial sites suggests that the labyrinth was symbolic of the pathway to the spirit world or served as a spirit trap to contain the souls of ancestors. Like their sister labyrinths in Arctic Russia, it is possible that these are the result of late-medieval contact with Pomor traders from northern Russia; they may also have been introduced by Norwegians traders, who colonized this coastline during the same period. Whatever their origin, their location at around 71° North makes these labyrinths the northernmost yet recorded.

Situated near to an old fishing station, the labyrinth at Umba on the south coast of the Kola peninsular in Arctic Russia is probably no more than 500 years old.

Labyrinths in Arctic Russia

The stone labyrinths found on islands in the White Sea and round the shoreline of the Kola Peninsular into the Barents Sea are the subject of controversial interpretation and dating. Some thirty or more labyrinths have been documented in the region, about half of which survive. Five or six along the northern shore of the Kola Peninsula have been destroyed, but all were situated at remote fishing stations established during the late and post-medieval periods. Two surviving labyrinths on the southern Kola coastline, at Kandalaksha and Umba, are not only next to fishing stations but are only 10-16 ft (3-5 m) above sea level. The rapid tectonic uplift in this region therefore rules out an origin much more than 500 years ago. Several labyrinths along the western shore of the White Sea share these locational features and were also constructed by fishing communities. The majority are of the classical or Baltic types and are quite small, typically formed of stones laid on soil or rock.

There were once two or three labyrinths at Ponoy, on the eastern shore of the Kola Peninsular, but today only one made of boulders survives. This labyrinth has been ascribed by Russian archaeologists[39] to the first millennium CE, but the design is typically medieval and points to an origin after the twelfth or thirteenth century.

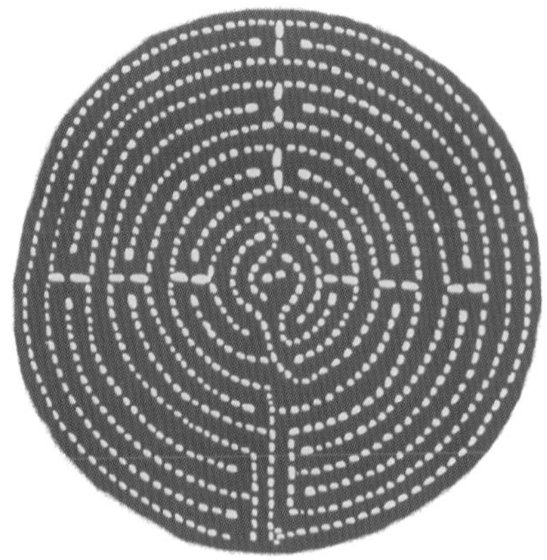

The labyrinth at Ponoy, on the eastern shore of the Kola peninsular, must be of post-medieval origin. The use of the medieval design in this remote location is remarkable.

The most dramatic labyrinths in the region are to be found on the Solovetski archipelago in the White Sea, just south of the Arctic Circle. Examples that obviously belong to the post-medieval tradition

Four surviving labyrinths on the small island of Zaiatski.

are found on a number of islands. One on Bolshoi Solovetski was restored in the 1970s and has subsequently accumulated several smaller replicas, built by visitors, alongside it. The island of Zaiatski has a remarkable collection of at least twelve labyrinths, falling into two different groups. The first are of post-medieval origin and can be distinguished by their varied designs, random orientation, and shoreline locations. The second group contains some of the most exciting labyrinths in the region. Three of these, the largest of which is nearly 82 ft (25 m) in diameter, are formed from banks of boulders creating knee-high walls. They are located on the southern flank of an extensive Saami ritual site dotted with hundreds of stone mounds. Some of these mounds have been investigated, but yielded little more than a few stone tools or bones. Such sites were sacrificial and ceremonial locations, where offerings were made to the spirits. They were rarely used for human burial and are extremely difficult to date.

There is evidence that this site on Zaiatski was in constant use from at least the second millennium BCE up to relatively recent times. How the labyrinths might fit this chronology is controversial. Local archaeologists have claimed that they are 4,000 or more years old[40] – which most researchers doubt. They may be contemporary with the apparently Iron Age labyrinths in southern Sweden, or they may be of medieval origin.

Labyrinths on Anzer and the nearby Kusova islands also belong to this group. They all have the eleven-path classical design with entrances to the south, all are built at least 33 ft (10 m) above sea level and, most importantly, all are directly associated with Saami ritual sites. It might also be significant that all are situated on a chain of islands that stretches across the White Sea around latitude 65° North, i.e. just south of the Arctic Circle, the boundary of the region where night and day can each last twenty-four hours.

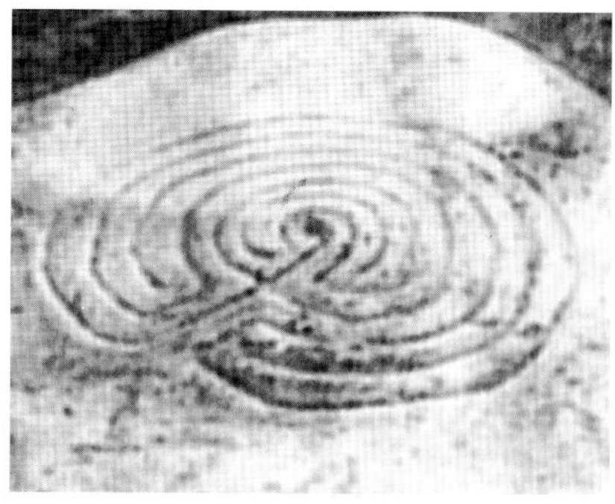
A classical labyrinth carved on a boulder near Makhchesk in the Ossetian Republic.

Central and Southern Russia

One final twist in this story remains to be told before we can move on, for the labyrinth is also found in the south of Russia. A labyrinth petroglyph, of typical classical form and measuring approximately 24 in (60 cm) in diameter, was found in 1938 carved on a granite boulder near Makhchesk in the Ossetian Republic. It has been claimed to date from the late second millennium BCE, though the sharp carving suggests a more recent origin. The local people of the Caucasus mountains regard the labyrinth as a symbol for the home of Syrdon, a mythical hero. A labyrinth carving has been found on a wooden box, probably no more than a hundred years old, collected in Dagestan. This, too, is a classical labyrinth with the outer circuits embellished with carved hatching that Kern interprets as a depiction of a fish trap.

The final example from this region poses the biggest question of all. During the late 1980s, careful excavation of a paved area in an ancient settlement at Mastische, near Voronezh in southern central Russia, uncovered a collection of granite boulders arranged in a series of concentric circles. Archaeologists interpreted the find as a stone labyrinth, and because the area was remarkably free from domestic debris, they suggested it was a ritual site.[41] Associated finds date this labyrinthine construction to the late third century or early second century BCE. If this is indeed the remains of a ruined stone labyrinth, preserved in an archaeological context, it provides the earliest evidence for this form of labyrinth in a rather unexpected location. Hopefully future excavation or development of new dating techniques will provide some answers.

But now we must leave these ancient labyrinths built of boulders in the remoter parts of Europe, and set off in search of the origin of the most familiar labyrinths of all – the puzzle mazes created from living hedges that grace parks and gardens all round the world.

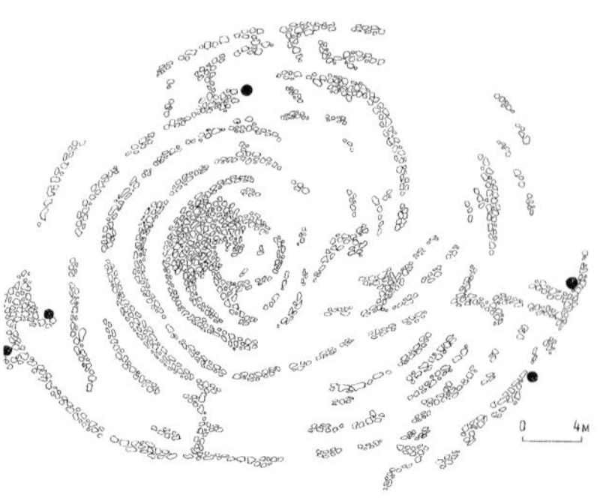
A plan of the unusual stone setting excavated at Mastische, near Voronezh. The jumbled concentric circles of boulders resemble the pattern left behind when overgrown stone labyrinths have been excavated in Scandinavia.

Although probably no older than the late nineteenth century, this wooden box collected in Dagestan shows a knowledge of the labyrinth in the Caucasus region of southern Russia in historic times.

Stone Labyrinths in Northern Europe

Country and Region	Number	Comments
England		
Scilly Islands	c. 15	1729 Original on St Agnes, recent copies on St Martin's and other islands
Sweden		
Western coastal region	50+	Two groups, in Bohuslän and around Gothenburg
Blekinge and Skåne	11	9 around Fridlevstad
Gotland	35+	A few 'ancient' examples, Visby and Fröjel both survive; many later copies
Småland and Östergötland	c. 19	Most on islands or near modern shoreline and relatively recent
Central region	c. 45	20+ in Stockholm archipelago and possibly ancient examples further inland
Northern coastal region	190+	150+ in Västerbotten alone, many surviving on small islands & headlands
Norway		
Oslofjord	9	Northern outpost of the Bohuslän group
West Coast	2	High in the mountains near Ørsta
Finnmark	8	On islands and headlands, near Saami burial grounds and fishing stations
Finland		
Northern region	50+	Some surviving on offshore islands
Åland	c. 35	Remarkable collection, most on small islands
Turku Archipelago	c. 20	On islands in the archipelago
Helsinki Archipelago	c. 30	Most on offshore islands
Estonia		
Coastal islands	5+	Possibly as many as 9; surviving examples at Kootsaare and Aksi
Iceland		
Northwest region	4	One surviving at Dritvik, Snæfellsnes
Russia		
Barents Sea Coast	6	6 recorded, all now destroyed
Kola Penninsula	5+	3 surviving: Kandalaksha and Umba on south coast, Ponoy on east coast
Southern White Sea	20+	Surviving examples on Zaiatski, Anzer, Kusova, and Bolshoi Solovetski
Voronezh	1?	Dated to 2nd/3rd C. BCE, interpretation uncertain

With over 500 examples documented, the stone labyrinths of northern Europe have a high survival rate and are certainly the most numerous of the labyrinths in the region. The accompanying map and table aim to provide an overview of their numbers and distribution. Although many regional studies have been published (see Bibliography), no complete catalogue has been compiled to date.

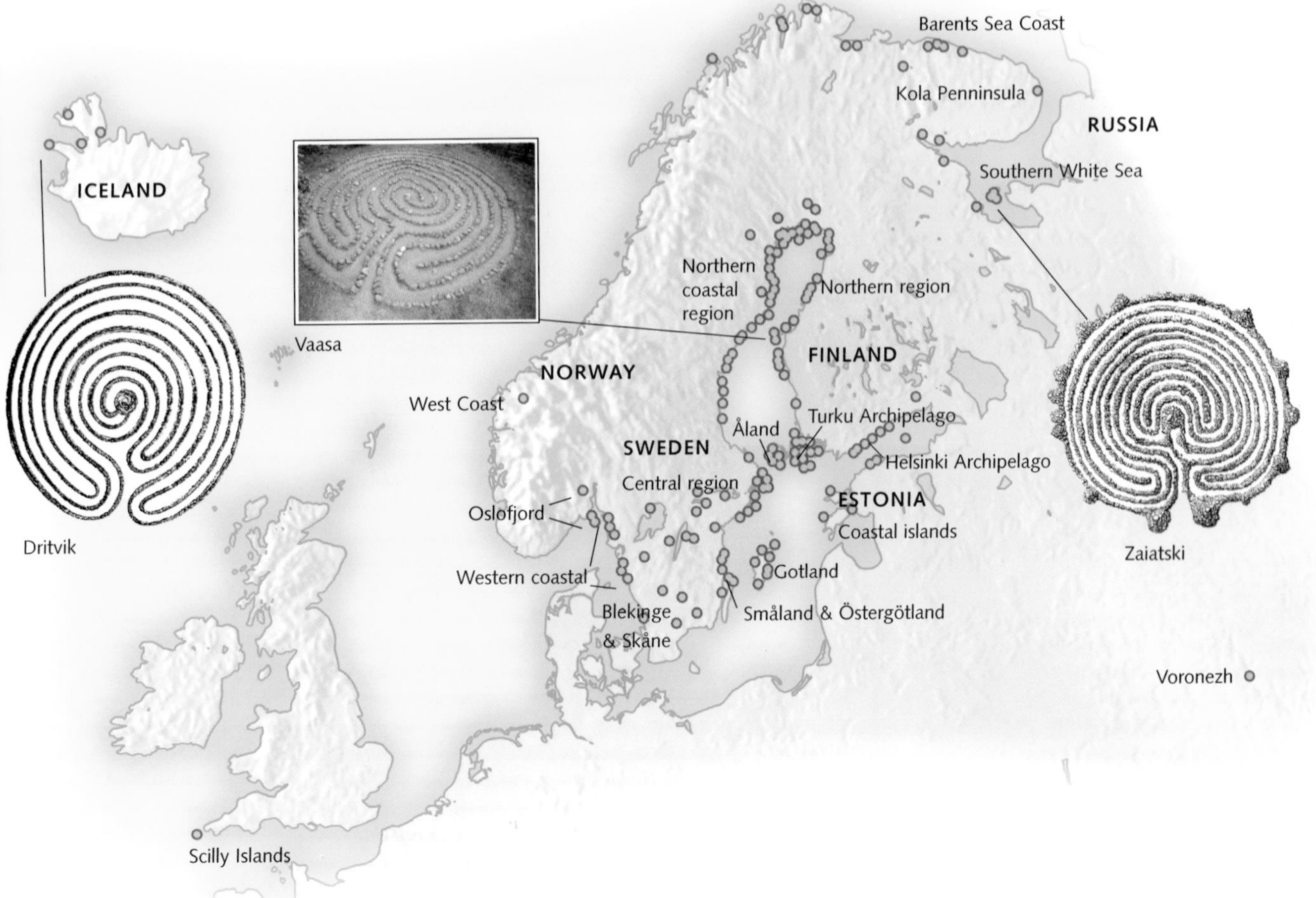

Chapter 5

Garden Labyrinths and Mazes

The thrill of entering a hedge maze, to deliberately get lost and confused, and wander paths between high hedges in search of a goal that may be glimpsed, but proves difficult to reach, has captivated many generations in many lands. As a quintessential element of the formal gardens of Europe, a plaything of the rich and titled, some mazes are famous worldwide, and have been widely copied. And yet, the fiendishly complex hedge mazes that can excite and terrify both children and adults are a fairly recent phenomenon. As with labyrinths, garden mazes started simply; indeed they grew directly from the designs of medieval labyrinths. Gradually they flowered into a multitude of ever more complex puzzles in private gardens and public parks around the world.

Originally planted *c.*1840, the hedge maze at Bridge End Gardens in the charming Essex town of Saffron Walden, England, was restored during the 1980s and is now once again in pristine condition.

The source of inspiration for the labyrinth as a medieval garden ornament probably goes back to the ancient world. Pliny the Elder praised the labyrinths of the classical era; in the early seventh century CE Isidore of Seville enthused about them in his influential *Etymologies* encyclopedia, which was widely circulated during the Middle Ages. Subsequent copyists of manuscripts and compilers of guides to medieval, historical, and topographical knowledge, such as Rabanus Maurus and Lambert of St Omer, all touch on the architectural artistry of Daedalus, usually in connection with the famous labyrinth of Crete. A number of works from the ninth to the fourteenth centuries are illustrated with diagrams of typical unicursal labyrinths to provide explanation.

We have already seen how these manuscripts provided inspiration for the construction of labyrinths in churches and cathedrals from the twelfth century onwards. So it is no surprise to find that at the same period the labyrinth became a popular feature in the gardens of royalty and the well-to-do, and that architects and designers drew on these same manuscripts and their classical sources for inspiration.

Medieval Garden Labyrinths

The medieval concept of the garden, inherited from the kitchen and medicinal gardens tended by monks in monasteries across Europe, was developed into the *hortus conclusus*, the walled garden of paradise, planted with flowers, fruit trees, and shady bowers for relaxation. The first references to labyrinths in these gardens date from the late twelfth century, around the same time that labyrinths were first appearing in cathedrals. The famous Rosamund's Bower at Woodstock, England, constructed by Henry II as a secret meeting place for his mistress, was probably a labyrinthine building, but no contemporary descriptions survive. Most early records of garden labyrinths come from France. One built at Ardres in Flanders was described *c.* 1195 as constructed "with a skill in woodwork little different from that of Daedalus". Records of repairs to a *maison dédalus* at Hesdin in 1338, and several similarly named structures during the same period, give no clues to the materials or designs employed, but these labyrinths were perhaps constructed of fencing or plant-supporting trelliswork.

The first evidence for a labyrinth formed of hedges is the recorded removal of "the hedge for the labyrinth, called the House of Daedalus" at the Hôtel des Tournelles in Paris in 1431. It is clear that the concept was familiar in England as early as *c.*1450, when an anonymous English author penned *The Assembly of Ladies*, a poem that describes a low hedge maze and the efforts of a group of ladies to reach the centre.[1]

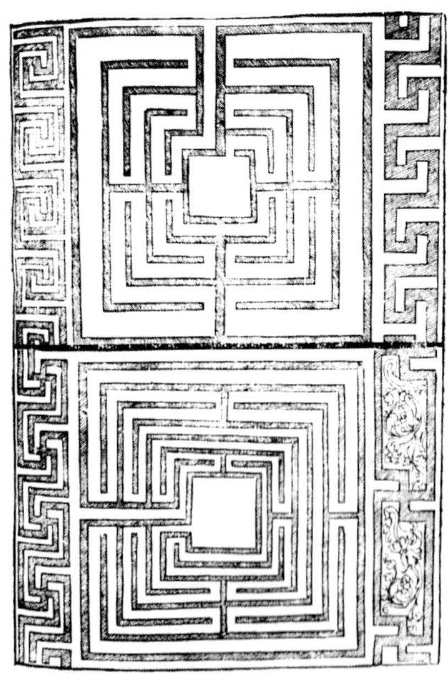

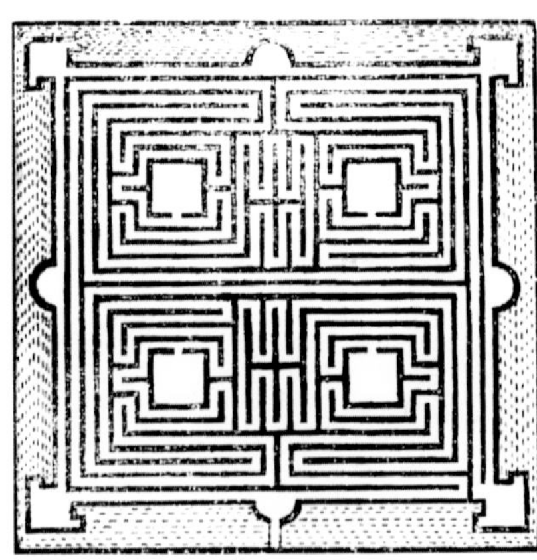

Early designs for garden labyrinths and mazes included these influential examples, from Serlio's *Libri cinque d'architettura,* first published 1537 (top); Loris's *Le Thesor Des Parterres De L'Uinvers,* 1579 (centre); and a design by Hans Puec in de Vries's *Hortorum viridariorumque elegentes et multiplicis formae,* 1592 (below).

Similar garden labyrinths are documented at the Château Baugé in Anjou (1477), and at the palace of Louise of Savoy (1513); and Francis I of France is reported to have spent time in his Maison de Dédalus in Cognac in 1520. Unfortunately no plans survive of any of these labyrinths, and it is not until the mid-1500s, with the advent of printing, that we have our first designs for garden mazes.

The two-dimensional church and turf labyrinths hardly ever offer a choice of pathway – pointless if the paths could be followed by eye – but three-dimensional hedging allows the multicursal maze to be developed from the unicursal labyrinth. Despite the potential that hedging offers, the surprising feature of the earliest depictions of hedge mazes is that many of them are in fact unicursal labyrinths. Some are simple adaptations of widespread medieval designs; others little more than interconnected concentric circles.

Sixteenth-Century Garden Labyrinths

The beginning of the sixteenth century coincided with the birth of the Renaissance, a period of cultural and political renewal across Europe and of the rebirth of classical art and architecture. The development of printing in the later years of the previous century brought the works of earlier authors to a new audience and allowed new ideas to circulate. Symmetry, architectural order, and complex symbolic forms were key to the vision of the ideal garden, and the garden labyrinth flourished. Labyrinth designs were often copied from plans in books detailing good gardening practice. These included Sebastiano Serlio's *Libri cinque d'architettura* (1537), Thomas Hill's *The Profitable Art of Gardening* (1568), and D. Loris's *Le Thesor Des Parterres De L'Univers* (1579). Loris gives more than twenty designs, many of them true mazes. His plates provided the models for many of the designs in Georg Boeckler's *Architectura Curiosa Nova* (1664), an influential source in the late seventeenth century. Important architectural pattern books were also produced by Johan Vredeman de Vries between 1555 and 1605. His *Hortorum viridariorumque elegentes et multiplicis formae* (1583) featured nine plates of garden labyrinths and mazes, mostly laid in parterre style with turf ridges or beds of dwarf shrubs or flowers. Later editions of De Vries's book contain additional mazes created by his student Hans Puec.

Garden mazes and labyrinths started to appear in paintings from the mid-sixteenth century onwards. One, painted in 1573, shows Lord Edward Russell standing in a small turf maze. This maze was re-created in 1983 at Chenies Manor, Buckinghamshire. The second, a full-length portrait of Sir George Delves

painted in 1577, shows a turf maze set in a large colonnaded garden with a tunnel arbour.[2] Paintings and engravings from the Netherlands and Italy (*c.* 1540–1600)[3] show proper hedge mazes populated with couples, although the hedges are rarely more than waist high. These "Labyrinths of Love" were designed for pleasurable dalliance; few provided more than the gentlest of puzzles and many are derived from the medieval labyrinth design, albeit with fewer circuits. Decorative fountains and shaded bowers around a central tree or maypole often feature at the centre. These romantic depictions reflect the fashion for garden labyrinths as a symbol of courtly love.

The powerful Gonzaga family of Mantua in Italy created labyrinths at several of their properties, of which a number survive. A mural painted *c.* 1510 in the Sala dei Cavalli in the Palazzo Ducale depicts a mountainous island with a spiral pathway leading to its summit, where a walled town is surrounded by a medieval-style labyrinth. This painting alludes to the labyrinth defenses of the island of Crete described by the Venetian philosopher Francesco Colonna in *The Dream of Poliphilus* (1499). Colonna was influential for his descriptions of garden ornaments and water features, many of which subsequently found their way into Renaissance gardens.

A turf maze appears in the background of the portrait of Sir George Delves, painted in England in 1577 (above), and a simple hedge maze features in the rendition of the meeting of David and Bathsheba, painted *c.*1545 in Antwerp (left).

The ceiling of the Sala del Labarinto in the Palazzo Ducale at Mantua, painted *c.*1601.

The mosaic floor of the Sala di Psiche in the Gonzaga family's Palazzo del Tè has eight small octagonal labyrinths within its design and adjacent frescos show Daedalus and other scenes from classical mythology. Two surviving decorated ceilings in another of their palaces, the Palazzo Ducale, also feature the labyrinth. One shows a scene from Ovid's *Metamorphoses* with a labyrinth in the background; the path of the other labyrinth is decorated with the motto of Vincenzo IV Gonzaga: "*Forse Che Si, Forse Che No*" ("Maybe yes, maybe no"). The centre of the labyrinth is inscribed "*Dedalei industrie et Theseii virtutis*" – no doubt qualities with which the Duke identified. The ceilings date from 1620 and 1601.

The Gonzaga also had plans for labyrinths in their gardens, but it is not clear whether they were ever actually built. The first, from *c.* 1525–34, shows a medieval-type labyrinth constructed within an open-sided octagonal stone structure, although no clues to the form of the labyrinth, hedges or otherwise, is given. The second is a design for a yew hedge maze, drawn *c.* 1550 to occupy the courtyard on the northern side of the Palazzo del Tè. Designed as a puzzle for guests, this must have been one of the first of its kind.

A hedge labyrinth planted in the 1570s in the gardens of Theobalds House, England, took its design directly from Serlio's influential book published in 1537.

Depictions of hedge mazes known to have been built appear from the 1560s, often as plans and engravings commissioned by the owners of the gardens. They include the hedge labyrinth planted in the 1570s at Theobalds in England for Lord Burghley, long-time adviser to Queen Elizabeth I. The design was identical to the plan provided in Serlio's book of 1537. A hedge maze in Henry VIII's gardens at Nonsuch, laid out in the 1540s, is first described in 1599 at a time when the hedges were too high to see over.[4] At least three examples are recorded from the palaces of France. A pair of labyrinths is depicted on the plans of the gardens of the Archbishop of Rouen at Gaillon, published in 1576 by their architect, Jacques Androuet de Cerceau. One square, the other circular with bastions at the corners, they are both of the Serlio design, as are two almost identical labyrinths, again by De Cerceau, planted in the 1560s for Renée, daughter of Louis XII, at Montargis in Loiret. Another of De Cerceau's creations, planted *c.* 1560 at the behest of Charles IX at Charleval in Normandy, is a true puzzle maze. Although not complex, it is arguably one of the first true hedge mazes recorded.

Two labyrinths, one square, the other circular, in the formal gardens at Gaillon in France, were modelled on Serlio's designs.

Italy's passion for labyrinths at this time was not restricted to the Gonzaga family. The labyrinths at Mantua span the sixteenth century, and the pavement labyrinths in the San Vitale basilica in Ravenna and the Castle Sant' Angelo in Rome date from the middle of the century. The gardens of the Villa d'Este at Tivoli, laid out during the 1560s, are frequently shown with four square labyrinths, although only two were actually built. Tivoli, Ravenna, and Rome are of the Serlio design, with low hedge walls and shrubs at the corners and centre. Other Italian garden labyrinths from this time are recorded, including an example in the hugely influential and innovative gardens of the Villa di Pratolino in Florence, but none of these has survived and few have plans preserved.

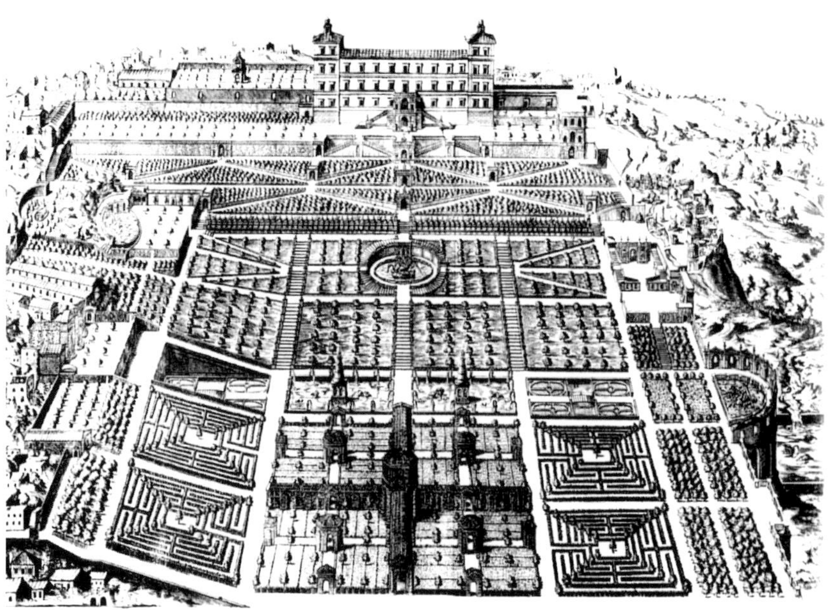

The extensive gardens of the Villa d'Este at Tivoli, Italy, laid out during the 1560s, featured labyrinths planted with low hedges. Once again, Serlio's plans were consulted for inspiration.

Unfortunately no hedge mazes from the sixteenth century have survived, but several re-creations of period gardens in the grounds of contemporary houses and palaces have consulted old engravings for inspiration, and added mazes to the layout to provide the visitor with an authentic surrounding. A notable example, planted in the 1980s with dwarf box bushes in the Tudor garden of Hatfield House in Hertfordshire, England, is based on designs found in sixteenth-century prints. This is a wonderful re-creation of an otherwise completely lost class of maze, and splendidly complements the full-height yew hedge maze planted in the grounds in 1840.

While the hedge mazes from this early period have not fared well, we do have at least one surviving garden labyrinth from these times. The Troy Town turf labyrinth at Somerton in Oxfordshire, England (see page 123), is the obvious example and illustrates well the fine dividing line between the different types of labyrinths in existence at this time, a period when garden mazes were starting to develop a separate identity and evolve into the traditional hedge mazes with which we are familiar today.

A re-creation of a typical sixteenth-century garden labyrinth, planted with low box hedging in the garden of Hatfield House in England during the 1980s, gives a good idea of the appearance of early garden labyrinths and mazes.

Seventeenth and Eighteenth Centuries

Many early garden labyrinths were influenced by classical reference and designed for contemplative exercise, but the rise of the Mannerist garden style in the seventeenth century signalled a change towards a more secular use of the labyrinth. A flurry of new plans and engravings spread across Europe. With full-height hedges and more complex designs, mazes soon became a puzzle and a challenge, a place for entertainment and an increasingly popular feature in the gardens of the wealthy.

In the Netherlands garden mazes were commonly known as Doolhof. Two such mazes, open to the public, were once situated in Amsterdam and known as the Oude Doolhof (*c.* 1610) and the Nieuwe Doolhof (*c.* 1630). The earlier of the two featured a bower at the centre with a statue of Theseus fighting the Minotaur. The remarkable hedge maze built in 1690 in the gardens of Sorgvliet Castle near The Hague featured a tree on a large flat-topped mount at its centre. A similar Doolhof with a tree and bower at its centre was planted in the courtyard of Leyden Castle around 1650 and probably survived until the early 1800s. Most of these seventeenth-century mazes derive from the medieval labyrinth design, although they are true mazes. Many more complex mazes were built during the eighteenth century, but none has survived.

Mazes in the gardens of palaces and great houses in Britain are often mentioned in visitors' accounts or financial records, but plans of them are rare. A small maze recorded in the early seventeenth-century garden of Tredegar House in Monmouthshire, Wales, was based on a design from Serlio, as was another in the garden of Yester House in East Lothian, Scotland, and two in the grounds of Wrest House in Bedfordshire, England.

At the start of the seventeenth century the work of Salomon de Caus and his younger brother Isaac brought a new fascination for grottos, hydraulic automata, and other water features to the garden owners of England and the Low Countries. De Caus had travelled to Italy and visited the famous gardens at Pratolino and the Villa d'Este in the late 1590s. He combined the best of these Renaissance garden styles with his own fascination for hydraulics in some of the most influential garden designs of the time. De Caus also installed

The hedge maze built in the 1690s in the gardens of Sorgvliet Castle in the Netherlands featured a central mount and was planted with trees. It is not difficult to imagine how mazes of this type may have influenced the design of turf labyrinths cut around this time in England and Germany.

Two surviving and recently restored hedge mazes, originally planted *c.*1691 in the gardens of Květná Zahrada in Kroměříž in Moravia vie with Hampton Court as the oldest surviving garden mazes in Europe.

mazes, including a simple concentric maze with a fountain at its centre in gardens at Heidelberg, Germany, which were unfortunately never completed due to the outbreak of the Thirty Years War.

The concept of a maze formed from water can be traced back to Colonna's *Hypnerotomachia Poliphili*, but the first evidence of the construction of such an audacious garden feature comes from the Queen's House at Greenwich, London.[3] The most likely candidate for designer of the Greenwich water maze was De Caus. From the records of its repairs and upkeep from 1615 until it was cleared towards the end of the century, we can surmise that this fascinating and innovative maze consisted of a flagstone pathway between lead-lined troughs. Water was pumped through the troughs from a cistern, and a fountain was added to the arrangement *c.* 1640. Regrettably no plan or drawing survives.

The famous hedge maze at Hampton Court, England, was planted in 1690 and can probably rightfully claim to be the world's oldest continuously surviving hedge maze.

From the end of the seventeenth century come the first surviving hedge mazes that are still growing on their original sites. Two mazes in the gardens of Květná Zahrade in Kroměříž in Moravia, originally planted *c.* 1691 and recently restored to good condition, are almost identical to two designs for garden mazes published in 1699 in J. van der Groen's *Den Nederlandtsen Hovenier*. The hedge maze at Hampton Court in England, arguably the most famous maze in the world and much copied around the globe, was originally planted with hornbeam bushes in 1690 for William of Orange, and can probably claim to be the oldest surviving hedge maze. Its unusual trapezoidal shape results from fitting a space in an earlier layout of the gardens, which may well have had a previous hedge maze dating back to the early sixteenth century. Adjacent to today's maze on early plans is a feature known as the "Plan-de-Troy" – tall espaliers are planted in a design of two simple meandering labyrinths bisected by a pathway. This feature has long since been replaced by a rockery, but it is recorded that a similar "Siege of Troy," formed of yew and holly clipped to resemble fortifications, graced King William's gardens at Kensington Palace. The maze at Hampton Court receives hundreds of thousands of visitors each year and the consequent wear and tear to the original hedges has necessitated a number of "patches" over the years. The use of different varieties of yew has resulted in uneven growth and there is talk of a complete re-plant in the near future to address current maintenance problems.

The long-surviving maze at Egeskov Castle in Denmark was planted in the early 1700s.

The hedge maze in the grounds of Egeskov Castle in Denmark, planted in the early 1700s to a plan almost identical to the Hampton Court maze, also survives in good condition. The close links between the English and Danish royal families at this time was no doubt responsible for the borrowing of this design, but hedge mazes had first appeared in Denmark in 1663, when one was planted in hornbeam in the King's Garden at Rosenborg Castle in Copenhagen. Several more mazes were planted in royal parks around Copenhagen during the early 1700s. A remarkable pair was planted in the 1720s at Vemmetofte in Sjælland in Denmark, of a three-circuit, classical design in dwarf box hedging. The only surviving example from the period, in the grounds of Fredensborg Palace, is unique. Known as the Sneglehøj (Snail Hill), it comprises a small mount encircled with a simple labyrinth of dwarf box hedges planted *c.* 1720. Mounts with paths spiralling to the summit to provide an overview of the garden were popular features among wealthy landowners of the time, but very few are recorded surrounded by a labyrinth.

The survival of historic hedge mazes is more a matter of chance than selection of the most important or exciting examples. In Italy, the mazes at the Villa Barbarigo in Vansanzibio and the Villa Pisani at Stra, both near Padua, are celebrated survivors from the many hedge mazes that once graced the gardens of villas throughout the country. The Villa Barbarigo maze was planted sometime between the 1670s and 1690s. The splendid maze at the Villa Pisani retains its ornamental central tower, with spiral staircase and statuary, and dates from 1720. Another maze in the garden of the Villa Altieri in Rome, dating from the 1670s, was less fortunate. It was uprooted *c.* 1870

At the unique Sneglehøj (Snail Hill) in the grounds of Fredensborg Palace, Denmark, the low box hedge encircling the mound forms a simple labyrinth.

Above: block maze at Versailles *c.*1699.
Below: block maze at Choisy-le-Roi, 1740.

because wild animals were living inside it. It was originally planted for Pope Clement X and it is recorded that he took great delight in sending his servants into the maze, then urgently summoning them and watching their attempts to find the exit.

From the late seventeenth century onwards a number of important developments in maze design took place in France. The garden constructed by André Le Nôtre, begun in 1662 at Louis XIV's palace at Versailles, featured a maze that was probably installed in 1669 by Le Nôtre's assistant James Hardouin-Mansart. Known as the Labyrinthe, it was not a hedge maze but a series of interconnecting paths leading through a large block of woodland. At each of the pathway intersections was a statue or water feature representing one of Aesop's fables. It offered not so much a puzzle as an entertaining promenade, although plotting the optimum course that took in all the fountains and features was still a challenge. Equally complex was the elaborate system of pipe-work, waterwheels, and pumps that diverted water from the River Seine to supply the fountains. The labyrinth was destroyed in 1774 to make way for a new garden feature, but its influence on subsequent maze design was considerable. Similar large woodland block mazes, planted *c.* 1739 at Chantilly as part of later improvements to André Le Notre's original layout of 1665, and at Choisy-le-Roi in 1740, feature dramatic swirling designs influenced by d'Argenville's *La Théorie et la pratique du jardinage* (1709).

By the early eighteenth century, the fashion for block mazes had spread to England, where notable examples included a smaller-scale replica of the Versailles maze, planted at Friar Park in Henley-on-Thames. This version had thirty-nine different sundials placed at the path intersections. A larger example filled a quarter of the gardens at Trinity College, Oxford, and another was located in the grounds of Badminton House, Gloucestershire. The dividing line between what might be considered a block maze, and what might better be described as a long walk through the woods, is well demonstrated by the "most surprizing labyrinth" cut into pre-existing woodland at Cookridge, near Leeds in England, by Thomas Kirke, around 1680.[6] Kirke had visited Versailles and had no doubt been influenced by the example there, but his extensive system of pathways, with sixty-five intersections, filled a much larger wooded area than did the

Below: Laberint d'Horta maze in Barcelona.

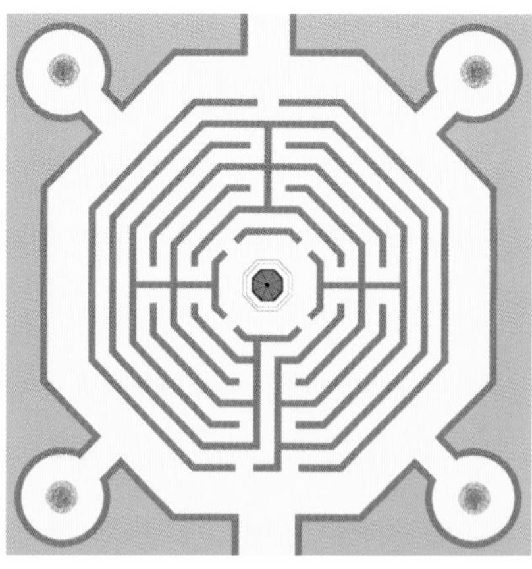

The octagonal hedge maze in Herrenhausen Gardens, Hanover, Germany, planted in 1936, is styled on a typical seventeenth-century garden maze.

Labyrinthe at Versailles. A surviving example of one of these labyrinthine pathway systems, originally laid out in 1735, is preserved in the Dwaalbos woods at Kernham, near Ede in the Netherlands. Woodland mazes were also popular in Germany. But as they were designed for the vistas that they offered rather than as a puzzle to solve, I will follow this path no further.

The maze at La Granja, in San Ildefonso, Spain, was planted during the mid-1700s, copied directly from d'Argenville's *La Théorie et la pratique du jardinage*. The recently restored gardens at the Laberint d'Horta park in Barcelona were originally planted by the Marquis of Alfarras *c.* 1791. Central to the layout of the garden is a splendid hedge maze formed of fragrant clipped cypress trees, enhanced with statues and fountains with a decorated grotto at the goal. In excellent condition once again, this is without doubt one of the most enticing mazes in Spain, indeed anywhere in Europe. The oldest surviving hedge maze in Germany, at Altjessnitz in Sachsen-Anhalt, was originally planted around 1750. It is still kept in good condition, although the castle in whose grounds it once stood has long since been destroyed. The octagonal hedge maze in the Herrenhausen Gardens in Hanover is often claimed to date from the 1670s. It was actually added during a restoration of the gardens in 1936, but is totally in keeping with the style of the gardens and is in all respects an authentic re-creation.

The varying fortunes of hedge mazes are well illustrated by the fate of the one in Schönbrunn Palace Gardens near Vienna in Austria, planted around 1750. This originally consisted of five or six separate design elements linked together to form one enormous maze with an overall length of nearly 2 miles (3 km) of meandering pathways. This curious arrangement may have been influenced by plans for similar "compound" mazes published in London in 1728 in Batty Langley's *New Principles of Gardening*. The upkeep of such a huge maze must have been daunting, and gradually the hedges at Schönbrunn decayed. By 1865 less than half remained and by the early years of the twentieth century it had almost disappeared, though the ground plan was still visible in the shapes of newly re-planted beds. During the late 1990s, one-quarter of the maze was restored, with the design subtly altered to provide a new entrance.

A similar re-creation project has recently taken place at Villandry in France. The original Renaissance gardens were destroyed during the nineteenth century to make way for a new garden, which in turn was replaced early in the twentieth century with a re-creation of the original layout. In the 1990s a copy of the Renaissance hedge maze was added. The maze at Villandry is a credible restoration in an authentic setting, and a sure sign that further reconstruction can be expected in similar historic gardens in the future.

This is the original layout of the vast hedge maze planted *c.*1750 in Schönbrunn Palace gardens near Vienna. The original maze has long since decayed and been removed, but the top left quarter of the design has recently been recreated in the gardens.

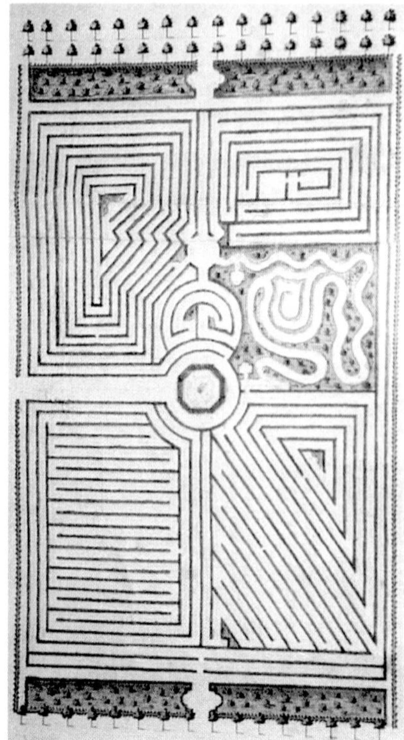

Nineteenth-Century Europe

The turn of the eighteenth century saw a decline in the fortune of garden mazes. Taste in the garden shifted to natural landscapes and picturesque vistas, and formal hedge mazes fell from fashion across much of Europe. However, the rise of public parks and recreation grounds provided new opportunities for hedge mazes to flourish.

During the 1820s Earl Stanhope, an eminent mathematician, designed at least three hedge mazes, including the surviving example in the grounds of Chevening House in Kent, England. Stanhope was the first maze designer to apply map theory to maze design. Until now most mazes could be solved by the "hand-on-wall method". By always turning in the same direction, the walker would eventually arrive at the goal, since most mazes consisted of a single wall, albeit with numerous branches. Stanhope's mazes contained a number of discrete sections of hedge stacked within the perimeter, which most importantly was not in contact with the goal. He produced mazes that were difficult to solve and contained few dead-ends along the way, producing a more fluid and exciting experience for the visitor. These are important factors in modern maze design. Stanhope's mazes were planted at Anerley Park and North Woolwich in London and at Beauport House near Hastings, but none has survived.

The Italianate gardening style – influenced by the Renaissance gardens of the great Italian villas – was popular in Britain around 1830 to 1850. It produced a number of interesting maze designs, of which several survive in excellent condition, including the recently restored yew maze in Bridge End Gardens, Saffron Walden, Essex (1839), and the Somerleyton Hall Maze near Lowestoft, Suffolk (1846), which has a delightful pavilion on a raised mound at its goal. A replica of the Somerleyton maze, planted 1886 in Worden Park in Leyland, Lancashire, has also been preserved. William Nesfield (1793-1881), a retired naval officer, designed a number of these mazes. The recently restored hedge maze at Shrublands Park in Suffolk is another splendid example of his work, which was widely imitated.

Other surviving hedge mazes from this period include one at Hatfield House in Hertfordshire, which was planted in 1840 and features a large traditional, rectangular design. Another, in the grounds of Woburn Abbey in Bedfordshire, was planted with hornbeam bushes *c.* 1831 and is notable for the Chinese Temple at

The preserved hedge maze in the private gardens of Chevening House, England, designed by Earl Stanhope and planted in the 1820s, was one of the first of a new class of more complex, multiply-connected mazes (see page 32).

Lord Astor's restoration of Hever Castle, England (right), included this hedge maze planted in 1905. The design is based on a 1623 woodcut, chosen to provide an authentic period maze for the gardens.

The Italianate-style maze (below) designed by William Nesfield and planted in the grounds of Somerleyton House, England, in 1846, is only a simple puzzle but provides a beautiful decorative addition to the gardens.

its centre. The hedge maze at Hever Castle in Kent has a seventeenth-century design, but dates from Lord Astor's restoration of the castle and grounds in 1905.

The swirling pathways of the laurel hedge maze at Glendurgan House in Cornwall were planted in 1833 and are now cared for by the National Trust. Built on a slope, the pathways alternately cut across and then follow the steep contours of the hillside.

The swirling pathways of the maze at Glendurgan House, England, were planted in 1833. The unusual design follows the contours of its sloping location.

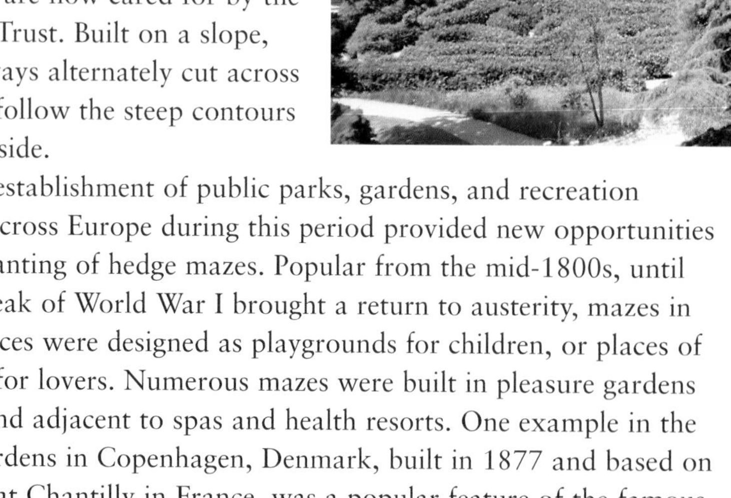

The establishment of public parks, gardens, and recreation grounds across Europe during this period provided new opportunities for the planting of hedge mazes. Popular from the mid-1800s, until the outbreak of World War I brought a return to austerity, mazes in public places were designed as playgrounds for children, or places of dalliance for lovers. Numerous mazes were built in pleasure gardens in cities and adjacent to spas and health resorts. One example in the Tivoli Gardens in Copenhagen, Denmark, built in 1877 and based on the maze at Chantilly in France, was a popular feature of the famous amusement park that survives to this day, although the maze itself was destroyed in 1905.

In Britain, hedge mazes were built in public parks such as Saltwell Park, Gateshead (*c.* 1860), in the Royal Horticultural Society's Gardens in South Kensington (*c.* 1862), at the Crystal Palace Park in Bromley, Kent (1865), and in Albert Park in Middlesbrough (1868). Both the Crystal Palace and Saltwell Park mazes have been replanted in recent years. The designs of many of these mazes were adaptations of old favourites, particularly Hampton Court – as at Tatton Park in Knutsford, Cheshire, and Rhinefield House, near Brockenhurst, Hampshire, both planted *c.*1890 and surviving. A little-known maze in the Iveagh Gardens in Dublin, Ireland, planted in 1863 along with a rustic grotto, fountains, and a rose garden, has now been returned to good condition. The hedges are only waist high and the design is quite simple, but this is probably the only surviving historic hedge maze in Ireland.

This plan of the maze in the Tivoli Gardens in Copenhagen comes from a guidebook to the pleasure gardens. Planted in 1877, the design was copied from a maze created at Chantilly, France, in 1739.

Elsewhere in Europe, a number of the hedge mazes planted during the nineteenth century in popular public parks and gardens have been preserved. A formal hedge maze of circular design with a central tree was added to the eighteenth-century gardens at Schönbusch in Germany in 1829. Another circular maze, planted in 1854 in the municipal park in Coutances in France, and one planted in 1873 at the Château de Loppem, near Bruges in Belgium, also featured a tree at the centre. The remarkable selection of hedge mazes that appeared in the Netherlands deserves mention, especially as a number of them survives. The huge maze at Ruurlo, a replica of the Hampton Court maze, but with much wider pathways, was planted *c.* 1889 and extensively restored in the early 1980s. Surviving mazes at Paterswolde (1825), Weldam (1885), and Sypesteyn (1901) are also based on the Hampton Court maze.[5] The hedge maze at Staverden, planted in 1907, employs the Chantilly design, which was intended for a wide area with broad pathways for easy strolling and space for fountains and statuary. Confined to a much smaller area, the Staverden maze has narrow pathways that are difficult to negotiate and easily become overgrown. Impatient walkers have forced shortcuts through the hedges at a number of points and unfortunately the gardeners have incorporated these breaks into the design. The hedge maze planted in the Koningin Julianatoren gardens at Apeldoorn in 1916 has lost half of its original hedgerows and now provides a backdrop to more modern attractions. Along with fine examples at Menkemaborg and Het Oude Loo, both planted in 1925, these are part of the remarkable collection of some twenty-five hedge mazes, old and new, to be found in the Netherlands.

William Nesfield designed the maze planted *c.*1862 in the gardens of the RHS (Royal Horticultural Society) in London.

This enormous hedge maze, a scaled-up version of the Hampton Court design, was planted *c.*1889 at Ruulo in the Netherlands.

Surviving Historic Garden Mazes and Labyrinths in Europe

Location	Planted	Comments
British Isles		
Aberdeen	1935	Hazlehead Park, large rectangular privet maze
Brockenhurst	*c.*1890	Rhinefield House Hotel, Hampton Court copy
Bromley	1865	Crystal Palace Park, circular maze, restored 1988
Castle Bromwich	*c.*1870	Holly hedge maze, restored 1990
Chatsworth House	1962	Recreation of 18th C. maze design
Chenies Manor	1983	Recreation of 1573 turf maze shown on painting
Chevening House	1820s	In private gardens, innovative design
Coddenham	1860s?	Shrubland Park, restored maze in private garden
Dublin	1863	Iveagh Gardens, circular maze, recently restored
Gateshead	*c.*1860	Saltwell Park, yew hedge maze, restored 1983
Glendurgan House	1833	Well preserved with unusual design
Hampton Court	1690	World-famous, the oldest certain survivor
Hatfield House	1840	Large rectangular maze in private garden
Hatfield House	1980s	Recreation of 16th C. low hedge maze
Hever Castle	1905	Recreation of 17th C. maze design
Knebworth House	mid-1800s	Yew maze destroyed, box replica planted 1994
Knutsford	*c.*1890	Tatton Park, rectangular Hampton Court copy
Leyland	1886	Worden park, copy of Somerleyton Hall maze
Madresfield Court	Late 1800s	Yew hedge maze preserved in private garden
Saffron Walden	1839	Bridge End Gardens, restored 1984
Somerleyton Hall	1846	Well maintained, with central pavilion
Woburn Abbey	*c.*1831	Large circular maze in private garden
France		
Beaumesnil	?	Château de Beaumesnil, on island in a lake
Chanonat	18th C.	Château de la Batisse, large maze in gardens
Coutances	1854	In town park, large circular maze
Paris	*c.*1734	Jardin des Plantes, restored 1990, central pavilion
Poncé-sur-le-Loir	*c.*1775	Château de Poncé, bizarre maze with central tree
Villandry	1990s	Authentic recreation of renaissance maze

Location	Planted	Comments
Belgium		
Bruges	1873	Château de Loppem, central tree
Netherlands		
Apeldoorn	1916	Köningin Julianatoren Gardens, only half survives
Apeldoorn	1925	Het Oude Loo, square maze, unusual design
Goor	1885	Kasteel Weldam, Hampton Court style
Oud-Loosdrecht	1901	Sypesteyn, Hampton Court style
Paterswolde	1825	De Braak, Hampton Court copy
Ruurlo	*c.*1889	Huge Hampton Court copy with central platform
Staverden	1907	Small copy of Chantilly design
Uithuizen	1925	Menkemaborg, large rectangular hedge maze
Denmark		
Egeskov Castle	*c.*1730	Rectangular version of Hampton Court
Fredensborg	*c.*1720	Sneglehøj, low box hedge labyrinth
Germany		
Aschaffenburg	1829	Schönbusch, circular maze with central tree
Altjessnitz	*c.*1750	Large square maze with viewing platform
Hanover	1936	Herrenhausen gardens, recreation of 17th C. maze
Probsteierhagen	1927	Irrgarten, popular puzzle maze
Czech Republic		
Kroměříž	*c.*1691	Květná Zahrade, two hedge mazes
Prague	1980s	Trojský Zámek Palace, maze in restored gardens
Austria		
Vienna	*c.*1750	Schönbrunn, restoration of part of original maze, late 1990s
Italy		
Collodi	18th C.	Villa Garzoni, square hedge maze
Stra	1720	Villa Pisani, splendid maze with tower
Valsanzibio	*c.*1688	Villa Barbarigo, one of the oldest
Verona	1786	Villa Giusti, rectangular maze, central fountain
Spain		
Barcelona	*c.*1791	Laberint d'Horta, recently restored and beautiful
San Ildefenso	mid-1700s	La Granja, spiralling Choisy-le-Roi design
Seville	1540	Alcazar Palace, modern re-interpretation of original maze

Many hundreds of garden mazes and labyrinths planted in the past have disappeared, as fashions for garden design have changed over the centuries, although details and plans are often documented. This map and the accompanying table show the historic examples that have survived, including those that have been replanted or restored in recent years, as well as a selection of authentic modern recreations of historically styled mazes and labyrinths in period gardens. A selection of the most notable modern hedge mazes is given in Chapter 6 (see page 206-8).

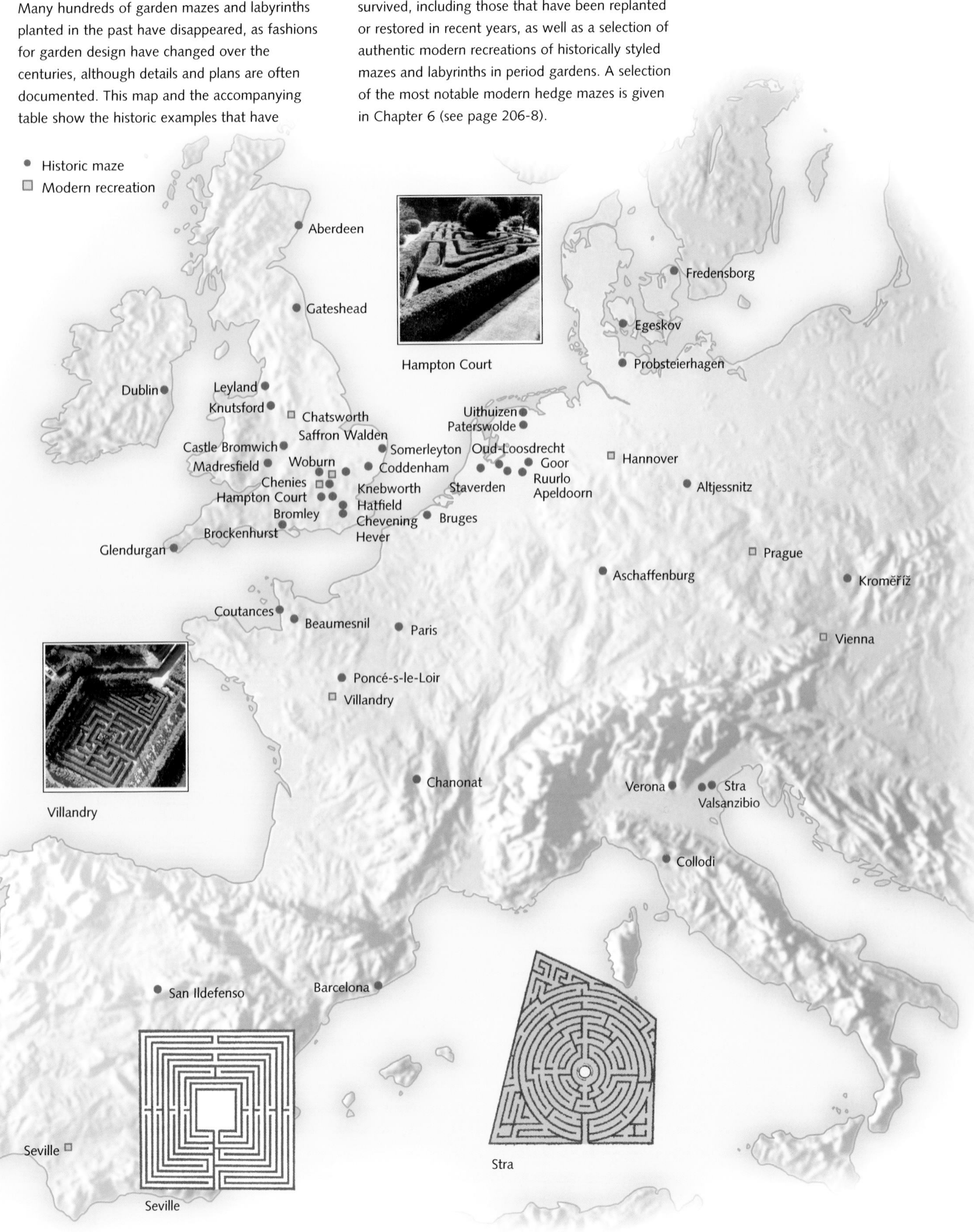

Restoration Project: Saffron Walden

In recent years hedge mazes have come again to be appreciated as an integral part of the design of historic gardens. The study of garden history has gone hand-in-hand with a number of imaginative projects to restore important historic gardens to their former glory after years of neglect, and several interesting and important hedge mazes have been rescued from states of terminal overgrowth or replanted, often on their original sites, from archival plans.

A pioneering project to restore an early nineteenth-century yew maze in Bridge End Gardens at Saffron Walden, Essex, England, has set an admirable precedent for careful recording and restoration. Early photos show a beautifully tended maze, but since the 1940s the hedges had become chronically overgrown.

Following an initial restoration proposal and survey in 1982 it was clear that the original yew bushes – now trees – were unlikely to regenerate if cut back hard, so a decision was taken to uproot and replant. This allowed an archaeological investigation of the site to be carried out, which revealed a number of important finds connected with the history and use of the maze. Sections taken from the trunks of the yew trees proved that it was planted in either 1838 or 1839.

This plan of the Bridge End Gardens maze (above) was used in the 1984 restoration.

Gardeners take a well-earned rest at the centre of the Bridge End maze in this photograph from 1907 (below).

After careful consultation of existing plans, old photographs, and the visible remains of the ground plan, the maze was replanted in 1984. It was officially re-opened to the public in 1991, and now, more than a decade later, the maze is fully grown and once again looking splendid. A replica of the original central viewing platform, installed in 2000, provides visitors with views across the maze and the adjacent gardens, which are also undergoing restoration to their former glory.

The Bridge End Gardens maze is pictured growing into shape in the mid-1990s (above left). By 2002 (above) the hedges were fully grown and the maze was in splendid condition once again. In 2000 a viewing platform was installed (below left). The design was based on old photographs and pillars from the original platform discovered in a nearby garden.

Community project work

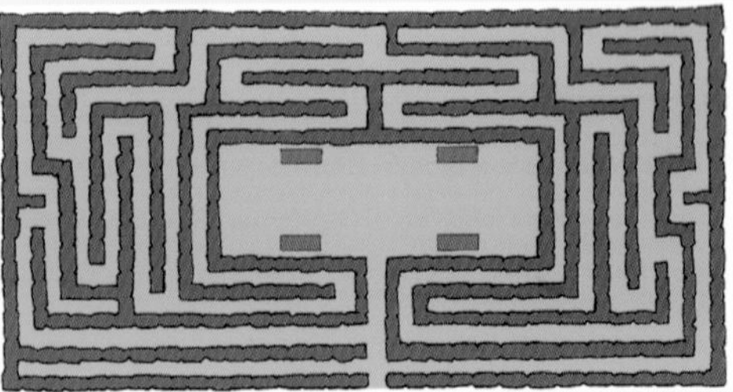

A project to restore an important eighteenth-century walled garden at Castle Bromwich Hall, near Birmingham, England, followed similar lines to the Bridge End project. It was discovered that the neglected holly maze in the grounds had been planted around 1870. This maze was also too overgrown to save, but a complete replant in 1989 (to the plan shown above) has now restored it to the ranks of the finest surviving historic hedge mazes. Both projects relied heavily on volunteers and donations, and show the admirable standard of work that can be achieved.

Mazes in the Colonies

The first recorded export of a garden maze to the colonies of the European seafaring nations describes not a hedge maze, but a maze constructed with high brick walls. Built *c.* 1766 in the gardens of the Imperial Court at Peking (Beijing), China, it also featured small groves of trees and a central pavilion. It was designed by the Italian Jesuit priest, architect, and painter, Giuseppe Castiglione, who worked as a missionary in China from 1737 to 1766. His commission to create a garden in the European style for the Emperor Qianlong at his summer palace included this remarkable maze that survived until 1860, when the soldiers of the Anglo-French expeditionary forces destroyed the gardens. Fortunately, a series of engravings (1783–86) record the details of the maze and show it to have been a unique blend of European design with Oriental architectural features added. Ironically, hedge mazes with "Chinese" pagodas at their goals became popular in Europe and America around the time that the Peking maze was destroyed.

The maze constructed *c.* 1766 in the garden of the Imperial Court at Peking in China.

By the early nineteenth century hedge mazes were beginning to appear in public and governmental parks and gardens in some unexpected places. One was planted at the beginning of the century in a garden in Pembroke on the British colonial island of Bermuda. Sadly long since destroyed, it was based on the Hampton Court maze. By the end of the century mazes had been planted as far away as Wilberforce near Freetown in Sierra Leone and in the grounds of a government residence at Barrackpore north of Calcutta in India. The first recorded example in Australia, another Hampton Court copy planted in 1862 in the Botanical Gardens at Ballarat, Victoria, was replanted in

The hedge maze at Wilberforce, near Freetown, Sierra Leone, in colonial Africa, was opened in 1905. A 1938 newspaper article complained that local people were no longer treating Whitsun as a religious holiday, but were visiting the maze instead.

the late 1880s and survived until 1954. Plans remain on file to restore it again in the future. Other early copies of British mazes include the concentric-style maze in Belair Park, Adelaide, planted in 1886, and the only survivor, but now very overgrown, and at Geelong Gardens in Victoria (1896). The first maze planted in New Zealand, in 1911 at the Dunedin Botanic Garden, was a circular design contained within a square frame. It was replanted in the 1930s, but removed in 1947. The design of these colonial hedge mazes was rarely adventurous; the challenge lay in choosing appropriate native plant species.

The first hedge maze known from New Zealand was this example planted in the Dunedin Botanical Gardens in 1911.

Colonial Garden Mazes

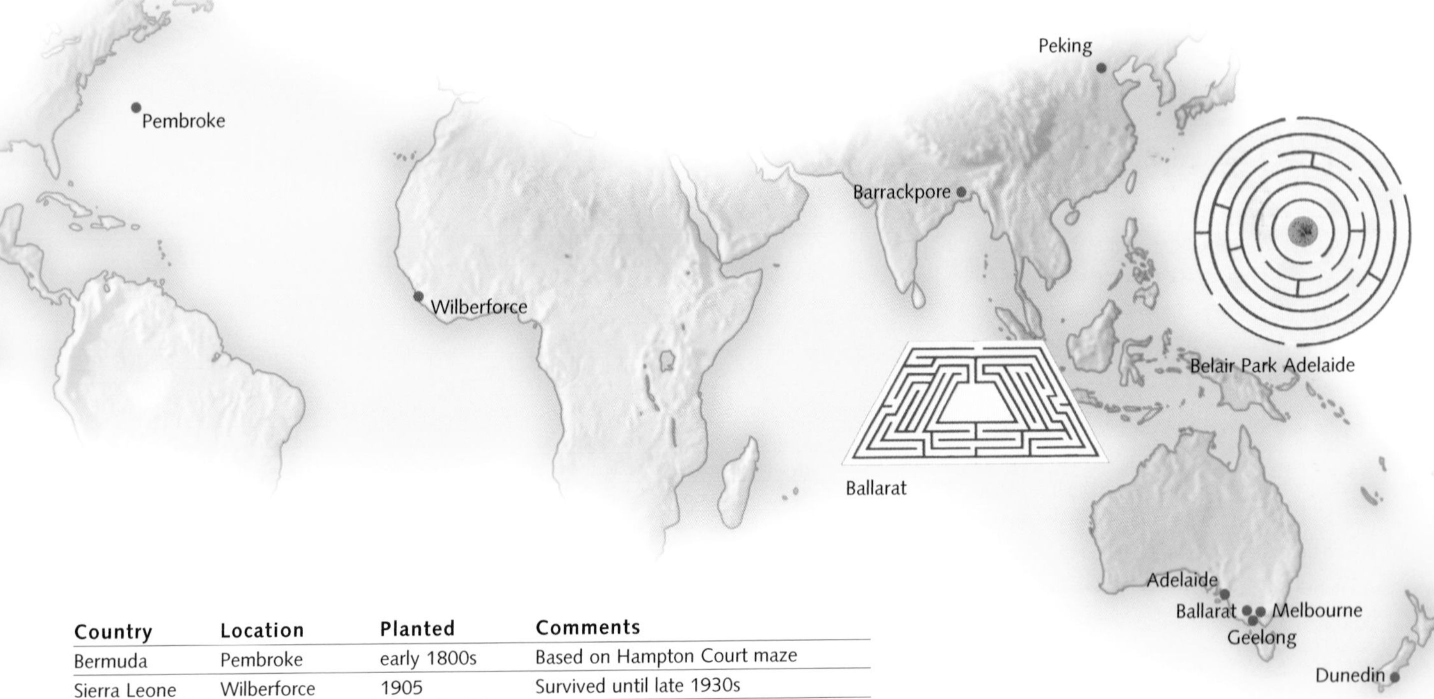

Country	Location	Planted	Comments
Bermuda	Pembroke	early 1800s	Based on Hampton Court maze
Sierra Leone	Wilberforce	1905	Survived until late 1930s
India	Barrackpore	late 1800s	In gardens of Governor's Palace
China	Peking	*c.*1766	Imperial Court gardens, destroyed 1860
Australia	Ballarat	1862	Hampton Court copy, uprooted 1954
Australia	Adelaide	1886	Belair Park, concentric design
Australia	Geelong	1896	Large rectangular maze
Australia	Melbourne	*c.*1890	Hampton Court copy
New Zealand	Dunedin	1911	Destroyed 1947

Undoubtedly more historic colonial mazes remain to be discovered scattered around the world in archives and on estate plans. Important examples are listed here, but regrettably none of these survive.

The third hedge labyrinth built by the Harmonists at Economy, Pennsylvania, *c.*1826, contained a few choices along the path, but still shows clearly that the design was derived from the classical labyrinth.

Hedge Mazes in America

Hedge mazes first reached the Americas in the early years of the nineteenth century. The first recorded example, built at Harmony, Pennsylvania, *c.* 1815, was in fact a hedge labyrinth of shrubs and vines with a single pathway to the centre. The Harmonists, a group of religious dissidents, left their native Germany in 1803 and set up three communities in Pennsylvania and Indiana between 1805 and 1825. At each settlement they built a similar labyrinth to symbolize their spiritual quest, based on a curious mix of mysticism, alchemy, and a belief in the imminent return of Christ. Each labyrinth had a stone grotto at its goal with rough stonework on the outside and delicate decoration within, reflecting the beauty of ultimate harmony. The second maze, built at Harmony, Indiana (1815) survived until the 1840s. The third, at Economy, Pennsylvania, was planted in 1825, and its central grotto survives.

The designs of all three Harmonist labyrinths are documented, although it is not certain which was planted where.[9] All were based on the classical form, but the reconstruction of one of them, based on the plan considered to be the second Harmonist labyrinth, and planted in 1941 in the former Harmonist village of New Harmony, Indiana, has ironically taken the original labyrinth design and with the addition of a few breaks in the walls, converted it into a maze!

Around the time that the Harmonists were building their first labyrinth, US president Thomas Jefferson drew a sketch of his estate at Monticello in Virginia (1806) and marked a spiralling arrangement of shrubs to the west of the house. It is not clear whether Jefferson intended it to be a labyrinth.

The fashion for landscape gardening, imported from Europe in the mid-nineteenth century, with its roots in seventeenth-century France and the garden layouts of the Italian Renaissance, gained widespread popularity during the 1880s among the newly wealthy industrialists and entrepreneurs of middle-class America. The development of holiday resorts and the establishment of public parks in cities across the nation resulted in the planting of a fair number of hedge mazes from the 1880s onwards. However, most were either copies of the Hampton Court maze or simply connected concentric designs.

The maze at Piedmont Park, near Oakland, California, was a large example of the concentric type, with a decorative "Japanese" pagoda

The hedge maze planted at New Harmony, Indiana, in 1941 was based on the design of the original Harmonist labyrinth planted when the town was founded in 1815. The recreation still survives in good condition.

standing at its centre. Built around 1900 near to the site of a renowned sulphur spring popular since the late 1860s, it was situated in a steep canyon along with a restaurant, bandstand, teahouse, exotic plants, and palm-lined pathways. This pleasure park, owned by a local property developer, was designed to attract Sunday visitors who might consider buying property adjacent to the park. The maze was destroyed *c.* 1920. A similar maze built in the Centennial Park in Nashville, Tennessee, once stood next to the replica of the Parthenon constructed for the 1897 Tennessee Centennial Exposition. It was planted *c.* 1902, when the exposition ground became a city park, landscaped for the enjoyment of the residents. Although the "Parthenon" still stands as a famous landmark in Nashville, the maze was uprooted *c.* 1930, when tastes had changed and the cost of maintaining it had become a burden.

The remarkable hedge maze in the grounds of the Hotel Del Monte at Monterey, California, was planted *c.* 1880, when the hotel and its accompanying golf course were built. Early photographs of the maze show it surrounded with floral plantings. It became a marvel of topiary and survived until the 1940s. The Great Maze at San Rafael was situated in the grounds of the Rafael Hotel, built in 1887, and was an especially large example of the concentric type. It was popular with holidaymakers from nearby San Francisco, escaping the cold, foggy weather that plagues the coast during the summer months. The hotel burnt down in 1928 and the maze was uprooted.

Piedmont Park, near Oakland, California, featured a pagoda at the centre of its maze. Postcards provide valuable information about the designs of these early American mazes.

Planted *c.*1902, the maze in Centennial Park in Nashville, Tennessee, provided gentle entertainment for citizens and visitors until it was uprooted *c.*1930.

The maze in the grounds of the Hotel Del Monte survived for over sixty years and eventually developed into a marvel of topiary before it was uprooted in the 1940s.

Based on the design of the Hampton Court maze, the Cedar Hill Maze at Waltham, Massachusetts, featured a Japanese-style ornamental pond at its goal.

The period known as the Country House Era lasted from the 1880s until *c.* 1930. During this time many private houses with spectacular gardens were built across America, and they occasionally featured hedge mazes.[9] Boxwood mazes with rambling designs were often planted in the southern states; the east coast and the Midwest favoured more traditional hedge mazes based on European models. Notable examples include the maze planted in 1896 at Cedar Hill, near Waltham in Massachusetts. This was a replica of the Hampton Court maze, with a rustic watchtower and a decorative pond at the goal. The privet hedge maze at Holly Croft, in Dayton, Ohio, was planted in 1927, after the estate owner had paid a visit to Hampton Court. It was kept in fine condition until it was sadly removed in the mid-1940s. The gardens planted at Vizcaya, near Miami, Florida, between 1916 and 1922, now owned and preserved by the city of Miami, were Italianate in style and included a small concentric hedge maze. Although hardly remarkable in its own right, it survives to this day, and is probably the oldest hedge maze in America. The sudden collapse of the stock market in 1929 and the subsequent depression brought an abrupt end to the building of expensive homes and gardens, and by the time the situation had improved, the fashion in garden design had moved on. Many hedge mazes were uprooted and few new ones were created after the 1930s.

There are, of course, some notable exceptions, including the 1941 planting of the re-created hedge maze at New Harmony, Indiana, mentioned above. The holly hedge maze planted in 1935 in the garden of the Governor's Palace at colonial Williamsburg, Virginia, also survives, although it is currently undergoing complete replanting to replace dead wood. The design is a squared-up version of the Hampton Court maze. Both of these mazes were planted as historical replicas in an era when the appreciation of the colonial history of America was starting to bloom; they should probably be classified quite separately from the landscape and pleasure park mazes planted between the 1880s and the 1920s.

More recently a small yew maze has been planted in the Missouri Botanical Gardens in St Louis. A replica of an original maze on the site, planted in the latter half of the nineteenth century in the garden of Henry Shaw, it too should be included in the historic recreation category.

The aptly named Great Maze at San Rafael, California, planted in 1887, was a popular attraction in the grounds of the Rafael Hotel. This photograph is from a stereo viewer card produced in 1895.

Historic American Garden Mazes and Labyrinths

Destroyed examples in italics

Location	State	Planted	Comments
Dayton	Ohio	1929	Holly Croft, destroyed 1940s
Economy	Pennsylvania	1825	3rd Harmonist labyrinth, central grotto survives
Fort Worth	Texas	?	In Botanical Gardens
Harmony	Pennsylvania	*c.*1815	1st Harmonist labyrinth, short-lived
Ipswich	Massachusetts	*c.*1927	Castle Hill, large rectangular maze
Monterey	California	*c.*1880	Hotel del Monte, destroyed 1940s
Monticello	Illinois	1920s	The Farms, Chinese garden box maze, replanted privet
Nashville	Tennessee	*c.*1902	Centennial Park, destroyed *c.*1930
New Harmony	Indiana	1815	2nd Harmonist labyrinth, destroyed 1840s
New Harmony	Indiana	1941	Adapted replica of the above
Newnan	Georgia	1929	Bankshaven, boxwood maze
Oakland	California	*c.*1900	Piedmont Park, large circular design, removed *c.*1920
S. Francisville	Louisiana	?	Afton Villa Gardens, boxwood maze
St Louis	Missouri	late 1800s	Recent replica planted in Botanical Gardens
San Rafael	California	*c.*1887	Rafael Hotel, large circular maze, destroyed *c.*1928
Santa Barbara	California	*c.*1920	Casa del Greco, boxwood maze
Shelter Island	New York	*c.*1900	Sylvester Manor, box maze in historic garden
Topeka	Kansas	1920s	Georgian Court, 50-acre estate with "maze garden"
Vizcaya	Florida	*c.*1916	Small circular maze, still survives
Waltham	Massachusetts	1896	Cedar Hill estate, Hampton Court copy
Williamsburg	Virginia	1935	Hampton Court type, undergoing replanting

From their introduction in the early nineteenth century until the early decades of the twentieth, the garden mazes of America tended to appear wherever the wealthy and industrious built their homes, or where holiday crowds gathered for entertainment. Practically all the early mazes in private and pleasure gardens have disappeared, but there have been several important historical recreations since the mid-1900s, and the map and chart include both of these categories.

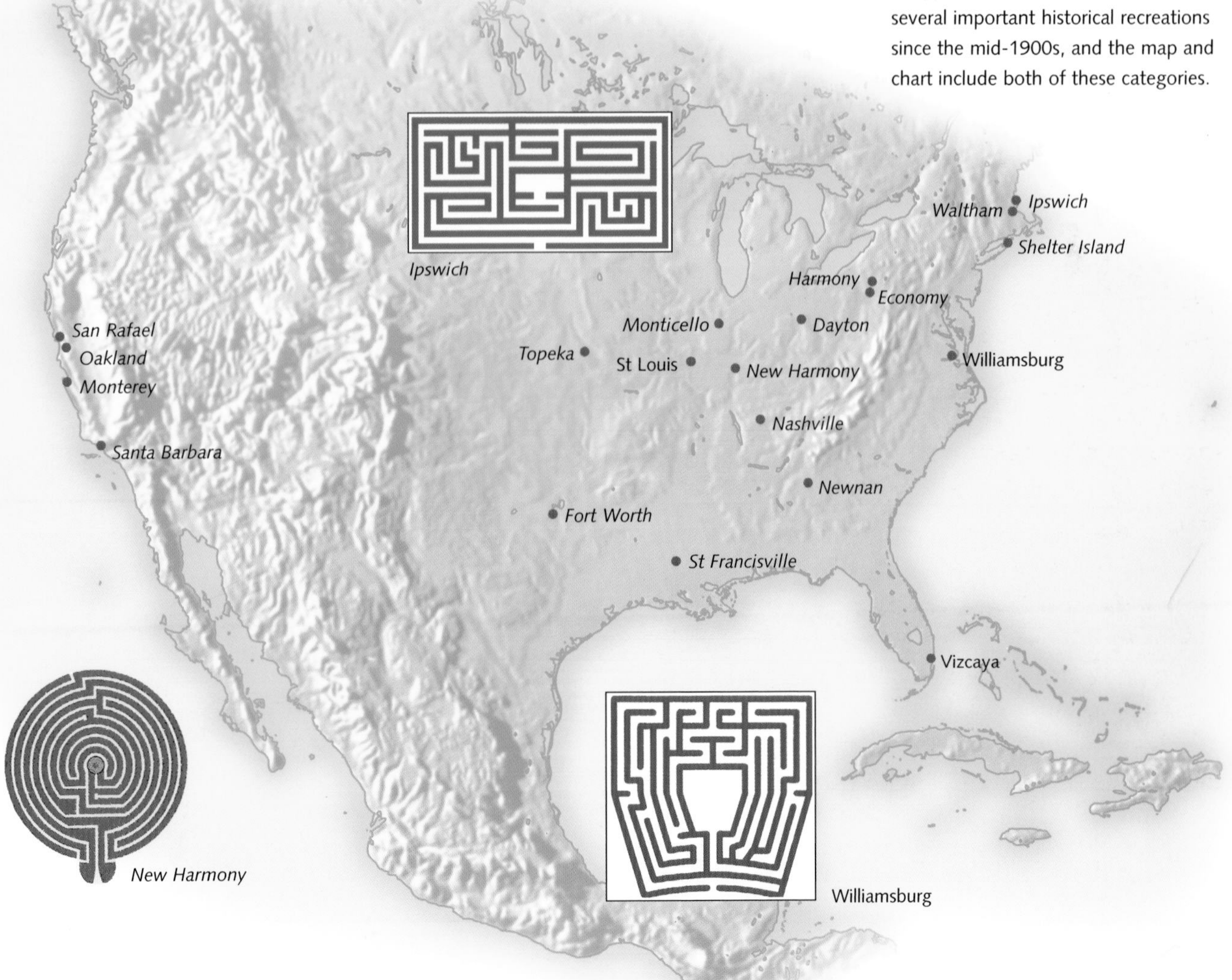

Chapter 6

The Modern Revival

The current revival of interest in both mazes and labyrinths has created a new recognition of the dual concepts of amusement and amazement. The need for chaos in an ordered world calls to us, as does a desire for calm in a world running ever faster. The temporary suspension of time and direction, an isolation from two of the most important principles by which the world and our life in it are ruled, has always been attainable within the concealing walls of the labyrinth, be they of tangled bushes, the simple circuitous lines cut into hilltop turf, or laid in stones on the ground. As the labyrinth symbol and its scattered family of offspring enter the twenty-first century they continue to prosper and provide us with both gentle relief and meaningful purpose.

Taking inspiration from the ancient stone labyrinths of Scandinavia and a design from the cathedral pavements of medieval France, this labyrinth in the grounds of the Buck Horn Inn near Gatlinburg, Tennessee, was installed as a memorial to a beloved daughter who died tragically young.

Over the course of their long history, labyrinths have undergone several revivals of fortune. As we have seen, each of these episodes has involved a resurgence of the traditional forms, coupled with the development of innovative varieties to suit new needs and locations. During the last thirty years, mazes have become a fundamental part of the leisure and entertainment industry, and countless new designs have been constructed in parks and playgrounds throughout the world. At the same time, the simple unicursal labyrinth has once again undergone a dramatic flowering, especially as a meditative and spiritual tool. Time alone will tell which of the many thousands of mazes and labyrinths created in recent years will become the monuments of tomorrow.

The Regrowth of Hedge Mazes

The resurgence of interest in hedge mazes began with the planting of a few new mazes in the 1950s and '60s, including two in the north of England at Scarborough. But the major turning point in their revival came in 1975 with the creation of the enormous maze at Longleat House in Wiltshire, which instantly entered the record books as the largest maze in the world.

The international boom in tourism in the late twentieth century imposed new demands on surviving historic hedge mazes, which were designed to provide gentle entertainment and exercise in parks and pleasure gardens. Not intended for a continuous stream of feet, some historic mazes suffered significant wear and tear due to increased visitor numbers. Rising maintenance costs forced owners to limit public access in an attempt to preserve these unique mazes from the enthusiasm of their visitors. In response to popular demand, more historic hedge mazes are being restored or replanted and many new designs are being created, often with wider paths and faster growing and more resilient hedging plants, specifically to cater for large visitor numbers.

Two distinct branches of development have appeared. Some new mazes have been built along familiar lines to provide an authentic attraction in the grounds of stately houses and public parks. At the same time, more adventurous designers have been experimenting with hedge mazes that meet the modern tourist's demands for instant,

The planting of the hedge maze at Longleat House in southern England in 1975 was a defining moment in the dramatic recent upturn of fortune for mazes as popular attractions worldwide. Its innovative design has inspired many further developments.

dramatic entertainment. This exciting departure successfully stretches the boundaries of a medium that many commentators had assumed was stuck in the past.

Leading the innovative trend was the hedge maze at Longleat, which was commissioned by Lord Weymouth (now Marquis of Bath) to add a further attraction to the famous safari park at his family home. The maze was designed by Greg Bright, who was already known for a series of maze puzzle books and a large maze at Worthy Farm in Pilton, Somerset.[1] This unusual "trench maze" was dug in 1971 to a depth of *c.* 6 ft (2 m). It soon became overgrown, but its swirling design was the inspiration for the maze at Longleat, which features complex spiralling pathways intended to disorientate walkers and bridges that link self-enclosed sections of the maze. It proved an instant hit with the public when it was opened in 1978 – and silenced cynics convinced that mazes had had their day as a visitor attraction.

Longleat no longer holds the record for world's largest maze – that was taken in the mid-1980s by the huge wooden panel mazes of Japan, and then in the mid-1990s by the maize mazes that sprang up across the cornfields of America, Europe, and the Far East. But Longleat remains one of the most challenging and pleasing hedge mazes in the world and solving it can take more than an hour, despite the provision of hints secreted in small boxes around the pathway. Recently the Marquis of Bath has added a further four mazes to his collection – two more hedge mazes with symbolic designs created by Randoll Coate; Adrian Fisher's lavishly decorated King Arthur's Mirror Maze; and Graham Burgess's Labyrinth of Love, planted with old-fashioned climbing roses. Longleat House now has one of the most impressive collections of mazes anywhere in Europe.

News of the success of the Longleat maze spread fast and within a decade new hedge mazes were beginning to appear in the gardens of other period houses and public attractions. A major element of the new popularity of hedge mazes is their nostalgia value; they create an atmosphere of past times and a safe and happy environment for good family entertainment. Fascinatingly, the nostalgia theme is popular in Australia, where traditionally styled hedge mazes in Victoria and Tasmania are accompanied by tea rooms.[2] The maze planted in the early 1980s, at Westbury, Tasmania, is modelled on the hedge maze in Hazlehead Park, Aberdeen, Scotland, and the remarkable

Tasmazia, situated near Lake Barrington in Tasmania, is typical of a new breed of popular attractions featuring a collection of mazes, both traditional forms and new ideas, opened to the public within the last two decades. Most are created by maze enthusiasts, happy to share their fascination with the visiting public.

collection of six mazes at "Tasmazia", also in Tasmania, includes a replica of the Hampton Court maze. These Australian mazes also feature design innovations, with family picnic places, barbecues, and miniature golf courses. The challenges of the Australian climate have also resulted in interesting mazes planted with fast-growing native creepers over trellis, instead of the traditional slow-growing bushes. In the same spirit, a hedge maze planted in 2002 at Soekershof near Robertson, South Africa, employs flowering hibiscus as well as cacti – surely the ultimate deterrent to taking short cuts!

The aMazing hedge maze at Symonds Yat, England, planted in 1977. The addition of a Museum of Mazes and a gift shop that specializes in puzzles has made it a popular destination for school parties and families.

In the past hedge mazes were just one element in a park or garden, but their popularity as a modern visitor attraction has enabled them to stand alone in their own right. The aMazing Hedge Maze at Symonds Yat West in the scenic landscape of the Herefordshire Welsh borders, is a splendid example. First opened in 1981, this beautifully tended maze is owned by the Heyes brothers, who dress in blazers and boaters to welcome their guests and have been known to ride unicycles around the maze! The addition of a maze museum and a puzzle shop provides interest and entertainment for all the family. A similar maze entertainment park known as Dúndelle opened at Bakkeveen in the Netherlands in 2001, with three puzzle mazes in stone, steel, and wooden panels.

Foremost among designers of modern hedge mazes must surely be Adrian Fisher. He built his first maze in his father's garden in southern England in 1975 and became a full-time maze designer in the early 1980s, since when he has built over four hundred mazes worldwide. Influenced by early partnerships with Randoll Coate and Graham Burgess, he has gone on to introduce radical interactive features and new construction materials to the maze design world. Working with mirrors, wooden fencing panels, brick pavement, coloured plastic tiles, and walls-of-water fountains, he brings a love of mathematics and an acute business sense to his vocation of creating unique and beautiful mazes. Famous for his pioneering designs for maize mazes and complex mathematical mazes, Fisher has also successfully turned his hand to more traditional hedge mazes, with installations at premier tourist sites around the world.

Adrian Fisher's Dreilandenpunt maze near Vaals in the Netherlands has a design based on heraldic beasts. Bridges and a number of interactive features offer further imaginative entertainment to the visitor.

Fisher's enormous hedge maze at Dreilandenpunt, near Vaals in the Netherlands (opened 1992) is based on the heraldic beasts of Germany, Belgium and the Netherlands, whose three borders meet at the location of the maze. His 1991 hedge maze at Blenheim Palace, Woodstock, Oxfordshire, England, is based on the heraldic stone sculptures adorning the palace building. Another heraldic hedge maze in the shape of a star is planted in interlocking rows of green and copper beech hedges to give the effect of tartan at Scone Palace near Perth, Scotland. In 1995 he planted a hedge maze in the grounds of the Château de Thoiry in France, taking his theme from the fifteenth-century *The Dream of Poliphilo* (see page 156). Sections of the maze are laid out to represent the various creatures in the story and in the centre is a giant eye overlaid with a five-pointed star representing the five senses.

The central tower of the hedge maze at Leeds Castle, England, leads into an underground grotto, which also provides a quick exit.

Although it appears a simple puzzle, moving through the Darwin Maze at Edinburgh Zoo (below right) is considerably complicated by a number of interactive gates and water jets.

The striking Tudor Rose pavement maze in the courtyard of Kentwell Hall at Long Melford, Suffolk (below left), was created by Adrian Fisher in 1985.

Fisher's collaboration with Randoll Coate and Vernon Gibberd in 1988 resulted in the planting of a remarkable hedge maze at Leeds Castle in Kent, England. The goal is occupied by a stone tower, which provides an overview of the maze, and also gives access to a splendid underground shell-lined grotto complete with water features. The grotto doubles as an exit tunnel, avoiding the need to retrace the maze. Fisher's Darwin Maze installed at Edinburgh Zoo, Scotland in 1995, has a choice of pathways for male and female visitors and a Chamber of Natural Selection, where the walker's height, weight, and other characteristics are assessed, introducing a new interactive element to the puzzle. Electronically controlled gates and water jets, operated by sensors hidden in the maze, determine whether the walker progresses or needs to return to the start to evolve further.

Not all Fisher's creations are made of hedges. His striking Tudor Rose Maze, laid in 1985, fills the main courtyard of Kentwell Hall in Suffolk, England, a moated Tudor house of some distinction. The folds of the petals form a simple maze pattern that can be followed to the central chequerboard, which is large enough to play chess with giant pieces. Fisher has also created paving pattern mazes in shopping malls, parks, and playgrounds.

A simple looping brick pathway maze is set into mown grass at Parham Park, England.

Drawing inspiration from the traditional turf labyrinths on village greens in England and Germany, he constructed other mazes in open grassy areas by setting bricks directly into the turf so that it is possible to run a lawnmower over the pathways without incurring any damage. A good example is provided by the brick-path maze in the garden at Parham Park, West Sussex, England. It was built into the lawn in 1991 in a looping pattern inspired by embroidery in the owner's house. It is difficult to follow with the eye and is to be walked with only one rule in mind – no turning back. Every fork in the path is a straightforward left or right decision and reaching the goal is dependent on arriving at the final junction from the correct direction. A similar maze, created by Fisher in 2000 in Higginson Park, Marlow, England, depicts a school of intertwined fish with the history of this riverside village portrayed in mosaic panels.

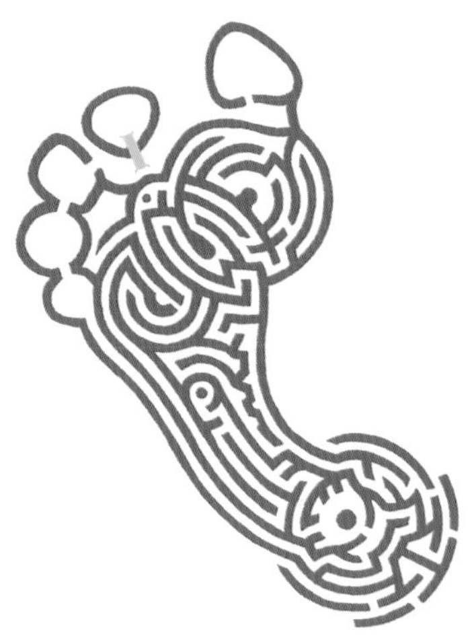

Randoll Coate's design for his Imprint of Man maze is formed from a multitude of individual symbolic elements.

Less well known, but equally influential in the resurgence of hedge mazes, is the work of a retired British diplomat, Randoll Coate. His first hedge maze, in a private garden in Gloucestershire, England in 1975, took the shape of a giant footprint entitled "The Imprint of Man". Entering at the heel, the path runs back and forth, visiting three small enclosed gardens before reaching the big toe, situated across a wooden bridge on a small island. The sinuous sweeps and loops of the yew hedges form the outlines of animals and symbols including the signs of the zodiac – 132 elements in all.

Coate's next maze, in the garden of the stately palace of Château de Beloeil in Belgium was planted to represent a pyramid; indeed the beech hedges have been trained to grow into an actual pyramid, 20 ft (6 m) high at the centre. The pattern of the pathway viewed from above traces out the name of the palace, "Beloeil", but the route to the centre spells out the anagram "Belle Io". According to classical mythology the beautiful nymph Io, relentlessly pursued by Zeus, changed into a female equivalent of the Minotaur, half-woman, half-cow, to escape his advances and flee to Egypt. Such are the sophisticated games that Randoll Coate plays with his maze designs. His "Creation" hedge maze designed for Baron Henric Falkenberg in Värmland Säby in Sweden in 1979 is based on the Swedish botanist Carl von Linné's motto "Omne Vivum Ex Ovo" ("All life comes from the egg") and appropriately takes the form of a giant egg. The complex interweaving hedges outline many images including Adam and Eve, a plan of the solar system and, of course, the owner's initials. In keeping with the theme, the maze has two entrances, one for Adams and one for Eves!

The intricate design of Randoll Coate's Alice in Wonderland Maze near Hurn, England, conceals many of the characters from Lewis Carroll's classic tale among its hedges.

The Sun Maze and Lunar Labyrinth at Longleat House, both designed by Randoll Coate, add two more fine examples to Lord Bath's splendid collection of mazes.

Coate has collaborated with other designers on a large number of public maze installations, especially in Britain. The hedge mazes at Blenheim Palace, Leeds Castle, and Newquay Zoo (in the shape of a dragon), all show his influence, as does the Alice in Wonderland Maze at Hurn in Dorset, England. It features characters from the classic children's tale, topiary figures for the suits of playing cards and a raised walkway at the entrance to provide an overview of the design. Opened in 1992, the maze is one of a number of Alice-themed attractions at the location, where the owners and staff dress in appropriate costume. Coate's eye for striking design is also evident in The Lion and Unicorn street pavement mazes in Worksop town centre (1989).

Coate has two mazes planted in low box hedging at Longleat. The first, The Lunar Labyrinth, is formed in the shape of a crescent moon. Designed as a true labyrinth with just a single pathway, it is embellished only by a pebble mosaic at the central goal. The adjacent Sun Maze, by contrast, is a riot of exuberant design and complex symbolism, with a few subtle jokes thrown in. All the characters of the Cretan Labyrinth are represented and the whole story is contained within a maze the shape of a glowering Minotaur's head surrounded by flames.

Other modern hedge mazes designed for family entertainment also employ unusual but easily recognized shapes. In 1982 a brick path maze was set in turf at the Lappa Valley Railway in St Newlyn, Cornwall, to represent the first locomotive. Walking the pathway, visitors turn to and fro on the cogs of the meshing drive wheels and children can run the flywheel in imitation of its whirling speed. Hidden within the design are giant letters and numerals that spell out names and dates for children's activity worksheets. A striking hedge maze at the Kristallwelt (Crystal World) attraction in the town of Wattens in the Austrian Tyrol is in the shape of a giant hand. A more complex yew hedge maze opened in 1997 at the Parc Meli theme park in Belgium takes the form of a giant seahorse, and the huge maze planted on the Dole Plantation at Wahiawa in Hawaii is based on the theme of pineapples!

A striking unicorn maze (below left) was laid as street paving in Worksop, England, in 1989. A yew maze at the Parc Meli amusement park in Belgium (below right) takes the form of a giant seahorse.

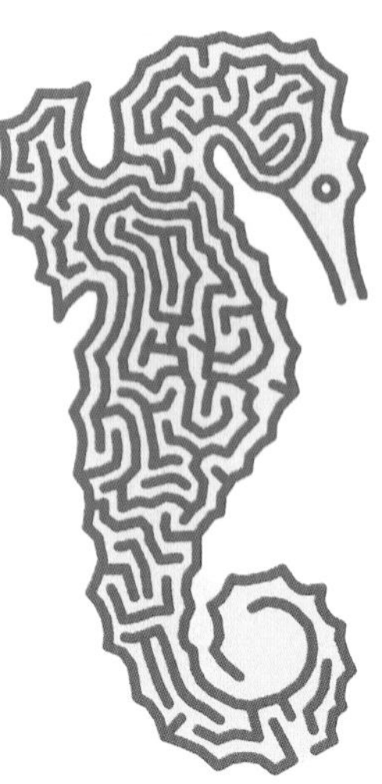

Wooden Panel Mazes

The pressure of seeing an immediate return on investment in the tourist industry often demands that mazes built today must be ready to receive paying visitors tomorrow. The mid-1980s saw a craze for wooden panel mazes that started in New Zealand, where the first was created at Wanaka in South Island in 1973 by entrepreneur Stuart Landsborough. Three years of studying the behaviour of the visitors to his maze provided Landsborough with insight into the psychology of the walkers. Based on his discoveries about their expectations and how long they were prepared to spend solving the puzzle before frustration set in, he added a series of wooden bridges to link different sections of the maze, thereby introducing further complexity without increasing the ground area. The bridges provide enticing overhead views, but are not necessarily helpful in solving the puzzle. The addition of extra goals – towers to climb in each corner of the maze – have extended average visitor time and satisfaction, with increased sales at the tea rooms and gift shop at the exit.[3]

Stuart Landsborough's pioneering wooden panel maze at Wanaka, New Zealand (above), was responsible for triggering maze mania in Japan.

By the early 1980s a number of similar panel mazes had appeared in New Zealand and Australia, but it was the export of Landsborough's design skills to Japan in 1985 that triggered true maze mania. Over a period of four years he designed twenty panel mazes, each larger and more complex than the last, at locations throughout the country. Their success was phenomenal and such large crowds visited that with each new commission Landsborough was pushed to discover more ways of increasing capacity while still keeping the public entertained. His later mazes could handle an incredible 1,500 people an hour without becoming congested. The challenge was to keep the visitors moving, especially at peak times, so he devised special "change points" where a few panels could be repositioned to increase flow for weekend and holiday crowds without seriously sacrificing complexity. He developed new ideas to entice visitors, including competitions against the clock and souvenir punch cards to prove the time in which the maze had been fully solved. Media coverage of record times kept interest at fever pitch, and within five years nearly two hundred mazes were built throughout Japan. Some panel mazes were not designed to last, but used simply a means of generating revenue from plots of land between construction projects. The craze had faded by the 1990s and many mazes were removed.

Panel mazes are quick to assemble and can be easily adapted. Above: Merlin's Magic Maze at Newquay, England. Below: the Labyrinthia maze in Rodelund, Denmark.

Panel mazes have made appearances in other parts of the world. In America they featured games of laser tag and overhead cable rides, and one was even constructed in the shape of a giant ringed planet. Merlin's Magic Maze at Newquay, Cornwall, England has a walk-through waterfall for extra effect. Labyrinthia in Rodelund, Denmark, has a red and white panel maze that resembles the Danish flag when viewed from above. The relatively simple construction and endless adaptability of panel mazes coupled with a potential quick return on investment, seems set to ensure their popularity for many years to come.

Maize Mazes

The latest craze to grip the imagination is for the maize mazes that have cropped up in cornfields since the early 1990s. For media attention, they rival the mysterious crop-circles that appear each summer, but maize mazes need no belief in aliens for explanation. Adrian Fisher and Don Frantz created the first such maze in 1993 at Annville, Pennsylvania, in the shape of a giant Stegosaurus. Traditional hedge mazes can take many years to grow, but maize grows fast, and the strength of its stems and the linear planting patterns available to modern farm machinery make the crop ideal for the maze creator. Maize mazes are doomed to wither and die at the end of the summer, but most are harvested along with the rest of the crop.

In some locations, such as the popular Labyrinthus attraction at Reignac-sur-Inde in France, the maize is planted to the same set pattern each year, but most mazes are designed to fit whatever field space is currently available. Created by removing rows of plants, the large and often complex designs provide both a satisfying puzzle for the walker and striking opportunities for aerial photography. Media popularity has allowed some maize mazes to attract over 50,000 paying visitors during their two- to three-month life span, proving maize to be a very profitable crop indeed!

Adrian Fisher's team has produced maize mazes at locations across Britain, Europe, North America, and Australia.

A maize maze in the form of a giant ship was built by Adrian Fisher's design team at Shippensburg, Pennsylvania, USA, in 1995. Maize mazes are usually known as corn mazes in America, thus missing the play on words. This huge maze held the world path length record until an even larger maize maze was planted the following summer.

Additional features include puzzles to solve along the way, wooden bridges to provide elevated viewpoints, sound systems, and even portable toilet facilities – these mazes can take a while to solve! Fisher's striking designs are ensured to receive maximum media coverage and provide opportunities for merchandising spin-offs. Laying out these huge mazes often involves complex mathematical and geometric calculation and several designers have now started to use the Global Positioning Satellite system to aid them with the initial layout in the otherwise featureless open fields. Each year new contenders come forward to claim world records for the largest maze in history – paths in excess of 7 km (4 miles) are now commonplace – but long before this point is reached the path can become a chore and no longer pleasurable. Providing an enjoyable experience should always be the aim when hoping to appeal to a family market.

Mirror Mazes

Mirror mazes, with their multiply reflected pathways, have been around since the late nineteenth century and were once a popular feature at fairgrounds. Often known in America as crystal mazes, they confuse the walker, typically appearing some five or six times larger than they really are. The most famous mirror maze was built at Geneva, Switzerland, in 1896, then reassembled at the Gletschergarten in Luzern in 1899, where it still stands. A similar mirror maze in the Palace of the Sultan at Constantinople (Istanbul) in Turkey was a popular attraction in the 1890s. Transformed by modern technology, today's mirror mazes appear at some of the most prestigious visitor attractions in Britain, Europe, and America and each one adds a new twist to an idea that many thought had seen its day. The leading designer of this new generation of mirror mazes is none other than Adrian Fisher, who is without any doubt the most prolific maze designer in the world today.

The difficulty of finding your way through a mirror maze is not dictated by a complicated layout, full of dead-ends and false turns, but by the illusions and deceptions of the mirrors. Improved glass manufacture produces large distortion-free mirrors and computer modelling has

This old postcard shows the mirror maze at the Gletschergarten in Luzern, Switzerland. Restored in the late 1980s, it is one of the few original mirror mazes of the late nineteenth century to have survived; another simpler example is preserved at Petřině in Prague, Czech Republic.

practically eliminated the corridor effect that characterised traditional mirror mazes. Digital lighting and sound effects enhance the sensual deception to a new degree. The installation of courtyard features within the maze – glimpsed repeatedly long before they are reached – and the use of revolving mirrors and back projections, triggered by movement within the maze, heighten the mystery of the experience.

Because a well designed mirror maze can appear to be six times its actual size, these mazes are a very attractive proposition for the potential owner. The mirror maze at Longleat is installed in an old coach-house, but provides the experience of wandering through an endless forest to stumble across a ruined medieval chapel in which the visitor may be lucky enough to glimpse the Holy Grail. Others are themed on ancient Egyptian temples or the original seaside pier environment in which these mazes first flourished a century ago. A recent addition to the genre at Navy Pier in Chicago, Illinois, simulates the subways and skyscrapers of the cityscape outside. The use of mirrors to deceive and confuse may be one of the oldest magic tricks in the book, but the old ideas are often the best.

Installed in 1991 by Adrian Fisher and Lesley Beck, the maze at Wookey Hole caves in Somerset, England, was the first of the new generation of mirror mazes. Themed to recreate a seaside pier environment, complete with the sounds of the sea, glimpses of fountains and figures secreted within the maze are caught long before they are reached.

Water Mazes

The idea of mazes with paths running between channels of water has been around for hundreds of years. Although long since destroyed, a maze of stone pathways winding between water-filled lead-lined troughs was built in a courtyard of the royal palace at Greenwich, England, during the early 1600s (see page 160). In Islamic palaces in North Africa and the Middle East courtyard water mazes based on simple labyrinth patterns were once popular decorative features, especially when combined with a fountain.

A simple water maze opened at Hever Castle in 1997 provides an additional attraction for visitors to the restored Tudor castle and takes pressure off the hedge maze, which has suffered in recent years from too many visitors.

Several small sculptural labyrinths with water running through their paths were installed in public settings in England, Denmark, and Germany during the 1970s and '80s. The example in Victoria Park, Bristol, has a shallow water channel set within a decorative brickwork enclosure. The modern revival of water mazes began in earnest with the innovative Beatles' Maze constructed by Minotaur Designs at the 1984 Liverpool Garden Festival. A brick pathway winding back and forth in a pool in the shape of an apple, linked by musical notes as stepping stones, provided access to a yellow submarine at the goal. The maze won design awards but was dismantled after the festival. A water maze opened in 1997 at Hever Castle in England (to compliment the traditional hedge maze planted in 1905) features a simple pathway that winds across a pond between dense rushes and leads to a central observation tower. Jets of water provide barriers to define the correct path and prove an irresistible challenge to children. A maze at De Pluimweide, at Hoedekenskerke in the Netherlands, consists of turfed embankment pathways set in a large lake. During the summer reeds grow to obscure the adjacent paths. Most such mazes are expensive to install and maintain and can offer only the simplest of puzzles.The water maze at St Helier on the island of Jersey, installed in 1997, marks a new departure. Occupying an open paved area, it comprises 208 water jets controlled by computer and precision valve technology to create walls of water that rise and fall to admit the walker to the next sector. Popular with children on warm days, it comes alive at nightfall with coloured fibre optic lighting. As the water from the fountain jets drains immediately through the grilles from whence it came, it is also free from the complex safety issues that surround other attractions where children and water are involved.

The innovative water maze at Les Jardins de la Mer in St Helier on the island of Jersey, off the northwest coast of France, was opened in 1997. The water jets that form the walls of this maze rise and fall according to a computer programme, draining away through the grilles inset into the pavement.

Novel Twists to the Story

In recent years modern plastics have been used to create a number of novel mazes. Portable mazes akin to inflatable bouncy castles are always popular with youngsters. A more interesting inflatable maze comprised of interconnected, enclosed modules of multi-coloured vinyl toured Europe in the mid-1990s. The use of clip-together flooring materials to create infinitely adaptable transportable mazes has been explored by a number of designers. They can be laid out in minutes to a printed plan and have proved popular for children's playgrounds and educational displays. Waterproof, washable, and slip-resistant, plastic mat mazes can be employed on ice-rinks, the decks of cruise ships, and in muddy fields.

Mat mazes are also useful for a class of mazes known as "mazes-with-rules" or "conditional movement mazes". Your move at any one point in the maze is conditional on your previous move or on the instructions given at this point. Such mazes look deceptively simple on the page or laid on the ground, but arriving at the finish is usually dependent on quite complex calculations. The maze with rules dates back to the work of eighteenth-century mathematicians – Leonhard Euler's famous Seven Bridges of Königsberg puzzle is frequently cited as a point of origin. Popularized in puzzle books produced by Sam Loyd and Lewis Carroll in the late nineteenth century, the maze with rules introduced concepts such as one-way streets long before they became a reality. Modern mathematics writers including Martin Gardner, Steve Ryan, and Robert Abbott, have developed intriguing new variations on the theme.[4]

Mat mazes formed from hundreds of plastic tiles can be clipped together easily following printed plans. These colourful portable mazes are suitable for any purpose and many locations.

Adrian Fisher has created many mazes with rules based on number sequences, both in portable mats and in permanent pavement designs. In recent years, Fisher has installed a number of these mazes in paving, in school playgrounds, and outside mathematics faculties at colleges in the UK and USA. The design of conditional movement mazes has direct analogies with the design of computer chip circuitry. Indeed, the algorithms developed to figure out how best to route the millions of connections in a computer chip were originally set up to solve simple maze designs.

The labyrinth has naturally become a central theme in many computer games. Cyber-heroes Lara Croft and Mario navigate complex multi-level mazes formed of digital code stored on silicon chips, in search of clues and prizes that allow the player to reach the next level. The imagery of the maze has appeared on the larger screen in several recent movies – Stanley Kubrick's *The Shining* and Jim Henson's *Labyrinth* both have complex mazes as key elements of the story. Cyber-mazes and mazes on film may feature imaginative special effects, but the true challenge of maze design surely lies in creating real mazes that contain ever more surprises for the visitor.

Educational Mazes and Labyrinths

A rich historical heritage and versatility of design, ranging from simple geometric symbols to complex mathematical puzzles, has ensured the popularity of mazes and labyrinths in many educational settings. In the last decade, particularly in Europe and America, designers have explored ways of incorporating modern conditional-movement mazes in mathematics lessons as well as in the teaching of history. Involving children in the planning and construction of the project can teach valuable lessons about design and co-operation. Children also take pride in looking after the finished product, and in leaving their mark for future pupils to admire and enjoy. Some teachers in America are also experimenting with using labyrinths in classrooms to help students with attention-focusing and conflict resolution, and have reported significant benefits.

Above: pavement mazes in the playground of Cliff School in Wakefield, England.

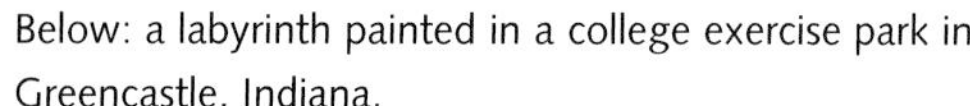

Below: a labyrinth painted in a college exercise park in Greencastle, Indiana.

Above: a simple maze painted in the shape of a snail in a school playground at Søndre Skole in Køge, Denmark.

Mazes with whimsical and entertaining designs appeal to children and adults alike. As long ago as the sixteenth century, the Paduan architect Francesco Segala published a series of designs for mazes in the form of animals, human figures, and ships. Today similar designs continue to be popular in school playgrounds and family pleasure parks. Several leading builders of mazes and labyrinths have made teaching materials available to schools and educational foundations, and this has proved so popular that they have subsequently been invited back to install their designs. The challenge of constructing hard-wearing maze installations suitable for children has produced some creative solutions, including several mazes designed specifically for disabled users.

Below: a labyrinth laid in a schoolyard in Plano, Illinois. Entitled "Growing a Better World", it was built by pupils and parents with donated paving stones and block pavers, each one painted by a child at the school with their name and wishes for the future.

Above: the labyrinth laid by Marty Kermeen in 2001 at the International Folk Art Museum in Santa Fe, New Mexico, is surrounded by an encircling wall that creates curious echoes and sound effects at the centre.

Below: based on the design of the labyrinth in St Omer, France, this colourful paving maze was created in 1995 by Adrian Fisher at St John's College School in Cambridge, England. It forms part of a larger paving scheme that includes a spider's web and various insects.

The Labyrinth Revival

The archetypal labyrinth symbol combines decorative design with layers of meaning, and its artistic and spiritual aspects make it popular both as decoration and as a reflection of the complexities of modern life. Many modern labyrinths employ traditional designs and materials, and are often based on the turf and stone labyrinths in northwestern Europe or the cathedral labyrinths of France. Private garden labyrinths can be now found in the Americas, Europe, and the Far East, as well as Australia, New Zealand, and South Africa. Replicas of historic labyrinths have also become a popular feature in public parks and gardens, as well as at tourist attractions with heritage themes. The labyrinth has also made a reappearance among spiritual communities, in churches and retreat centres. In tracing the sources of this new interest in the labyrinth we can follow three main threads – the historic, the artistic, and the spiritual.

The Thread of History

The historical and cultural importance of mazes and labyrinths has been debated in academic circles since the mid-nineteenth century. The first important summary of knowledge was W.H. Matthews' pioneering study, *Mazes & Labyrinths*, published in 1922. The reprinting of this classic work in 1970 brought the topic back into popular circulation, especially among those interested in ancient mysteries, earth energies, geomancy, and sacred geometry. Janet Bord's *Mazes and Labyrinths of the World* appeared in 1976 and around this time Nigel Pennick began publishing his own influential research in a series of books and pamphlets. The exploits of Greg Bright, designer of the Longleat hedge maze, helped trigger the new interest in puzzle mazes. During this time, keen amateurs often built temporary labyrinths at fairs and music festivals, where they became a popular attraction. In 1980 enthusiasts were brought together for the first time to exchange ideas when the present author founded *Caerdroia, the Journal of Mazes and Labyrinths*.

From the mid-1970s, the work of a new generation of labyrinth enthusiasts flourished. John Kraft, Bo Stjernström, and Jørgen Thordrup diligently researched, located, and catalogued a large number of sites, predominantly stone labyrinths, throughout Scandinavia. Their findings were widely published, and generated much interest in the subject. The installation of a stone labyrinth at the popular Iron Age village at Lejre in Denmark in 1979 led to a number of copies being constructed in parks and playgrounds, often in connection with local cultural projects.

The mid-1980s saw Noel Broadbent and Rabbe Sjöberg's application of archaeological dating techniques to Scandinavian stone labyrinths. They revolutionized the understanding of these enigmatic monuments and brought them to the attention of the archaeological community, generating further research, as well as official recognition and conservation orders for the surviving examples.

In 1982 Hermann Kern, art historian and director of the Haus der Kunst in Munich, published his encyclopaedic *Labyrinthe*, a study of historic labyrinths from around the world. At this time the partition of Germany was causing serious problems for researchers attempting to look beyond the Iron Curtain. Kern was convinced that important turf labyrinths at Steigra and Graitschen in East Germany had vanished, since no reference to them had been published in Western literature for forty years. A visit to both these labyrinths by the present author in 1983 proved otherwise and opened the door for further research by Nigel Pennick, John Kraft and Kurt Krüger; and in recent years local enthusiasts have rediscovered a number of other labyrinths in Germany.

The designation of 1991 as "The Year of the Maze" by the English Tourist Board saw a flurry of new mazes installed and the publication of several academic books as well as popular titles by Nigel Pennick, Adrian Fisher, and Sig Lonegren, which introduced the subject to a new generation of readers. Heightened media awareness ensured publicity for many maze-related events, including Labyrinth '91, an international conference based in Saffron Walden, where maze and labyrinth enthusiasts from the UK, USA, and Europe gathered to celebrate the restoration of the important Bridge End Gardens hedge maze.

Glowing under ultra-violet lighting, a labyrinth painted with phosphorescent paint featured at the 1996 American labyrinth enthusiasts' conference held at the Omega Centre in Rhinebeck, New York.

In America, a new interest in labyrinths led to the launch in 1994 of a magazine entitled *The Labyrinth Letter*, edited by Jean Lutz in Scottsdale, Arizona. Although no longer published, the magazine sponsored national labyrinth conferences in 1995 and 1996, which brought together enthusiasts from across the United States. Further labyrinth conferences sponsored by The St Louis Labyrinth Project in 1997 and 1998 resulted in the founding of The Labyrinth Society to promote labyrinth education, research, and events (see page 216 for details). At one of these meetings, the current author and Robert Ferré pledged to guide the translation of the late Hermann Kern's definitive study of the subject into English. His *Through the Labyrinth* was published in 2000, and typifies the international co-operation between enthusiasts and academics that has developed in recent years to provide a new understanding of the history of mazes and labyrinths.

The Artistic Thread

Many artists have flirted with labyrinths during their careers; some make it a central theme of their work, for others it is simply a by-way to explore. The popularity of Greek mythology in the late nineteenth century resulted in numerous depictions of Theseus and the Minotaur. The theme continued into the twentieth century and is especially noticeable in the earlier works of Picasso. Other artists have interpreted the labyrinth in three dimensions. In 1971 English land artist Richard Long built a stone labyrinth, modelled on the Scilly Isles Troy-town, in Connemara, Ireland. American artist Richard Fleischner installed his Sod Maze in 1974 at Château-sur-Mer in Newport, Rhode Island; it is a turf labyrinth in all but name. Joe Tilson, working in England, constructed a series of wooden labyrinth installations during the 1970s, and his work has introduced the labyrinth symbol to many in the art world.

Labyrinthos, one of a series of wooden labyrinth art installation pieces created by Joe Tilson in the 1970s, helped bring new recognition for the labyrinth in the art world.

The English sculptor Michael Ayrton, another artist obsessed with the theme of the Minotaur and the labyrinth, is especially important. His remarkable installation constructed of high brick walls at Arkville, New York State, in 1966, was created to simulate the Cretan labyrinth of legend. The design is set in the wooded landscape like a giant thumbprint. The high walls produce an intentionally claustrophobic effect and the long winding paths lead to two separate goals, containing Ayrton's bronze sculptures of a particularly fearsome Minotaur and Icarus taking flight, surrounded by polished metal panels. The Minotaur story was a recurrent theme in Ayrton's work and his etchings, sculptures and writings around it are extensive. The Arkville Maze was the culmination of his work and a bronze maquette of the maze adorns his tombstone in Hadstock churchyard in Essex, England.

In 1990 the Italian artist Italo Lanfredini created a labyrinth high in the hills above Castel di Tusa on the island of Sicily. Entitled Arianna, this large labyrinth is formed with cast terracotta coloured concrete walls to blend harmoniously into the landscape. A tall archway, reminiscent of the pierced monoliths guarding the entrance to ancient stone tombs in the area, spans the mouth of the labyrinth and symbolizes the entry into the world from the womb. At the end of the winding path, a small pool of water at the centre provides a literal chance to reflect on life. Labyrinth installations set firmly in the landscape such as these are often categorized as land art, and the work of several other land artists is worthy of mention.

Michael Ayrton's interpretation of the Cretan Labyrinth was built in 1966 in stone with high brick walls at Arkville in the Catskill Mountains, New York, for Armand G. Erpf. Two of Ayrton's bronzes stand at the two goals in the labyrinth.

California-based Alex Champion is rapidly becoming the most prolific modern labyrinth land artist. His output has been prodigious since he constructed his first labyrinth in 1987. His interest in labyrinths was kindled at conferences held by the American Society of Dowsers. Since the mid-1980s fellow dowsers Sig Lonegren, Richard Feather Anderson, and Nicolas Finck had been making experimental labyrinths with chalk dust at the conferences, and they noted that people generally felt energized after walking or running their designs. Several experimenters had also reported positive health improvements, both short and long-term, after repeated walking of the labyrinths. Fascinated by these findings, Champion decided to build a labyrinth of his own to experiment further.

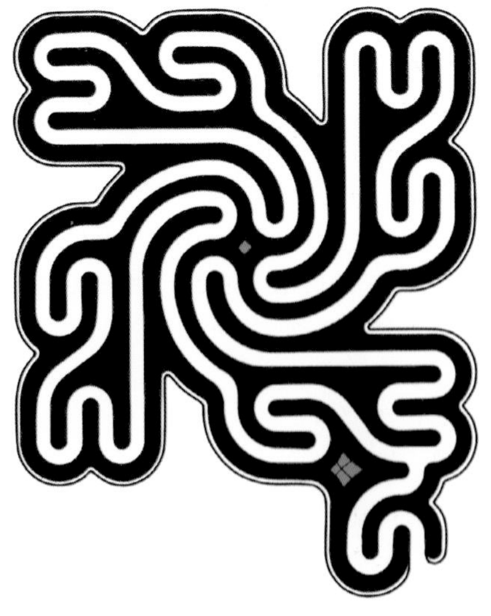

The dramatic swirling design of Alex Champion's Viking Age Horse Trapping (VAHT) Maze. Champion built this maze in earthen mounds on a private property in California. He has also constructed other similar installations with far simpler designs.

The first was simply mown into long grass on his property in Mendocino County in northern California, but following a visit to the famous Serpent Mound in Ohio, an ancient earthwork in the shape of a giant snake, he decided to make his labyrinth more permanent. Inspired also by the Neolithic henge monuments of Britain, he set about creating a labyrinth with a hollow pathway bordered by earth embankments. Digging the labyrinth by hand, Champion moulded some thirty tonnes of hard clay into a striking earth sculpture. The mounds separating the paths were planted with daffodils. This labyrinth, of the familiar seven-path classical design, is still covered in blooms each spring. Champion has subsequently built dozens of similar Earth Mazes in public and private settings and has developed a number of interesting and challenging labyrinthine designs; his VAHT Maze is a mass of whirling pathways, while others are minimalist, little more than loops and spirals.

Working mostly in his native Scotland, Jim Buchanan has also taken the symbol of the labyrinth as a core theme for his distinctive land art installations. Fascinated by spirals and maze designs since he was a child, Buchanan received his first commission to build a public labyrinth in 1996. On a hillside in Tapton Park near Chesterfield, England, he used a dumper truck to bank 7,000 tonnes of sub-soil from an adjacent building project into a series of concentric rings, linked up to form a huge classical labyrinth with an overall diameter of 400 ft (122 m). The result is best appreciated from the opposite side of the valley and can be seen clearly up to 2 miles (3 km) away. Trees already growing on the hillside have been incorporated into the design and add essential vertical interest to what is without doubt one of the largest permanent labyrinths in the world. The low fertility of the sub-soil was ideal for wild flowers and the labyrinth is covered in blooms alive with bees and butterflies each summer. The long winding

Jim Buchanan's Wildflower Labyrinth in Tapton Park, England. Constructed on a steep hillside, the labyrinth is visible from a considerable distance and is quite possibly the world's largest permanent labyrinth – with the possible exception of the putative Glastonbury Tor labyrinth, also in England.

path has proved popular with dog-walkers, and winter snows see the labyrinth teeming with children on sledges. Buchanan is always looking for new locations and challenges. Recent projects include mowing huge labyrinthine patterns on to playing fields in Western Scotland. Visible only from the air, they are based on interlocking Celtic spirals and prehistoric rock art. His Millennium Labyrinth, located in a boggy clearing in the Galloway Forest, southwest Scotland, is a simple twisting pathway of crushed granite leading to a mound of stones at the centre and forms a labyrinth of the simplest kind. With no signposts to mark its presence, the labyrinth is only just visible from the road, glimpsed through a line of pine trees. The surrounding landscape is dotted with standing stones and Neolithic chambered tombs, and the first impression is that this too is some prehistoric relic hidden deep in the forest.

Mazes are rare in land art, for they fall firmly within the realm of entertainment. A labyrinth, even with a single path, can illustrate the principles of choice and confusion, and this ambiguity is part of the appeal for the artist. Couple this with the mythology and symbolism of the labyrinth and it is not difficult to understand its fascination as an art form that is as popular today as at any time in its colourful and complex past.

An interesting Christian interpretation of the classical labyrinth appears on the door handles of the church of St Regnus, built in the late 1960s in Burt, County Donegal, Ireland. This is an early instance of the current trend for the labyrinth appearing in a spiritual context.

The Spiritual Thread

To walk a labyrinth is to make a journey towards the goal, whether literally or metaphorically. The appeal that this symbol holds as an allegory for the complexities of the journey through life is long established, but in many ways, life is more like a maze, with its dead-ends and surprises. The current revival of spiritual interest in the labyrinth was heralded by the creation of several mazes in the second half of the twentieth century that owed their origin to religious symbolism revealed to their creators in dreams or visions.

The Archbishop's Maze, installed in 1981 at Greys Court in England, was inspired by a dream recalled by the then Archbishop of Canterbury, Robert Runcie. Designed by Adrian Fisher, it can be walked as either a maze or a labyrinth.

Canon Harry Cheales' planting of a simple hedge maze in the garden of his rectory at Wyck Rissington in Gloucestershire, England, during the 1950s was probably the first of the new trend. The winding path led to a tree at the goal and was the scene of annual pilgrimages for parishioners and visitors until it was uprooted when he retired in 1980. A plan of the maze survives as a mosaic replica set into the wall of the church, dedicated as a memorial to the canon in 1988. A similar hedge maze, opened in 1968 in the garden of the Van Buuren Museum in Brussels, Belgium, has a cedar tree at its goal. A simple pathway leads through a series of alcoves containing sculptures that illustrate the Bible's Song of Songs.

In his enthronement address as Archbishop of Canterbury in 1980, Robert Runcie told how he had seen a maze in a dream where people near the centre could not find their way, while those in the

Right: Marty Kermeen's block paver replica of the labyrinth in Chartres Cathedral was installed in 1998 in Riverwalk Park in Naperville, Illinois.

This small labyrinth was laid in 1977 in black and white marble on the landing leading into the crypt of Cologne Cathedral.

outer circuits soon reached the goal. This sermon inspired the building of the Archbishop's Maze at Greys Court in Oxfordshire the following year. The design, adapted from medieval cathedral labyrinths, can be followed to a sundial at the centre, standing on a Byzantine-style stone cross inset with a Roman cross in contrasting stone. The reconciliation of the various branches of the Christian Church was central to Runcie's life and work and the design of the maze abounds with Christian symbolism. In many ways it typifies the resurgence of the labyrinth as a tool for spiritual renewal.

During the 1970s and early '80s, several new labyrinths were installed in churches and cathedrals. They include one created in the crypt of Cologne Cathedral in 1977, and a copy of the Ely Cathedral labyrinth built in the Anglican Cathedral at Pietermaritzburg in South Africa in 1981. Another pavement labyrinth, set in the floor of Batheaston Church, near Bath, is a half-size replica of the labyrinth formerly in the Abbey of St Bertin in St Omer, France. The parish priest, who had an interest in labyrinths and their association with sacred and religious dance patterns, installed it in 1985.

On the other side of the Atlantic, Jean Houston was renowned for teaching the labyrinth in the 1980s in her Mystery Schools, where she made a particular study of Chartres Cathedral. Her work inspired the Rev. Dr Lauren Artress, Canon for Special Ministries at Grace Cathedral in San Francisco, California, to recreate the famous Chartres Cathedral labyrinth on canvas. It was laid in the nave of Grace Cathedral for the 1992 New Year event led by the Rev. Artress. Thousands walked the labyrinth that night, the first such event in a Christian church to gain widespread media coverage in America. The fame of the labyrinth at Grace Cathedral spread as visiting pilgrims related the powerful experiences and positive benefits that walking the labyrinth had brought them. Before long, Lauren Artress was travelling with her portable labyrinth to churches throughout America, and her book *Walking A Sacred Path: Rediscovering the Labyrinth as a Spiritual Tool*, soon became the standard work for the meditative use of the labyrinth.

The woven labyrinth carpet in Grace Cathedral, San Francisco, replaced the original canvas labyrinth first laid out for New Year's Eve 1992. Without doubt, this labyrinth has been the most influential in the current spiritual revival of labyrinths.

Veriditas, the World-Wide Labyrinth Project, a non-profit foundation based at Grace Cathedral, has since trained hundreds of "labyrinth facilitators" to teach others how to use the labyrinth as a spiritual tool. Many return to their churches or communities and make a labyrinth of their own, which then inspires others. This has resulted in a phenomenal expansion of the labyrinth network in North America. Veriditas, under the umbrella of the Episcopalian church, has also established a connection with the Catholic administration of Chartres Cathedral, and now leads annual pilgrimages to France to walk the original labyrinth by candlelight. For many years, the Chartres labyrinth has languished beneath the chairs in the nave, but of late, the cathedral authorities have begun to organize days on which the labyrinth is uncovered for walking.

Eventually the canvas labyrinth in Grace Cathedral was replaced with a woven carpet of the same design and today the cathedral labyrinth is rarely without somebody either walking the paths or contemplating the meaning of the symbol. In 1995 a further replica of the Chartres Cathedral labyrinth was installed in terrazzo paving in front of Grace Cathedral, offering access to visitors and pilgrims twenty-four hours a day.

The portable Chartres replica popularized by Lauren Artress is now conveniently made from overlapping canvs strips held together with Velcro. Packed into plastic boxes, these kits have travelled to Europe, Southern Africa, and the Far East for presentations, religious retreats, and residential courses exploring the spiritual and meditative uses of the labyrinth. Hundreds of portable labyrinths have been produced over the last ten years and many hundreds of thousands of people have walked them. While many labyrinths are created by individuals or community groups for local use, several enthusiasts, notably Robert Ferré in St Louis and John Ridder in Indianapolis, have built a veritable cottage industry producing hand-painted labyrinths to order in a range of styles and materials.

Replicas of the Chartres labyrinth are popular with more traditional Christian communities, while the classical labyrinth pattern figures more often outside the customary religious settings, especially among New Age or Pagan communities. Although these groups are often exploring the same spiritual paths, they sometimes prefer to use a less overtly Christian labyrinth. The seven concentric paths of the classical labyrinth have become associated with the seven colours of the rainbow and the seven chakras, the energy centres of the human body, and portable labyrinths with paths painted in a spectrum of colours to "channel the energies" are now popular.

In America, enthusiasts have often put the labyrinth to other innovative uses. Robert Ferré's construction of a large indoor labyrinth from cans of food donated to a homeless charity ensured

Portable canvas labyrinths suitable for use outdoors in dry weather are often found in church and community halls. Hundreds of portable labyrinths, painted on a variety of materials, have been produced since the early 1990s. This example is the Santa Rosa design, a seven-circuit adaptation of the medieval type created by Lea Goode-Harris.

wide and entertaining coverage. Lea Goode-Harris's Santa Rosa labyrinth combines a seven-circuit design with medieval-like turns and proportions, and has proved particularly popular where space is at a premium or wider paths suitable for wheelchair access are required. Her recent installation of a simple labyrinthine pathway in the shape of Snoopy's head in the gardens of the Charles Schultz Museum in Santa Rosa, California, is bound to bring the labyrinth to a whole new audience.

This precise replica of the Chartres Cathedral labyrinth was etched on to interlocking blocks of polished granite and installed in 1997 in a small park in the historic town of New Harmony, Indiana, which is also home to a notable hedge maze.

Labyrinths designed to symbolize a spiritual quest have of course appeared in America before. The re-created hedge maze at New Harmony, Indiana, planted in 1941 and based on the plan of the original hedge labyrinth at New Harmony (see page 174), has now been joined by a stunning modern replica of the Chartres labyrinth. Commissioned by Jane Blaffer Owen, a descendant of the Owen family that purchased the town from the Harmonists in 1824, it is a full-scale copy precisely created with computer technology, and etched on to polished interlocking blocks of granite, set in a small park in the town. Fittingly, it was dedicated by Canon Legaux, Rector of Chartres Cathedral, in 1997.

Modern techniques for staining concrete paving blocks with permanent colours have been used to interesting effect in the pavement labyrinth built in 1998 by Marty Kermeen in Riverwalk Park at Naperville, Illinois. This replica of the Chartres labyrinth surrounded by amphitheatre-style seating in a splendid riverside setting among pine trees has become a popular meeting place for families, and, before the visitors arrive, for ducks and geese from the river. The construction of this labyrinth took over 1,000 hours of labour. Many of the paving blocks were hand-cut to produce the complex shapes of the decoration surrounding the outer perimeter and the trefoils in the central goal, resulting in a pavement labyrinth to rival the technical expertise of its medieval counterpart.

Kermeen has also created a number of labyrinths in churches at Knoxville, Tennessee; Destin, Florida; Austin, Texas; Naperville, Illinois; and Long Beach, California. Tailored to fit the available space and budget, his hand-built paver labyrinths cover a broad range of styles from the traditional to the contemporary and reflect the loving and meticulous craftsmanship that has become his trademark. These church labyrinths are valued for their beauty, and even more so for the function they fulfil in the community.

This striking labyrinth was created by Marty Kermeen with coloured block pavers in the garden of St Thomas the Apostle Church in Naperville, Illinois.

The Knoxville labyrinth was the scene of a remarkable spontaneous gathering that occurred immediately after the terrorist attacks on 11 September 2001. On hearing the news, people flooded to the church where they walked the spiralling paths in an effort to come to grips with their tumultuous emotions. Similar spontaneous gatherings were reported at other labyrinths throughout America.

Enthusiasts worldwide have created numerous spontaneous labyrinths from rocks and boulders on remote headlands, hilltops, and beaches. Many of these survive, as new visitors replace dislodged stones and tidy debris left behind by others. Other simple materials such as bricks, rocks, and turf-cut slots are often used to make labyrinths for contemplation in the grounds of spas and health resorts, among other locations.

The construction of a replica of the Chartres labyrinth in 1993 at the Trappist monastery of St Remy in Rochefort, Belgium, is typical of the current interest in the labyrinth pattern in Europe. In Germany a simple tiled labyrinth in the church at Hohenberg in Ellwangen was laid in 1985. Gernot Candolini, working mainly in his native Austria, has built a number of temporary labyrinths at schools and events for the Innsbruck Catholic Youth Service. Several labyrinths have been installed in Lutheran churches and seminaries in Austria and Germany, and many are the work of women's groups. Ilse Seified, based in Vienna, has staged important labyrinth exhibitions; the Zurich-based Labyrinth Project International has created labyrinths in churches, both Catholic and Protestant, in town squares and the grounds of retreat centres. Artists Agnes Barmettler, Marianna Ewaldt, Rosmarie Schmidt, and Susanne Kramer-Friedrich are among the most productive workers in the region. Their recent installations in women's prisons bring the contemplative and spiritual aspects of the labyrinth into the lives of long-term inmates. Prisoners are encouraged to tend the labyrinth formed of plants and stones in the exercise yard, and the positive reports from prison staff parallel the stories coming from the "prison ministries" in America where volunteers take canvas labyrinths into high-security prisons.

Within the last few years the spiritual labyrinth revival has reached Australia and New Zealand with several beautiful outdoor Chartres replicas installed in the grounds of religious retreats. A splendid illustration of the dedication and community spirit fostered by the construction of these labyrinths is provided by the Frederick

Built with volunteer labour over an eight-month period, this labyrinth in the grounds of the Frederick Wallace House retreat centre at Lower Hutt, New Zealand, is a beautiful example of the Chartres Cathedral replicas that have appeared all over the world since 1992.

Wallis House retreat at Lower Hutt, on the outskirts of Wellington, New Zealand. Drawing largely on volunteer labour, the intricate mosaic that forms the walls of the labyrinth took a thousand hours of work over an eight-month period, and was completed in 1999.

The medieval design has become the labyrinth of first choice for many of today's builders. Modern labyrinths are often presented as a reflective island of tranquillity in a chaotic world, a quiet spot to sit in contemplation. The winding path of the labyrinth invites the walker to clear the mind, quieten the pace, and refresh the soul. The recent appearance of several permanent labyrinths in the grounds of hospitals, medical schools, and hospices in America, is explained by a doctor who was heard to remark: "Medicine can cure the body, but this is a tool for curing the soul." Perhaps his words give new credence to claims of the benefits of labyrinth-walking that have been circulating during the last decade.

By far the most touching of the recent labyrinth installations are those created as memorials to loved ones taken before their time. The tortuous path of the labyrinth, a path that leads relentlessly to its conclusion with no opportunity for turning back, has proved a powerful metaphor for people seeking to come to terms with the painful loss of friends or family members. The installation of a labyrinth as a memorial provides the opportunity to walk the path of life. The labyrinth becomes a contained space for a quiet and contemplative exercise, a place to let down one's guard and fully experience the depth of one's emotions. It offers the chance to rekindle happy memories and creates an interface between this world and the beyond. The ancient stone labyrinths to be found in Sweden and Arctic Russia, situated alongside prehistoric grave fields, are considered by some scholars to have served exactly the same purpose.

The Search for Meaning

The remarkable renaissance of the labyrinth within the last decade must surely beg the biggest question of all. Just what is it about this most ancient of symbols that has suddenly found relevance in the lives of modern people?

For religious communities and congregations, especially in America, it is the heritage of the labyrinth and the practices associated with it. The fact that the labyrinth symbol was in widespread use in the Christian church 800 years ago allows the modern pilgrim to participate in an "authentic" medieval ritual. Walking the same pattern of pathways in the labyrinth provides a direct connection to worshippers of the past in a continuity that transcends time, language, and differing liturgical traditions. The labyrinth invites people to share a common experience. The importance of its role in building a community should not be underestimated, and reconciling the interests of a diverse congregation is one of the biggest challenges facing churches today.

For those seeking a less overtly, or even non-Christian, experience, the classical labyrinth likewise offers a long history to draw on for inspiration. The worldwide distribution of this form and the wealth of folklore and traditions that accompany it wherever it occurs show its timeless adaptability. The multi-cultural approach provides numerous opportunities to reach out and build bridges between seemingly disparate sections of the community.

But what do people experience when they walk the labyrinth? Many report a change for the better, saying that that walking the labyrinth has brought them increased calm, clarified insight, and spiritual rejuvenation. The labyrinth can be a pathway of prayer, an opportunity to connect with the Divine and contemplate the magic and mystery of existence. The chance to walk the same pathway travelled by our ancestors, indeed to tread in the very same footsteps of countless visitors before us, continues to draw new pilgrims. The labyrinth's charms invite playfulness as well as soulfulness, delight and curiosity as well as contemplation. Perhaps it is this interaction with mystery, with what cannot be understood and explained, yet is contained within the circuitous paths of a simple design marked on the ground, that so appeals to the modern imagination.

The attraction of the ever more complex mazes of modern times is surely the thrill of getting lost in an environment that we know is ultimately controlled and safe; a place where time and direction are suspended, but where chaos reigns for only as long as we choose to entertain it. The lure of the labyrinth, as well as the magic of the maze, has ensnared humankind for thousands of years. As we enter this new millennium, that fascination has certainly not abated, indeed it shows every sign of continuation.

After a history spanning some four millennia, the archetypal labyrinth symbol continues to draw new pilgrims to walk its circuitous path. This example was laid as an installation at the Das Labyrinth exhibition held in St Pölten, Austria, between November 1999 and January 2000. Along with a number of others built to mark the occasion, it helped to carry the labyrinth tradition into yet another millennium.

Modern Mazes and Labyrinths

The modern revival of mazes and labyrinths started in the 1950s, and has accelerated dramatically since the 1970s. In such a dynamic environment, cataloguing is not easy; this map gives a representative selection of important or interesting examples only. Of the hundreds of new mazes that have been constructed worldwide, some, such as maize mazes, are not intended to last, and others disappear as fashions change. Details of those designed as tourist attractions can be accessed via the Internet. Several thousand new labyrinths have been constructed in recent years, but many are in private locations and finding information on these is more difficult. Once again, the Internet is often the best guide – see page 216 for suggested web sites.

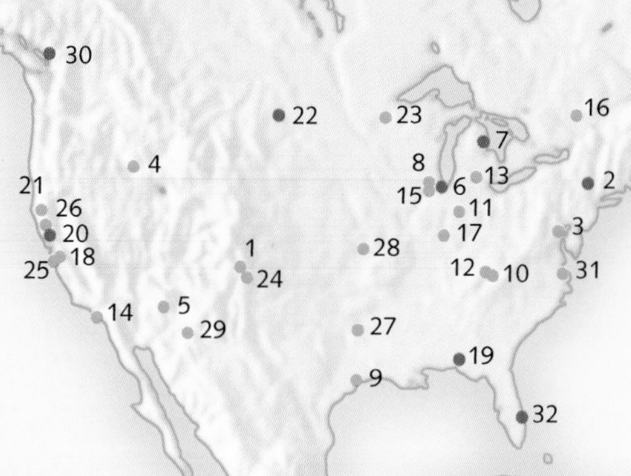

America and Canada

1 Abiquiu, NM; Ghost Ranch labyrinth
2 Arkville, NY; Ayrton's brick wall maze
3 Baltimore, MD; Bayview Medical Centre labyrinth
4 Buhl, ID; Arts Centre garden labyrinth
5 Carefree, AZ; Golden Door Spa labyrinth
6 Chicago, IL; Navy Pier, mirror maze
7 East Tawas, MI; Maze of the Planets, panel maze
8 Elgin, IL; Unitarian Universalist Church labyrinth
9 Galveston, TX; Texas Uni. Medical Centre gardens
10 Gatlinburg, TN; Buck Horn Inn, stone labyrinth
11 Greencastle, IA; painted pavement labyrinth
12 Knoxville, TN; St John's Episcopal Church labyrinth
13 Lansing, MI; Sparrow Hospital, pavement labyrinth
14 Long Beach, CA; replica of Chartres labyrinth
15 Naperville, IL; Riverwalk Park pavement labyrinth
16 Nepean, ON; Bells Corner United Church labyrinth
17 New Harmony, IN; replica of Chartres labyrinth
18 Oakland, CA; Sibley Park stone labyrinths
19 Panama City, FL; Coconut Creek panel maze
20 Petaluma, CA; regular corn maze beside interstate 101
21 Philo, CA; Alex Champion's "Earth Mazes"
22 Rapid City, SD; Black Hills Maze, panel maze
23 St Paul, MN; Wisdom Ways turf labyrinth
24 Santa Fe, NM; Folk Art Museum, paving labyrinth
25 San Francisco, CA; Grace Cathedral labyrinths
26 Santa Rosa, CA; Schultz Museum, Snoopy labyrinth
27 Shreveport, LA; St Luke's Church labyrinth
28 Sibley, MO; Prairie Labyrinth cut into tall grass
29 Tucson, AZ; Speedway, Man in Maze labyrinth
30 Vancouver, BC; Vandusen Gardens, hedge maze
31 Virginia Beach, VA; Edgar Cayce Centre labyrinth
32 West Palm Beach, FL; Norton Museum paving maze

Hawaii

33 Wahiawa; Dole Plantation hedge maze

Euorpe and UK
see page 208
Hong Kong
34 Kowloon Park; rooftop hedge maze
South Korea
35 Cheju; huge hedge maze
Japan
36 Fushimi-Ku; Daigo Gran panel maze
37 Mito; Mito panel maze
38 Numakuma; Mirokunosato panel maze
39 Sayama; Chichibu Muse Park maze
40 Shiga; Shiga-Rittou panel maze
41 Shimane; Hikimi panel maze
42 Tohaku; Misasa panel maze
Australia
43 Ballarat, Victoria; Kryal Castle brick wall maze
44 Bullsbrook, WA; Sequoia Park panel maze
45 Cowes, Victoria; A Maze'n Things panel maze
46 Dromana, Victoria; Arthur's Seat hedge maze
47 Healesville, Victoria; Hedgend hedge maze
48 Mullumbimby, NSW; Crystal Castle stone labyrinth
49 Promised Land, Tasmania; Tasmazia maze collection
50 Richmond, Tasmania; Richmond panel mazes
51 Shoreham, Victoria; Ashcombe hedge maze
52 Tanawha, Queensland; Bellingham hedge maze
53 Westbury, Tasmania; hedge maze and tearooms
New Zealand
54 Lower Hutt, N Is; Frederick Wallis paving labyrinth
55 Rotorua, N Is; panel and hedge mazes
56 Wanaka, S Is; Great Maze, the original panel maze
South Africa
57 Pietermaritzburg Cathedral; pavement labyrinth
58 Robertson; Soekershof hedge maze & labyrinth
59 Sizanani, Pretoria; terraced wall labyrinth
42 40 37
41 39
35 38 36
34
59
57
58
52
48
44
43 47
46 51 45
55
49 53
54
50
56

Modern Mazes and Labyrinths continued

- Mazes
- Labyrinths

England

1 Bath; Beazer Gardens stone paved maze
2 Batheaston; pavement labyrinth in parish church
3 Bicton Park; foot-shaped log maze
4 Blackpool; Pleasure Beach, feature-filled maze
5 Chesterfield; Tapton Park, huge land art labyrinth
6 Glastonbury Tor; huge 3-D labyrinth encircling a hill
7 Henley-on-Thames; Grey's Court symbolic maze
8 Hever Castle; simple water maze with central tower
9 Holywell Bay; Merlin's Magic Maze panel maze
10 Hurn; Merritown House, Alice in Wonderland maze
11 Ilkley; Darwin Garden paving maze
12 Leeds Castle; hedge maze & underground grotto
13 Long Melford; Kentwall Hall pavement maze
14 Longleat House; collection of mirror & hedge mazes
15 Pulborough; Parham Park, brick pathway maze
16 Symonds Yat West; hedge maze & maze museum
17 Turners Hill; Tulleys Farm, annual maize maze site
18 Windsor; three hedge and panel mazes at Legoland
19 Worksop; pavement mazes in town centre
20 Wyck Rissington; site of spiritual hedge maze

Jersey

21 St Hellier; hi-tech water maze in seafront park

Scotland

22 Edinburgh Zoo; interactive hedge maze
23 Galloway Forest; Raiders Road land art labyrinth
24 Strathpeffer; Touchstone gravel path labyrinth

Northern Ireland

25 Castlewellan Country Park; Peacemaze hedge maze

Ireland

26 Burt, Co Donegal; labyrinths in unusual church
27 Dunbrody Abbey; Celtic cross-shaped hedge maze
28 Russborough House; hedge maze with central pillar

Austria

29 Wattens; Kristallwelten hedge maze
30 Innsbruck; regular labyrinths at garden festival

Belgium

31 Brussels; Van Burren Museum hedge maze
32 Parc Meli; seahorse-shaped hedge maze
33 Trois Ponts; Puzzle Planet panel maze

Czech Republic

34 Prague; restored historic mirror maze

Denmark

35 Lejre Historic Centre; influential stone labyrinth
36 Rodelund; Labyrinthia collection of mazes
37 Copenhagen; Valbypark stone labyrinth

Finland

38 Vaasa; Brågaden stone labyrinth

France

39 Marne-la-Vallee; Euro Disney Wonderland maze
40 Peaugres; Safari Park mirror maze
41 Reignac-sur-Indre; Labyrinthus maize maze
42 Yvoire; Labyrinthe aux Oiseaux hedge maze

Germany

43 Augsburg; St.Sebastian stone paved labyrinth
44 Bad Birneck; pavement labyrinth
45 Bad Waldliesborn; health resort hedge maze
46 Cologne Cathedral; small pavement labyrinth
47 Kleinwelka; complex hedge maze

Italy

48 Castel di Lucio, Sicily; Arianna labyrinth
49 Genoa; Parco Labarinto garden maze
50 Rome; traditional hedge maze on Palatine hill

Netherlands

51 Bakkeveen; 3 mazes in Dundelle puzzle park
52 Hellendoorn; pleasure park hedge maze
53 Vlaardingen; Oranjepark hedge maze
54 Vaals; Drielandenpunt hedge maze

Norway

55 Alta; Arctic Museum stone labyrinth
56 Tromso University; huge stone labyrinth

Sweden

57 Gothenburg; Lisebergparken mirror maze
58 Varmlands Saby; symbolic hedge maze

Switzerland

59 Lucerne; restored historic mirror maze
60 Mannedorf; Boldern retreat centre turf labyrinth
61 Zurich; Zeughaushof flower garden labyrinth

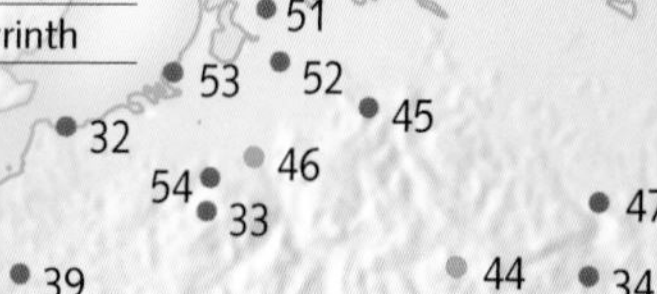
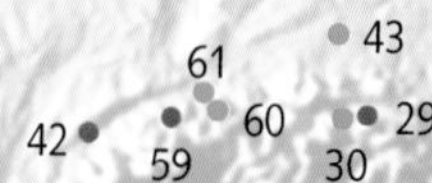
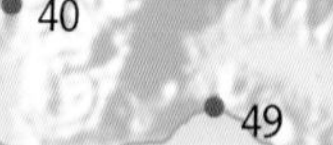

References

Introduction

1. MacGillivray, 2000
2. Wood, 1985
3. Kern, 2000
4. Bancroft, 1875
5. Lonegren, 1991
6. Paliga, 1989
7. Castleden, 1990
8. Bietak, 1995; Morgan, 1995
9. Kern, 2000
10. Matthews, 1922
11. Gimbutas, 1982
12. Kern, 2000
13. Lawler, 1964
14. Gimbutas, 1982
15. Kern, 2000
16. Abbott, 1998
17. e.g. Heller & Cairns, 1969
18. Kern, 1982; West, 2000
19. Saward, 2001
20. Phillips, 1992
21. Daszewski, 1977; Kraft, 1985
22. Saward, 2001
23. Fisher & Gerster, 1990; Abbott, 1998
24. Landsborough, 1992

Chapter 1

1 Saward, 2001
2 Bradley, 1997
3 Peña Santos & Vázquez Varela, 1979; Costas Goberna, Hidalgo Cuñarro & Peña Santos, 1999
4 Anati, 1964
5 Zanettin, 1975
6 Meunié & Allain, 1956
7 Lundén, 1996
8 Deecke, 1881
9 von Salis, 1930; Gallini, 1959
10 Kern, 1982
11 Kraft, 1997
12 Kuhlmann, 1983
13 Lundén, 1996
14 Daszewski, 1977; Kern, 2000

Chapter 2

1. Kern, 2000
2. Nath, 2001
3. Scerrato, 1983
4. Lundén, 1998
5. Cimino, 1995
6. Kern, 2000
7. Layard, 1937
8. Kern, 2000
9. Kidd, 1906
10. James, 1902; Kissell, 1916
11. Saward, 2001
12. Shaw, 1968
13. Schuster, 1988
14. Waters, 1963
15. Schuster, 1988
16. Schuster, 1988
17. Griffin-Pierce, 2000
18. Aveni, 2000
19. Saward, 2003
20. Schuster, 1988

Chapter 3

1. Rypson, 1986
2. Reed Doob, 1990
3. Harbison, 1991
4. Lundén, 1996
5. Bradley, 1997
6. Saward, 2000; Lundén, 2003
7. Roder, 1971
8. Lundén, 2003
9. Kern, 2000
10. Clayton, 1990
11. Haubrichs, 1980
12. Wright, 2001
13. Critchlow et al, 1975; Villette, 1984; Ketley Laporte, 1997
14. Eastes, 1990
15. Saward, 2001
16. Kraft, 1991; Saward & Thordrup, 1993
17. Schaefers, 2001

Chapter 4

1. Gerritsen & van Melle 1998
2. Stukeley, 1724
3. Behrend, 1984
4. Kraft, 1983
5. Barker, 1990
6. Morrell, 1990
7. Allcroft, 1908
8. Harte, 1986
9. Halliday, 1989
10. Sowan, 1980
11. Braybrooke, 1836
12. Mitchell, 1962; Fisher & Gerser, 1990
13. Trollope, 1858
14. Lane, 1946,
15. Hunke, 1940
16. Magdalinski, 1921
17. Lotze, 1878
18. Massmann, 1844
19. Kraft, 1984
20. Brusewitz, 1953
21. Sjöberg, 1996
22. Kraft, 1986
23. Kraft, 1985
24. Stjernström, 1991
25. Kraft, 1985
26. Simek, 1993
27. De Santillana & von Dechend, 1969
28. Kraft, 1986
29. Westerdahl 1992
30. Nance, 1923
31. Kraft, 1983
32. Coles, 1990
33. Hultin, 1999
34. Lonegren, 1993
35. Broadbent, 1989
36. Bäcksbacka, 1972
37. Saward, 1998
38. Olsen, 1991
39. Gourina, 1957
40. Kuratov, 1970
41. Vinnikov & Sinyuk, 1990

Chapter 5

1. Reed Doob, 1990
2. Strong, 2000
3. Kern, 2000
4. Strong, 1979
5. Robey, 1998
6. Crossley, 1999
7. Schaefers, 2001
8. Laishley, 2001
9. Griswold & Weller, 1991

Chapter 6

1. Bright, 1973
2. Saward, 1998
3. Landsborough, 1992
4. Abbott, 1997

Bibliography

Introduction

Abbott, Robert. "Supermazes!" *Caerdroia* 29 (1998), pp.52-57.

Bancroft, Hubert Howe. *Antiquities of Arizona and New Mexico*. Leipzig: 1875.

Bietak, Manfred. "Connections Between Egypt and the Minoan World: New Results from Tell el-Dab'a / Avaris" in *Egypt, the Aegean and the Levant*. ed. W. Vivian Davies & Louise Schofield. London: British Museum, 1995

Castleden, Rodney. *The Knossos Labyrinth*. London: Routledge, 1990.

Daszewski, Wictor. *Nea Paphos II, La Mosaique de Thésée, Etudes sur les mosaiques avec representations du Labyrinth, de Thésée et du Minotaur*. Varsovie: PWN editions scientifiques de Pologne, 1977.

Fisher, Adrian & Georg Gerster. *The Art of the Maze*. London: Weidenfeld & Nicolson, 1990.

Gimbutas, Maria. *The Goddesses and Gods of Old Europe*. London: Thames & Hudson, revised edition, 1982.

Heller, John L. & Stewart S. Cairns. "To Draw a Labyrinth" in *Classical Studies Presented to Ben Edwin Perry*. Chicago: University of Illinois Press, 1969.

Kern, Hermann. *Labyrinthe*. Munich: Prestel, 1982.

Kern, Hermann. *Through the Labyrinth*, ed. Robert Ferré & Jeff Saward. Munich: Prestel, 2000.

Kraft, John. "The Cretan Labyrinth and the Walls of Troy: an analysis of Roman labyrinth designs" *Opuscula Romana* XV:6, (1985), pp79-86.

Krause, Ernst. *Die Trojaburgen Nordeuropas*. Glogau: 1893.

Landsborough, Stuart. "The Great Maze at Wanaka" *Caerdroia* 25 (1992), pp.14-16.

Lawler, Lillian B. *The Dance in Ancient Greece*. London: Adam & Charles Black, 1964.

Lonegren, Sig. *Labyrinths – Ancient Myths & Modern Uses*. Glastonbury: Gothic Image, 1991.

Lonegren, Sig. "Come to Terms" *Caerdroia* 24 (1991), p.11.

MacGillivray, J. Alexander. *Minotaur – Sir Arthur Evans and the Archaeology of the Minoan Myth*. London: Jonathan Cape, 2000.

Matthews, W.H. *Mazes and Labyrinths – A General Account of their History and Developments*. London: Longmans, Green & Co., 1922.

Morgan, Lyvia. "Minoan Painting and Egypt: The Case of Tell el-Dab'a" in *Egypt, the Aegean and the Levant*. ed. W. Vivian Davies & Louise Schofield. London: British Museum, 1995

Paliga, Sorin. "Types of Mazes" *Linguistica* XXIX (1989), pp.57-70.

Phillips, Anthony. "The Topology of Roman Mosaic Mazes" *Leonardo* vol.25, no.3/4 (1992), pp.321-329.

Rigoglioso, Marguerite. "The Oldest Labyrinth in the World? The Polyphemus Cave Paintings" *Caerdroia* 29 (1998), pp.14-22.

Saward, Jeff. "The Pavement Labyrinth in Gent Town Hall, Belgium" *Caerdroia* 32 (2001) pp.59-61.

Saward, Jeff. "An Unusual Pima Labyrinth" *Caerdroia* 32 (2001) pp.4–7.

Ward, Anne.G. (ed.). *The Quest for Theseus*. London: Pall Mall Press, 1970.

West, Melissa Gayle. *Exploring the Labyrinth*. New York: Broadway Books, 2000.

Wood, Michael. *In Search of the Trojan War*. London: B.B.C., 1985.

Chapter 1

Anati, Emmanuel. *Camonica Valley*. London: Jonathan Cape, 1964.

Anati, Emmanuel. *Evoluzione e stile nell'Arte rupestre camuna*. Capo di Ponte, Italy: Edizioni del Centro, 1975.

Bradley, Richard. *Rock Art and the Prehistory of Atlantic Europe*. London & New York: Routledge, 1997.

Costas Goberna, Fernando Javier; José Manuel Hidalgo Cuñarro & Antonio de la Peña Santos. *Arte Rupestre no Sur da Ría de Vigo*. Vigo, Spain: Instituto de Estudios Vigueses, 1999.

Deecke, Wilhelm. "Le Iscrizioni Etrusche del Vaso di Tragliatella" *Annali dell'Istituto di Corrispondenza Archeologica* 35 (1881), p.160-168.

Gallini, Clara. "Potinija Dapuritoio" *Acmè, Annali della Facoltà di Filosofia e lettere dell'Università Statale di Milano* 12 59), p.149-176.

Kern, Hermann. *Labyrinthe*. Munich: Prestel, 1982.

Kern, Hermann. *Through the Labyrinth*, ed. Robert Ferré & Jeff Saward. Munich: Prestel, 2000.

Kraft, John. "Labyrinth Construction" *Caerdroia* 25 (1992), p.41.

Kraft, John. "The Queen's Medals" *Caerdroia* 28 (1997), pp.24-25.

Kuhlmann, K.P. "Eine Labyrinth-artige Darstellung" *Göttinger Miszellen* 40 (1980), p.41, pl.1.

Lundén, Staffan. "Labyrinth Construction" *Caerdroia* 24 (1991), pp.24-26.

Lundén, Staffan. "The Labyrinth in the Mediterranean" *Caerdroia* 27 (1996), pp.28-54; *Caerdroia* 28 (1997), pp.28-34 and *Caerdroia* 29 (1998), pp.38-42.

Meunié J. & C. Allain. "Quelques gravures et monuments funéraires de l'extrême sud-est Morocain" *Hesperis* 43 (1956), pp.51-88.

Peña Santos, Antonio de la & J.M.Vázquez Varela. *Los Petroglifos Gallegos*. La Coruña, Spain: Edicios Do Castro, 1979.

Peña Santos, Antonio de la & Fernando J. Costas Goberna. "Los laberintos de tipo cretense en los grabados rupestre galaicos" *Boletín del Instituto de Estudios Vigueses* VI: 6 (2000), pp.283-306.

Salis, Arnold von. *Theseus und Ariadne*. Berlin: 1930.

Saward, Abegael. "The Rocky Valley Labyrinths" *Caerdroia* 32 (2001), pp.21-27.

Zanettin, A.-M. "Il significato magico-religioso del labirinto nell'arte rupestre Camuna", in: *The intellectual expressions of prehistoric man: art and religion, Acts of the Valcamonica Symposium '79*, ed. E. Anati & A. Beltran. Capo di Ponte, Italy: 1983.

Zanettin, A.-M. *Il tema del labirinto nell'arte rupestre Camuna e sue possibili comparazion*. Unpublished thesis at University of Rome, 1975.

Roman Labyrinths

Daszewski, Wictor. *Nea Paphos II, La Mosaique de Thésée, Etudes sur les mosaiques avec representations du Labyrinth, de Thésée et du Minotaur*. Varsovie: PWN editions scientifiques de Pologne, 1977.

Kern, Hermann. *Through the Labyrinth*, ed. Robert Ferré & Jeff Saward. Munich: Prestel, 2000. (Chapter VI provides the most complete catalogue of Roman mosaic labyrinths published.)

Kraft, John. "The Cretan Labyrinth and the Walls of Troy: an analysis of Roman labyrinth designs" *Opuscula Romana* XV:6, (1985), pp79-86.

Ling, Roger. *Ancient Mosaics*. London: British Museum Press, 1998.

Lundén, Staffan. "The Labyrinth in the Mediterranean" *Caerdroia* 27 (1996), pp.28-54; *Caerdroia* 28 (1997), pp.28-34 and *Caerdroia* 29 (1998), pp.38-42.

Lundén, Staffan & John Kraft. "A Labyrinth Mosaic at Mieza, Macedonia" *Caerdroia* 28 (1997), pp.13-16.

Neal, David S. *Roman Mosaics in Britain*. Gloucester, England: Alan Sutton, 1981.

Phillips, Anthony. "The Topology of Roman Mosaic Mazes" *Leonardo*, vol.25, no.3/4 (1992), pp321-329.

Chapter 2

The Labyrinth in India and Asia

Brooke, S.C. "The Labyrinth Pattern in India" *Folklore* LXIV (1953), pp.463-472.

Cimino, Rosa Maria. "A Short Note on a New Nepalese Labyrinth" *East and West* 45 (1995), pp.381-385.

Hyland, Paul. "The Ondavalli Labyrinth" *Caerdroia* 26 (1993), pp.11-12.

Kern, Hermann. *Through the Labyrinth*, ed. Robert Ferré & Jeff Saward. Munich: Prestel, 2000.

Layard, John. "Labyrinth Ritual in Southern India" *Folklore* XLVIII (1937), pp.116-182.

Lundén, Staffan. "A Nepalese Labyrinth" *Caerdroia* 26 (1993), pp.13-22.

Lundén, Staffan. "A Nepalese Labyrinth" *East and West* 48 (1998), pp.117-134.

Nath, Ashoke. "Hoary Past of Goa" *India Perspectives* vol.14/1 (2001), pp.2-5.

Scerrato, Umberto. "Labyrinths in the Wooden Mosques of North Pakistan" *East and West* 33 (1983), pp.21-29.

Schuster, Carl. *Social Symbolism in Ancient & Tribal Art*, Volume 3, Book 2, ed. Edmund Carpenter. New York: Rock Foundation, 1988.

Sibeth, Achim. *The Batak*. London: Thames & Hudson, 1991.

The Labyrinth in Southern Africa

Kidd, Dudley. *Savage Childhood*. London: Adam & Charles Black, 1906.

Samuelson, L.H. *Some Zulu Customs and Folk-lore*. London: 1912.

Saward, Jeff. "The Labyrinth in Southern Africa" *Caerdroia* 25 (1992), pp.42-43.

The Labyrinth in the American Southwest

Breazeale, J.F. *The Pima and His Basket*. Tucson, Arizona Archaeological and Historical Society, 1923.

DeWald, Terry. *The Papago Indians and Their Basketry*. Tucson: Terry DeWald, 1979.

Griffin-Pierce, Trudy. *Native Peoples of the Southwest*. Albuquerque: University of New Mexico, 2000.

James, George Wharton. *Indian Basketry*. Pasadena, California: privately printed,1902; reprinted New York: Dover, 1972.

Kern, Hermann. *Through the Labyrinth*. ed. Robert Ferré & Jeff Saward. Munich: Prestel, 2000.

Kessell, John L. *Spain in the Southwest*. Norman, Oklahoma: University of Oklahoma, 2002.

Kissell, Mary Lois. *Basketry of the Papago and Pima*. New York: Anthropological Papers of the American Museum of Natural History, vol.17, no.4, 1916.

Saward, Jeff. "The House of Iitoi" *Caerdroia* 22 (1989), pp.30-38.

Saward, Jeff. "An Unusual Pima Labyrinth" *Caerdroia* 32 (2001), pp.4-7.

Schuster, Carl. *Social Symbolism in Ancient & Tribal Art*, Volume 3, Book 2, ed. Edmund Carpenter. New York: Rock Foundation, 1988.

Shaw, Anna Moore. *Pima Indian Legends*. Tucson: University of Arizona, 1968.

Tanner, Clara Lee. *Indian Baskets of the Southwest*. Tucson, University of Arizona, 1983.

Waters, Frank. *Book of the Hopi*. New York: Viking, 1963.

The Labyrinth in South America

Aveni, Anthony F. *Nasca - Eighth Wonder of the World?* London: British Museum, 2000.

Saward, Jeff. "The Curious Cuenca Labyrinths" *Caerdroia* 33 (2003), in press.

Schuster, Carl. *Social Symbolism in Ancient & Tribal Art*, Volume 3, Book 2, ed. Edmund Carpenter. New York: Rock Foundation, 1988.

Von Däniken, Erich. *The Gold of the Gods*. London: Souvenir Press, 1973.

Chapter 3

Amé, Emile. *Les Carrelages émaillés du Moyen Age*. Paris, 1859.

Bradley, Richard. *Rock Art and the Prehistory of Atlantic Europe*. London & New York: Routledge, 1997. (see p.33)

Clayton, Mary. *The Cult of the Virgin Mary in Anglo-Saxon England*. Cambridge: Cambridge University Press, 1990.

Critchlow, Keith, Jane Carroll and Llewylyn Vaughan Lee. *Chartres Maze – a model of the universe?* London: RILKO Occasional Paper No.1, 1975.

Durand, Julien. "Les Pavés Mosaïques en Italie et en France." *Annales Archéologiques*, XIV & XVII, Paris, 1855 & 1857.

Eastes, Zeta. "My Father, W.H.Matthews" *Caerdroia* 23 (1990), pp.6-8.

Ferré, Robert. *Origin, Symbolism and Design of the Chartres Labyrinth*. St.Louis, MO: One Way Press, 2001.

Gailhabaurd, Jules. *L'Architecture du Ve au XVIIIe siecle*. Paris, 1858.

Harbison, Peter. *Pilgrimage in Ireland*. London: Barrie & Jenkins, 1991. (see pp.118-124, pp.141-144.)

Haubrichs, Wolfgang. "Error inextricabilis. Form and Function der Labyrinthabbildung in mittelalterlichen Handscriften." *Text und Bild: Aspecte des Zusammenwirkens zweier Künste in Mittelalter und früher Neuzeit*. Wiesbaden, 1980, pp.63-174.

James, John. *The Master Masons of Chartres*. Leura, NSW Australia: West Grinstead Publishing, 1990.

Kern, Hermann. *Through the Labyrinth*. ed. Robert Ferré & Jeff Saward. Munich: Prestel, 2000. (Chapter VII provides the most complete catalogue of labyrinth manuscripts published.)

Ketley-Laporte, John and Odette. *Chartres – le labyrinthe déchiffré*. Chartres: Éditions Garnier, 1997.

Kraft, John. "Labyrinths in Nordic Churches" *Caerdroia* 24 (1991), pp.29-37.

Lundén, Staffan. "The Labyrinth in the Mediterranean" *Caerdroia* 27 (1996), pp.28-54.

Lundén, Staffan. "A Labyrinth Inscription at Knidos" *Caerdroia* 33 (2003), in press.

Mastrigli, Manuela. "The Volterra Lectern Labyrinth" *Caerdroia* 30 (1999), pp.6-9.

Mastrigli, Manuela & Fulvio Pompili. "A Labyrinth in the Centre of Rome" *Caerdroia* 30 (1999), pp.10-16.

Matthews, W.H. *Mazes and Labyrinths – A General Account of their History and Developments*. London: Longmans, Green & Co., 1922.

Pugin, Augustas, W.N. *The True Principles of Pointed or Christian Architecture*. London, 1841

Reed Doob, Penelope. *The Idea of the Labyrinth from Classical Antiquity through the Middle Ages*. Ithaca, NY: Cornell University Press, 1990. (see pp.81-82).

Richards, E.G. *Mapping Time - The Calendar and its History*. Oxford: Oxford University Press, 1998. (see pp.354-378).

Röder, J. "Marmor Phrygium. Die antiken Marmorbrüche von Iscehisar in westanatolien" *Jahrbuch des Deutschen Archäologischen Instituts* 86 (1971) pp.252-312.

Ruskin, John. *The Seven Lamps of Architecture*. London, 1849.

Ruskin, John. *The Stones of Venice*. London, 1851-3.

Rypson, Piotr. "The Labyrinth Poem" *Visible Language*, XX 1 (1986), pp.65-95.

Saint-Hilaire, Paul de. *L'universe Secret du Labyrinthe*. Paris: Robert Laffont, 1992.

Saward, Jeff. "Three Newly Discovered Labyrinths" *Caerdroia* 31 (2000), pp.54-55.

Saward, Jeff. "The Pavement Labyrinth in Gent Town Hall, Belgium" *Caerdroia* 32 (2001), pp.59-61.

Saward, Jeff & Jørgen Thordrup. "Mazes & Labyrinths of Denmark III" *Caerdroia* 26 (1993), pp.57-59.

Schaefers, Fons. "A Catalogue of Labyrinths & Mazes in the Netherlands" *Caerdroia* 32 (2001), pp.28-35.

Soyez, Edmond. *Les Labyrinthes D'Églises*. Amiens: Yvert & Tellier, 1896.

Trollope, Rev. Edward. "Notices of Ancient and Mediaeval Labyrinths" *The Archaeological Journal* XV (1858), pp.216-235.

Verbrugge, Rév.Père A.-R. "L'énigme des labyrinths" *Atlantis* 365 (1991), pp.200-279.

Villette, Jean. "L'énigme du labyrinthe de la cathédrale" *Notre-Dame de Chartres* 58 (1984), pp.4-13.

Wallet, Emanuel. *Description d'une crypte et d'un pavé mosaïque de l'église St-Bertin à Saint-Omer*. St.Omer and Douai, 1843.

Watts, Mrs.G.F. (Mary). *The Word in the Pattern – A Key to the Symbols on the Walls of the Chapel at Compton*. London: Ward & Co., 1904.

Wright, Craig. *The Maze and the Warrior*. Cambridge, Massachusetts: Harvard University Press, 2001.

Chapter 4

Turf Labyrinths

Allcott, Trevor. "A Scottish Turf Labyrinth" *Caerdroia* 32 (2001), pp.39-40.

Allcroft, A. Hadrian. *Earthworks of England*. London: Macmillan & Co., 1908.

Barker, Katherine. "The Mizmaze at Leigh" *Caerdroia* 23 (1990), pp.9-14.

Behrend, Michael. "Julian Bowers" *Caerdroia* 15 (1984), pp.4-7.

Behrend, Michael. "Julian's Bower and Troy Names" *Caerdroia* 27 (1996), pp.18-23.

Braybrooke, Lord. *Audley End and Saffron Walden* (1836), manuscript insertion (1859) in Saffron Walden Museum, Essex, England.

Brusewitz, G. "Anteckningar under vandringar I sodra Halland sommaren 1865" *Samfundet Hallands biblioteks vanners publikationer*, III. Halmstad, Sweden, 1953.

Duffy, Christopher. *Siege Warfare*. London: Routledge, Keegan & Paul, 1979. (see p.182.)

Fisher, Adrian & Georg Gerster. *The Art of the Maze*. London: Wiedenfeld & Nicolson, 1990.

Gerritsen, Willem P. & Anthony G.van Melle. *A Dictionary of Medieval Heros*. Woodbridge, England: Boydell Press, 1998.

Halliday, Robert. "Three Cambridgeshire Mazes" *Caerdroia* 22 (1989), pp.44-47.

Harte, Jeremy. "Dorset's Maypoles and Mazes" *Dorset County Magazine*, vol.113 (1986).

Hawkes, C.F.C., J.N.L. Myres & C.G. Stevens. *Saint Catherine's Hill Winchester*. Proceedings of the Hampshire Field Club and Archaeological Society, vol.XI. Winchester: Warren & Son Ltd., 1930.

Hunke, Waltraud. *Die Trojaburgen und ihre Bedeutung*. Unpublished dissertation, 1940.

Kraft, John. "Wunderburg and Jerusalem" *Caerdroia* 13 (1983), pp.11-19.

Kraft, John. "German Turf Labyrinths" *Caerdroia* 14 (1984), pp.11-18.

Kraft, John. "Turf Labyrinths in Southern Scandinavia" *Caerdroia* 15 (1984), pp.14-22.

Krüger, Kurt. *Rasenlabyrinthe*. Marburg, Germany: privately published, 1995.

Lane, Margaret. *The Tale of Beatrix Potter*. Harmonsworth, England: Frederick Warne, 1946.

Leonhardt, K.Fr. "Das Rad in der Eilenriede" *Hannoversche Geschichtsblätter* (1938), pp.65-76.

Lotze, Wilhelm. *Geschichte der Stadt Dransfeld*. 1878.

Magdalinski, Pastor. "Die Windelbahn von Stolp in Pommern" *Mannus* 1921 (Leipzig 1922), pp.197-205.

Matthews, W.H. *Mazes and Labyrinths – A General Account of their History and Developments*. London: Longmans, Green & Co., 1922.

Massman, H.F. *Wunderkreis und Irrgärten für Turnplätze und Gartenanlagen*. Leipzig, Germany: 1844.

Mitchell, T.J. "Some Observations on Turf Mazes" *Scarborough and District Archaeological Society Transactions*, vol.1, no.5 (1962) pp.7-14.

Morrell, R.W. *Nottingham's Mysterious Mazes*. Nottingham, England: APRA Press, 1990.

Mullard, Jonathan. *Caerdroia Salopia*. Telford, England: Mizmaze Publications, 1983.

Pennick, Nigel. *Mazes and Labyrinths*. London: Robert Hale, 1990.

Saward, Jeff & Deb Saward. "Labyrinths of Ireland" *Caerdroia* 14 (1984), pp.4-10.

Sowan, Paul. "Non-Industrial Use of Firestone Quarries in the Early 18th Century" *Unit 2 Newsletter*, no.2 (1980), pp.11-14.

Stukeley, William. *Itinerarium Curiosum*. 1724.

Thompson, Ian. *Julian's Bower – a Guide to the Alkborough Turf Maze*. Scunthorpe, England: Bluestone Books, 1999.

Trollope, Rev. Edward. "Notices of Ancient and Mediaeval Labyrinths" *The Archaeological Journal* XV (1858), pp.216-235.

Tyack, Rev. George S. "Mazes" in *Ecclesiastical Curiosities*, ed. William Andrews. London: Andrews & Co., 1899.

Wall, John. "Lincolnshire Turf Mazes." *Caerdroia* 26 (1993), pp.24-38.

Williams, Damon. "Three Cowley Troytowns" *Caerdroia* 22 (1989), pp.58-60.

Stone Labyrinths

Bäcksbacka, Christina. "Stenlabyrinter i Finland" *Finska Fornminnesföreningens Månadsblad* (1972), pp.64-73.

Broadbent, Noel. *Lichenometry and Archaeology*. Research Reports nr.2. Centre for Arctic Cultural Research, Umeå University (1987).

Broadbent, Noel. "Datering av rösen och labyrinter på Åland" *Åländsk Odling* 49 (1989), pp.99-105.

Campbell, Fiona. "A Swedish Labyrinth Database" *Caerdroia* 31 (2000), p.23.

Coles, John. *Images of the Past*. Uddevalla, Sweden: Bohusläns Museuem Skrifter, nr.32, 1990.

Damell, David. "Rösaring and a Viking Age Cult Road" *Archaeology and Environment* 4 (1985), pp.171-185.

De Santillana, Giorgio & Hertha von Dechend. *Hamlet's Mill*. Jaffrey, New Hampshire: Godine, 1969.

Gourina, N.N. "Sur la Datation des Labyrinthes de Pierre de la Mer Blanche et de la Mer de Barentz" *Annales du Centre d'Etudes et de Documentation Paleontologiques*, 1957, pp.345-356.

Hultin, Johan. "The Bjorkskar Labyrinth." *Caerdroia* 30 (1999), pp.34-36.

Kern, Hermann. *Through the Labyrinth*, ed. Robert Ferré & Jeff Saward. Munich: Prestel, 2000.

Kraft, John. "Gotlands Trojeborgar" *Gotländskt Arkiv* 1983, pp.59-90.

Kraft, John. *The Goddess in the Labyrinth*. Turku, Finland: Åbo Akademis, 1985.

Kraft, John. "Labyrintnamn – från Troja till Trelleborg" *Sydsvenska Ortnamnssällskapets, Årsskrift 1986*, pp.8-72.

Kraft, John. "The Magic Labyrinth" *Caerdroia* 19 (1986), pp.14-19.

Kraft, John. "Labyrinths in Pagan Sweden" *Caerdroia* 21 (1987), pp.12-24.

Kraft, John. "The First Labyrinths in Scandinavia" *Caerdroia* 31 (2000), pp.18-22.

Kraft, John & Urmas Selirand. "Labyrinths in Estonia" *Caerdroia* 23 (1990), pp.32-37.

Kuratov, A.A. "On the Stone Labyrinths of Northern Europe" *Sovetskaia Arkheologiia* 1970, no.1, pp.34-47.

Lonegren, Sig. "From Labyrinths to Mazes" *Caerdroia* 26 (1993), pp.39-43.

Nance, R. Morton. "Troy Town" *Journal of the Royal Institute of Cornwall* vol.XXI (1923), pp.260-279.

Olsen, Bjørnar. "Material Metaphors and Historical Practice: A Structural Analysis of Stone Labyrinths in coastal Finnmark, Arctic Norway" *Fennoscandia Archaeologica* VIII (1991), pp.51-58.

Saward, Jeff. "Labyrinths of the Scillies" *Caerdroia* 23 (1990), pp.43-47.

Saward, Jeff & Deb Saward. "The Labyrinth in Iceland" *Caerdroia* 29 (1998), pp.58-60.

Simek, Rudolf. "Völunderhús – Domus Daedali: Labyrinths in Old Norse Manuscripts" *Nowele* vol.21-22 (1993) Odense University Press, pp.323-368.

Sjöberg, Rabbe. "Lichenometric Dating of Boulder Labyrinths on the Upper Norrland Coast, Sweden" *Caerdroia* 27 (1996), pp.10-17.

Stjernström, Bo. "Ålands Labyrinter" *Åländsk Odling* 49 (1989), pp.107-115.

Stjernström, Bo. "Baltic Labyrinths" *Caerdroia* 24 (1991), pp.14-17.

Stjernström, Bo & Anita Stjernström. "Magiska instrument längs leden" in *Dalarö-leden, Skärgårdsstiftelsens Årsbok* (1998), pp.90-99.

Vinnikov, A.Z. & A.T.Sinyuk. *Following the Paths of the Past Centuries*. Voronezh, Russia: 1990.

Westerdahl, Christer. "Navigational Aspects of Stone Labyrinths and Compass Cards" *Caerdroia* 25 (1992), pp.32-40.

Chapter 5

Carpeggiani, Paolo. "Labyrinths in the Gardens of the Renaissance" in *The History of Garden Design*, ed. Monique Mosser & Georges Teyssot. London: Thames & Hudson, 1991.

Collins, Tony & John Bosworth. "A Victorian Maze Restored" *Caerdroia* 16 (1985).

Crossley, Richard. "Thomas Kirke's Most Suprizing Labyrinth" *Caerdroia* 30 (1999), pp.37-38.

Griswold, Mac & Eleanor Weller. *The Golden Age of American Gardens*. New York: Harry N. Abrams, 1991.

Fisher, Adrian & Georg Gerster. *The Art of the Maze*. London: Weidenfeld & Nicolson, 1990.

Kern, Hermann. *Through the Labyrinth*, ed. Robert Ferré & Jeff Saward. Munich: Prestel, 2000.

Laishley, Lilan. "The Harmonist Labyrinths" *Caerdroia* 32 (2001), pp.8-20.

Locock, Martin. "A Holly Maze Restored" *Caerdroia* 23 (1990), p.19.

Matthews, W.H. *Mazes and Labyrinths – A General Account of their History and Developments*. London: Longmans, Green & Co., 1922.

Pizzoni, Filippo. *The Garden – A History in Landscape and Art*. London: Aurum Press, 1999.

Reed Doob, Penelope. *The Idea of the Labyrinth from Classical Antiquity through the Middle Ages*. Ithaca, NY: Cornell University Press, 1990.

Robey, Ann. "A 17th Century Water Maze at Greenwich" *Caerdroia* 29 (1998), pp.33.

Schafers, Fons. "A Catalogue of Labyrinths & Mazes in the Netherlands" *Caerdroia* 32 (2001), pp.28-35.

Strong, Roy. *The Renaissance Garden in England*. London: Thames & Hudson, 1979.

Strong, Roy. *The Artist & the Garden*. New Haven & London: Yale University Press. 2000.

Thordrup, Jørgen. *Alle Tiders Labyrinter*. Silkeborg, Denmark: Dixit, 2002.

Chapter 6

Abbott, Robert. *Supermazes*. Rocklin, California: Prima Publishing, 1997.

Artress, Lauren. *Walking a Sacred Path – Rediscovering the Labyrinth as a Spiritual Tool*. New York: Riverhead Books, 1995.

Bord, Janet. *Mazes and Labyrinths of the World*. London: Latimer, 1976,

Bright, Greg. *Greg Bright's Maze Book*. London: Latimer, 1973.

Candolini, Gernot. *Das Geheimnisvolle Labyrinth*. Augsburg, Germany: Pattloch, 1999.

Champion, Alex. *Earth Mazes*. Albany, California: Earth Maze Publishing, 1990.

Curry, Helen. *The Way of the Labyrinth: A Powerful Meditation for Everyday Life*. New York: Penguin Compass, 2000.

Ferré, Robert. *The Labyrinth Revival*. St. Louis, Missouri: One Way Press, 1996, revised 2002.

Fisher, Adrian. *Your Land is His Canvas*. Portsmouth, England: Adrian Fisher Maze Design, 1997.

Fisher, Adrian & Georg Gerster. *The Art of the Maze*. London: Weidenfeld & Nicolson, 1990.

Fisher, Adrian & Howard Loxton. *Secrets of the Maze*. London: Thames & Hudson, 1997.

Fisher, Adrian & Jeff Saward. *The British Maze Guide*. St. Alban's, England: Minotaur Designs, 1991.

Granger, Penny. "Religious Symbolism in Mazes" *Caerdroia* 29 (1998), pp.11-13.

Lonegren, Sig. "New Labyrinths in the Eastern USA" *Caerdroia* 25 (1992), pp.9-13.

Landsborough, Stuart. "The Great Maze at Wanaka" *Caerdroia* 25 (1992), pp.14-16.

Matthews, W.H. *Mazes and Labyrinths – A General Account of their History and Developments*. London: Longmans, Green & Co., 1922.

Saward, Jeff. "Mazes in Australia & New Zealand" *Caerdroia* 29 (1998), pp.23-29.

Saward, Jeff. *Magical Paths – Labyrinths & Mazes in the 21st Century*. London: Mitchell Beazley, 2002.

West, Melissa Gayle. *Exploring the Labyrinth*. New York: Broadway Books, 2000.

Westbury, Virginia. *Labyrinths – Ancient Paths of Wisdom and Peace*. Sydney, Australia: Lansdowne Publishing, 2001.

Select Further Reading

The following titles, mostly still in print or available through libraries, are recommended for both history and current developments in the field of mazes and labyrinths. Between them they provide a selection to suit all tastes and interests.

Artress, Lauren. *Walking a Sacred Path – Rediscovering the Labyrinth as a Spiritual Tool*. New York: Riverhead Books, 1995. A classic introduction to the labyrinth and its role in the field of spiritual psychology, hugely influential in the current spiritual revival of labyrinths.

Attali, Jacques. *The Labyrinth in Culture and Society*. Berkeley, California: North Atlantic Books, 1999. Historically muddled but thought-provoking study of the philosophy and function of mazes and labyrinths.

Caerdroia – the Journal of Mazes & Labyrinths. First published in 1980, this international annual journal provides a forum for scholars and enthusiasts alike. Details available from Labyrinthos, 53 Thundersley Grove, Thundersley, Essex SS7 3EB, UK, or www.labyrinthos.net

Candolini, Gernot. *Labyrinthe*. Augsburg, Germany: Pattloch, 1999. Potted history and full page plans of different labyrinth designs for drawing exercises.

Candolini, Gernot. *Das Geheimnisvolle Labyrinth*. Augsburg, Germany: Pattloch, 1999. Well illustrated German-language study of labyrinths, ancient and modern.

Curry, Helen. *The Way of the Labyrinth: A Powerful Meditation for Everyday Life*. New York: Penguin Compass, 2000. A guide to using the labyrinth in personal spiritual practice as well as in ceremony and ritual for larger groups and communities.

Field, Robert. *Mazes: Ancient & Modern*. Diss, England: Tarquin Publications, 1999. Colourful introduction to mazes and labyrinths.

Fisher, Adrian & Georg Gerster. *The Art of the Maze*. London: Weidenfeld & Nicolson, 1990. Reprinted by Seven Dials, London, 2000. Fully illustrated guide to mazes and labyrinths worldwide, with good detail of Adrian Fisher and Randoll Coate's early works. Published in the USA as *Labyrinth – Solving the Riddle of the Maze* by Harmony Books, 1990.

Fisher, Adrian & Howard Loxton. *Secrets of the Maze*. London: Thames & Hudson, 1997. Large format book of mazes from around the world, with puzzles and solutions.

Geoffrion, Jill Kimberly Hartwell. *Praying the Labyrinth & Living the Labyrinth*. Cleveland, Ohio: Pilgrim Press, 1999/2000. A guide to the pilgrim's journey on the labyrinth with scriptural selections to broaden the context.

Kern, Hermann. *Through the Labyrinth*, ed. Robert Ferré & Jeff Saward. Munich: Prestel, 2000. Definitive scholarly catalogue of historic labyrinths from around the world, now translated into English and updated.

Kraft, John. *The Goddess in the Labyrinth*. Turku, Finland: Åbo Akademis, 1985. Excellent study of the folklore and traditions associated with labyrinths.

Jaskolski, Helmut. *The Labyrinth: Symbol of Fear, Rebirth, and Liberation*. Boston, Massachusetts and London: Shambhala, 1997. Reflective and playful study of the labyrinth motif from ancient myths and medieval tales to modern fiction.

Lonegren, Sig. *Labyrinths: Ancient Myths & Modern Uses*. New York: Sterling Publishing, 2001. Instructional labyrinth workbook with wide-ranging study of labyrinth mythology, earth energies, and suggestions for practical usage.

Matthews, W.H. *Mazes and Labyrinths – Their History & Development*. Reprinted, New York: Dover Publications, 1970. The 1922 classic study of the subject and still full of facts and surprising snippets of information.

Pennick, Nigel. *Mazes and Labyrinths*. London: Robert Hale, 1990. A wide-ranging study of maze and labyrinth history, especially in the UK and Europe.

Reed Doob, Penelope. *The Idea of the Labyrinth from Classical Antiquity through the Middle Ages*. Ithaca, NY: Cornell University Press, 1990.
Scholarly study of labyrinths from classical antiquity through the medieval, especially in texts and literature.

Saint-Hilaire, Paul de. *L'universe Secret du Labyrinthe*. Paris: Robert Laffont, 1992. French language guide to mazes and labyrinths, especially in Europe. Historically unreliable, but with extensive gazetteer.

Sands, Helen Raphael. *Labyrinth: Pathway to Meditation and Healing*. London: Gaia, 2000. Beautifully illustrated discussion of labyrinth design, history and use. Includes clear instructions for creating labyrinths and open-ended suggestions for possible construction materials. Published in the USA as *The Healing Labyrinth* by Barrons.

Saward, Jeff. *Magical Paths – Labyrinths & Mazes in the 21st Century*. London: Mitchell Beazley, 2002. Lavishly illustrated study of the current resurgence of mazes and labyrinths around the world.

Seifried, Ilse M. *Das Labyrinth - oder Die Kunst zu Wandeln*. Innsbruck, Austria: Haymon, 2002.
Well-illustrated German-language study of the modern labyrinth revival, with contributions from a number of artists and labyrinth builders.

Simpson, Liz. *Finding Fulfilment*. London: Piatkus, 2000. A broad outline for a self-guided process using the labyrinth to promote healthy change in one's life.

Thordrup, Jørgen. *Alle Tiders Labyrinter*. Silkeborg, Denmark: Dixit, 2002. Danish-language guide to labyrinths and mazes, beautifully illustrated and with very comprehensive coverage of sites in Denmark and Scandinavia.

Westbury, Virginia. *Labyrinths – Ancient Paths of Wisdom and Peace*. Sydney, Australia: Lansdowne Publishing, 2001. Nicely illustrated introduction to the labyrinth revival, with insight into the characters and reasons behind it all.

Wright, Craig. *The Maze and the Warrior*. Cambridge, Massachusetts: Harvard University Press, 2001. Scholarly study of the labyrinth symbol in medieval and Renaissance architecture, theology and music.

Resources

Organizations

The Labyrinth Society: The international society for labyrinth enthusiasts organizes conferences and events etc. P.O. Box 144, New Canaan, CT 06840-0144, USA. E-mail: info@labyrinthsociety.org

Labyrinthos: The Maze and Labyrinth Resource Centre, Photographic Library and Archive. Publisher of *Caerdroia – the Journal of Mazes & Labyrinths*. Labyrinthos, 53 Thundersley Grove, Thundersley, Essex SS7 3EB, UK. E-mail: info@labyrinthos.net

Stichting Doolhof en Labyrint: Netherlands-based maze and labyrinth enthusiasts society. c/o Noorddammerveg 100-102, 1187 ZV Amstelveen, The Netherlands.

Websites

The phenomenal success of the Internet has seen many hundreds of maze- and labyrinth-related websites appearing in recent years. The following list of recommended sites will provide a range of information and links to further sites.

Information

The Labyrinth Society: www.labyrinthsociety.org
Excellent and extensive website, with much information, details of events, discussion forum and links to other sites, worldwide labyrinth locator website.

Labyrinthos: www.labyrinthos.net
International maze and labyrinth resource centre, photo library and archive. Maze and labyrinth events, consultancy and tours. Publisher of *Caerdroia*.

Mid Atlantic Geomancy: www.geomancy.org
Sig Lonegren's website with excellent information on labyrinths and much more besides.

Maze World: www.maze-world.com
Adrian Fisher's extensive World Maze Guide.

Jo Edkin's Maze Pages: www.gwydir.demon.co.uk/jo/maze
Interesting information and plans of mazes and labyrinths.

The Egyptian Labyrinth:
www.casa.ucl.ac.uk/digital_egypt/hawara
Fascinating documentation and reconstruction of the Egyptian Labyrinth of legend.

Amazing Stuff: www.amazing-stuff.com
On-line puzzle maze magazine.

Think Labyrinth: www.astrolog.org/labyrinth
Good links to maze and mathematics sites.

A Web of Labyrinths: www.mcli.dist.maricopa.edu/smc/labyrinth
Arizona-based information and links.

Labirintus: www.labirintus.lap.hu
Hungarian website with many articles and links.

Ashland: www.ashlandweb.com/labyrinth
Information and discussion forum.

Freemazes: www.freemazes.com
Links to many maze- related sites.

Labyrinths in Austria: www.labyrinthe.at.

Labyrinths in Austria: www.das-labyrinth.at

Labyrinths in Germany: www.begehbare-labyrinthe.de

Labyrinths in the Netherlands: www.smartbits.nl/labyrinth

Labyrinths in Switzerland: www.labyrinth-project.ch

Labyrinth Services

Labyrinth Project of Connecticut: www.Ctlabyrinth.org
Labyrinth workshops, portable floor labyrinths and ceremonies.

Labyrinth Online: www.labyrinthonline.com
Information, books and products.

Paxworks: www.paxworks.com
Portable labyrinths and more.

Relax For Life: www.relax4life.com
Finger labyrinths and more.

Santa Rosa Labyrinth Foundation:
www.srlabyrinthfoundation.com
Labyrinth workshops and consultancy. Home of the Santa Rosa labyrinth design.

St.Louis Labyrinth Project: www.labyrinthproject.com
Portable and permanent labyrinths, One Way Press publications and extensive links pages to other websites.

Veriditas: www.gracecathedral.com
Labyrinth facilitator training and pilgrimages, worldwide labyrinth locator website.

Maze and Labyrinth Attractions

The aMazeing Hedge Maze, Symonds Yat, England:
www.btinternet.com/~mazes

Labyrinthia, Rodelund, Denmark: www.labyrinthia.dk

Puzzle Planet, Trois-Ponts, Belgium: www.puzzleplanet.be

Longleat House, Wiltshire, England: www.longleat.co.uk

Puzzling World, Wanaka, New Zealand:
www.puzzlingworld.co.nz

Maze and Labyrinth Builders

Adrian Fisher: www.mazemaker.com
Maze design, development and management; mirror, colour, and maize mazes.
Portman Lodge, nr Blandford, Dorset DT11 0QA, UK.

Marty Kermeen: www.artpaver.com
Custom built labyrinths in pavement and stone, replicas of historic labyrinths.
800 Big Rock Avenue, Plano, IL 60545, USA.

Alex Champion: www.earthsymbols.com
Land art, labyrinth design and construction.

Jim Buchanan: www.landartist.co.uk
Land art and labyrinths.

The Labyrinth Company: www.labyrinthcompany.com
Portable and permanent labyrinths.

Cornmazes: www.cornmazes.com
Maize mazes.

Index

Where national boundaries have changed, place names are given under the modern country. Italics indicate picture captions.

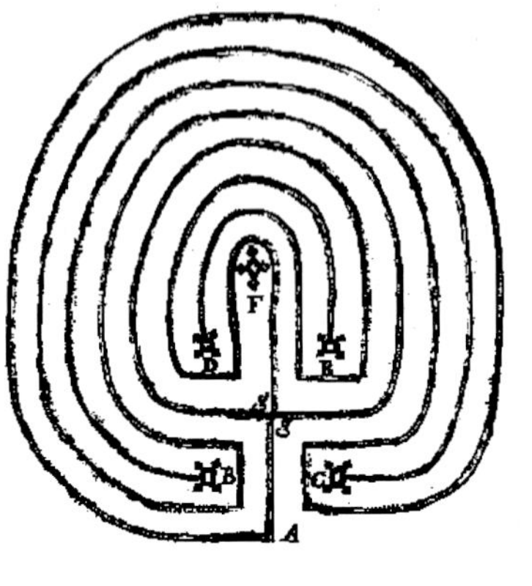

T

U

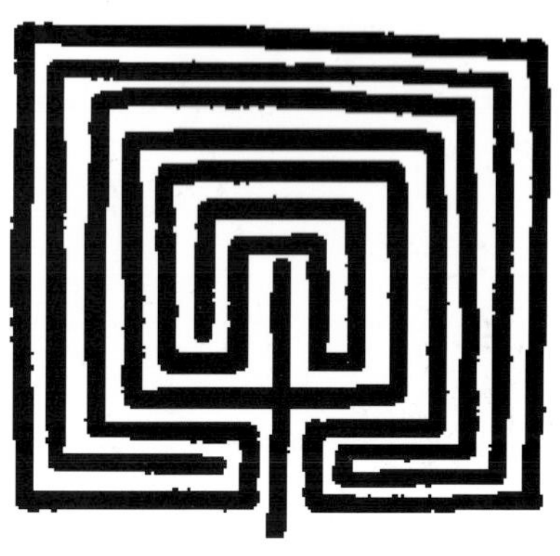

Photo and Illustration Credits: Jeff Saward/Labyrinthos Archive: 8, 10, 11, 12 L & R, 13 T, 13 C (after Selirand), 14 T, 15 T (after Cassiano), 15 B, 16 (all), 17 (all but CL), 22, 23, 24 T (courtesy of Mark Wilson), 24 C (after Krause), 26, 27, 28 C & B, 29 T (after Jünemann), 29 C & B, 30 T, 31 T, C & B, 32 T & B, 34, 36, 37 T, 37 B, 40 T & B, 41 T (after Meunié & Allain), 41 B, 42 T, 44 T (after Kern), 44 B, 45 T (after Lundén), 45 B (after Kuhlmann), 46 T, 46 C (after Lundén), 46 B (after Museo Borbonico), 48 T, 48-49, 49, 50, 51, 53 B, 54 T (after Gandolphe), 54 C & B, 55 T, 56 C, 57 C & B, 60 T, 61 T (after Cassiano), 61 B (after Galdieri), 62 T (after Kern), 62 C, 62 B (after Layard), 65 B (L&R), 66 C, 67 T (after Samuelson), 68 T & B, 69 T & B, 70 T & B, 71 T (after Nentvig), 71 B (after Schuster), 72 T & C (after Waters), 72 B (courtesy of Heard Museum), 73, 74 (after Schuster), 75 C & R, 76 (all), 77 (all), 78, 79 T (after Lévi-Strauss), 79 C, 80, 82, 83, 84 T, 84 C (after Barnea), 85 L & C, 87 T (after Kern), 88 C (after Kern), 91 B (after Kern), 92 (all), 93 (all), 94 B, 95 T, C & B, 97 T & B, 98 T, C & B, 99 T & C, 100 T & C, 101, 102 T, C & B, 103 T, 104, 105 T, 106 T, C & BL, 107, 108 T & C, 109 TL, TR & B, 110, 111 (all), 112, 113, 114 T & B, 115 (all), 116 T & C, 117 (all), 118, 121,122 T & C, 123 T & C, 124 T & B, 125 T & B, 126 T & C, 127 T, C & B, 128 T & B, 129 T, C & B, 130, 131 T (after Kraft), 131 B, 132 T (after Jünemann), 132 C, 133 T & B, 134 T & B, 136 C & BR, 137 (all), 141 C & B, 142 T, C & B, 143, 144 T & B, 145 T, 146 T & B, 147, 148 T (after Olsen), 148 C, 148 B (after Vinogradov), 149 (all), 150 B (after Richthofen), 151 L & C, 155, 157 (all), 158, 159, 160 (all), 161 B, 162 T & C, 163 T, 164 T, 166 T & B; 167 T, 169 T, BL & BR, 170 T, 171 TL & BR, 172 T, 173 BC & BR, 174 T & B, 175 T, C & B, 176 T & B, 177 (all), 178, 182 B (after Fisher), 183 BL, 184 C (after Coate), 184 B (after Fisher), 185 BR (after Fisher), 186 C, 188, 189, 190 T, 192 B, 193 T & CL, 195, 196 T, 198 T, 200 T & B, 201, 202, 205.

Additional images supplied (with thanks) by: 14 B, Bayerische Staatsbibliothek, Munich; 17 CL, after Kern; 30 B, Bayerische Staatsbibliothek, Munich; 33 T, Ole Jensen, Labyrinthia; 33 C, Steve Ryan; 33 B, Adrian Fisher; 37 C, David Singmaster; 38, 39, after Costas Goberna & Peña Santos; 42 C, courtesy University of Pennsylvania Museum; 43, Musei Capitolini, Rome/Picture research: IKONA, Rome; 47 T, Zeta Eastes; 47 B, courtesy of Louvre Museum & Staffan Lundén; 48 CL, Andrew Collins; 52 T, courtesy of V. Allamani; 52 C & B, Silvia Regolati; 53 T, Musée Archéologique de Nimes; 53 C, Museo Civico, Cremona; 55 B, Kunsthistorisches Museum, Vienna; 56 B, Robert Field; 58, Leiden University Library; 60 C, Ashoke Nath; 60 B, courtesy of Umberto Scerrato/IsMEO; 63 T, Carl Schuster Archive, Basel; 63 C, courtesy of Jean-Louis Bourgeois; 63 B, Richard Gombrich; 64 T, Leiden University Library; 64 B, Jan Brouwer; 65 T & 66 T, Rijksmuseum voor Volkenkunde, Leiden; 66 B, India Office Library; 67 C, Dudley Kidd; 75 B, Museum of Northern Arizona; 75 BR, 79 B, Carl Schuster Archive, Basel; 85 R, Prof. Christine Özgen; 86, Badische Landesbibliothek, Karlsruhe; 87 B, Österreichischen Nationalbibliothek, Vienna; 88 T, Cambridge University Library; 89, Bayerische Staatsbibliothek, Munich; 90, The Dean & Chapter of Hereford Cathedral and the Hereford Mappa Mundi Trust; 91 T, Bayerische Staatsbibliothek, Munich; 94, Gernot Candolini; 96, Helene Pühringer; 103 B & 105 C, Manuela Mastrigli & Fulvio Pompili; 105 B, Silvia Regolati; 106 BR, Carlos Soreto; 109 TC, Jørgen Thordrup; 116, Cardiff Castle; 132, Paul Goldstein; 136 BL, Adrian Fisher; 145 C, John Kraft; 145 B, Bo Stjernström; 146 C, J. Röömus; 150 T, E.J. Krupnov; 150 C, after Vinnikov & Sinyuk; 151 R, Prof. Stolyarov; 152, Jürgen Hohmuth, Zeitort; 156 T, Board of Trustees of the National Museums & Galleries on Merseyside (Walker Art Gallery, Liverpool); 156 B, Isabella Stewart Gardner Museum, Boston, Mass./Bridgeman Art Library; 161 T, Jørgen Thordrup; 162 B, Georg Gerster/Network; 163 B, Gernot Candolini; 164 B, Jürgen Hohmuth, Zeitort; 165, Harpur Garden Library; 167 B, Béa Verheul; 169 C, Jürgen Hohmuth, Zeitort; 170 B, courtesy of Uttlesford District Council; 171 TR, Jürgen Hohmuth, Zeitort; 171 BL, Ben Smeedon; 172 B, Cambridge University Library/James Carmichael Smith Photo Collection, Royal Commonwealth Society Deposit; 173 T, Dunedin City Council Archives; 180, Adrian Fisher; 181, B&L Inder; 182, Jürgen Hohmuth, Zeitort; 183 T & BR, Adrian Fisher; 184 T, Adrian Fisher; 185 T, Longleat House Estate; 185 BL, Adrian Fisher; 186 T, Stuart Landsborough; 186 B, Ole Jensen, Labyrinthia; 187, 190 B, 191, 192 T, Adrian Fisher; 193 BL, Penny Granger; 193 BR, Marty Kermeen, Artpavers; 196 B, Scott Campbell; 197 T, Alex Champion; 197 B, Jim Buchanan; 198 B, Adrian Fisher; 199, David Weinlader, Artpavers; 203, Marty Kermeen, Artpavers; 204, Lyn Bavin.